Performance, Embodiment and Cultural Memory

Edited by

Colin Counsell and Roberta Mock

CAMBRIDGE
SCHOLARS

PUBLISHING

Performance, Embodiment and Cultural Memory,
Edited by Colin Counsell and Roberta Mock

This book first published 2009

Cambridge Scholars Publishing

12 Back Chapman Street, Newcastle upon Tyne, NE6 2XX, UK

British Library Cataloguing in Publication Data
A catalogue record for this book is available from the British Library

ISBN (10): 1-4438-1120-3, ISBN (13): 978-1-4438-1120-0

CONTENTS

Contents

INTRODUCTION

COLIN COUNSELL

Even acknowledging the operation of will, affect and individual desire, it is evident that the bulk of our behaviours are socially constructed. Manners and etiquette, deportment, vestimentary codes, the constraints of propriety and conventions for expressing sexuality, gender and power – all predate the particular act, are the realisation of inherited schemes. In this sense, they constitute embodiments of memory, and a memory that is collective. This has long been recognised in the academy, for when anthropologists of the late nineteenth and early twentieth centuries considered the rituals of "primitive" peoples, they implicitly viewed the bodies involved as the bearers of pre-existing significance – even as, conversely, they tacitly assumed Western, "civilised" bodies acted in ways that were largely ideationally neutral.[1]

This recognition was not always relegated to the implicit, however. Writing in 1934 of the "techniques of the body,"[2] Marcel Mauss attempted a general theorisation of the relationship between corporeal practices and a wider *habitus*,[3] while Norbert Elias's compendious study of the "civilising process" demonstrated the impact of large-scale historical developments upon the *soma*.[4] In his 1941 account of carnival, Mikhail Bakhtin described the celebratory body's symbolic participation in the subversion of social hierarchy.[5] By the mid twentieth century there was already a theorised understanding of the body as a vehicle for extant cultural meaning, its forms and actions a mnemonics of what had gone before.

It is this – the cultural coding of the *soma* and its behaviours, the way it reproduces, modifies or challenges inherited formulations – that is the subject of this volume of essays. In introducing the volume, I want first to consider some of the conceptual frames within which such acts of embodied remembering have been understood. Rather than try to be comprehensive, I will focus here on just three bodies of writing that have had particular impact on the modern study of the body in performance.

The first is that pool of writings that comprises modern Structuralism. For the "father" of Structuralism, Claude Lévi-Strauss, the significance granted acts and artefacts is the product of semiotic "sets" that are culturally specific.[6] Composed of elements that typically take a binary, oppositional form – male versus female, raw versus cooked – these paradigmatic structures provide the thetic scaffolding within which all particular meanings are generated. At the core of Lévi-Strauss's Structural Anthropology, therefore, is a conception of human action as always already culturally charged, and charged alike for both actor and (culturally competent) observer. Although most subsequent structuralist writings would focus on language as the primary medium of culture, Lévi-Strauss thereby prepared the ground for a view of corporeal practice as partaking of, drawing significance *from*, inherited cognitive systems.

It was on this basis that the early work of ethnologist Pierre Bourdieu proceeded. Writing of the people of Kabylia (Algeria), Bourdieu explained how their gendered behaviours – the groundward-leaning posture of women, connoting a "proper" modesty, versus the upright stances of men; male visibility in public spaces and female restriction to the enclosed space of the home – were born of their culture's founding sexual *habitus*, the very shapes their bodies adopted deriving their logic from systems of oppositions peculiar to Kabylian life. For Bourdieu, the subject who acts and the subject who perceives the act function within the same inherited frames, their behaviours constituting a form of corporeal remembering.[7]

In the work of the early Bourdieu, then, actor and observer exist in a perceptual relationship determined by specific species of cognition. For both, the act is rendered a sign, a concretisation of constructions peculiar to that culture. It is this broadly structuralist proposition that Michel Foucault developed so successfully. Writing of what he termed the "episteme" of "surveillance" in his vastly influential *Discipline and Punish* (1975), Foucault attributed to behaviour a similarly mnemonic status.[8] For while much of the piece's rhetorical force derives from his tracing of the episteme's imprint on diverse cultural artefacts – architecture, discourses of penology and education, modes of social organisation – its final point of impact is bodily practices. Foucault's account of those practices is distinct, however, in putting politics at its centre. The "micro-physics of power" he detailed ultimately rests on a three-part economy of perception of the kind resonant of Structuralism *per se*, but in which power was always already embedded: as subjects act, their acts are perceived by onlookers through the lens of one or other hegemonic discourse, are "known" in the terms that discourse provides. Knowledge for Foucault is always "power/knowledge," with somatic practices inescapably implicated in a politics of social control.

Although interest in Structuralism *per se* has waned in recent years, elements of its perspective continue to inform cultural theory. In relation to questions of performance and embodiment, it is arguably Judith Butler who, while in no sense a structuralist, has done most to develop the insights provided by such as Foucault. In her much quoted *Gender Trouble* (1990) Butler argues that identity, and notably gendered and sexual identity, is itself the product of somatic shaping.[9] Prevailing Cartesian models of the self insist on a division between mind and body, valorising the former as the repository of the subject's essence and relegating the latter to the role of "automaton," merely the instrument for expressing what lies within. Butler in effect inverts this explanation: "essential" selfhood, she argues, is a chimera, for subjects in reality enact an identity via existing corporeal codes, "stylised acts" that possess given semic freight. If this embeds hegemonic models of the self in both everyday and staged behaviours, it also renders those models vulnerable to challenge. For in refusing the usual conflation of (gendered) behaviour and "essence," performances such as drag acts subvert any automatic equation of identity with stylised act. Although embodiment is the medium of received constructions of selfhood, for Butler it is also the arena in which these can be contested, and it is possible to extend her conclusions regarding gender and sexuality to other species of social identity.[10]

In recent years models of culture rooted in structuralist assumptions have been subject to widespread critique. It has been noted, for example, that Structuralism does not easily admit diversity: that in viewing culture as a single semic "system," it obscures the plurality of positions and identities all real cultures – indeed, all real *subjects* – manifest. It therefore offers no place for theories of ethnicity or sexual dissidence, say, founded as they are in notions of difference. For those concerned with embodiment and performance, however, there is perhaps a more pressing problem, albeit a related one. For the Foucault of *Discipline and Punish*, embodiment always takes a negative form, consisting of the imposition of corporeal regimes that serve the interests of a diffuse, Nietzschean power. In this period of his writing, at least, he admits no possibility of effective somatic resistance – bodily practices able to oppose prevailing hegemonies

– for even dissident acts are perceptually constructed within the terms of the prevailing episteme.[11]

This is in large part the result of the synchronic perspective at the heart of structuralist thought. To view a culture synchronically is to render the relations between its parts static, and to freeze what may in reality be ongoing, temporally-based, dialectical *processes* into apparently fixed patterns of dichotomies. Structuralism's own analytical posture, and its consequent aestheticisation of thesis into systems of oppositions, thus produces a vision of culture as monolithic – and, for the middle-period Foucault, one in which all is inescapably part of the dominating order.[12] Butler's work is not entirely free from this limitation. The "stylised acts" detailed in *Gender Trouble* also exist in systematic relations, defining identity according to patterns of ideologically-weighted polarities. As a consequence, resistance can only take the form of a *subversion of* hegemonic regimes. There is little sense in which the body might be the site of independent, autonomous constructions such as would characterise a genuinely polyphonous cultural terrain.

Additionally, while Structuralism offers a way of conceptualising the body in culture, it has less to say about the inheritance thus embodied, that which is corporeally remembered. In so far as memory features at all, it resides in the semiotic *langue*, the network of arbitrary relations that link signifier to signified, act to concept. It was from sociological writing that an account of cultural memory was initially to emerge. Memory has been a tacit object of study since the inception of modern Sociology, of course, for when Durkheim wrote in 1912 of religious ceremonies and rituals, he addressed those concrete acts as the bearers of values rooted in actual and notional pasts – more precisely, mythological values derived from a real past.[13] But it was a follower of Durkheim, Maurice Halbwachs, who first considered the question of memory directly, viewing it from the outset as a social property.

Moreover, while Durkheim and others considered societies their object of study, Halbwachs wrote specifically of "groups." The distinction is not insignificant, for in doing so he acknowledged the pluralism characteristic of any modern social whole, its composition as an amalgam of different collectives, and its resulting potential to manifest multiple, possibly conflicting identities and positions. Thus in his *Social Frameworks of Memory* (1934) it is smaller-scale social aggregates, in the form of families, religious groups and social classes, that he proposes as the breeding ground of distinct bodies of memory.[14] Halbwachs's choice of collectives may be subject to critique, seen as reflecting the cultural assumptions of his time, and the modern scholar might wish to propose different – indeed, less strictly bounded – collective forms; but he nevertheless saw the *group* as memory's proper environment.

The historical value of Halbwachs's work resides in large part in its recognition of memory as a social artefact. Generalising in its observations, and discursive in form, it is eminently quotable but perhaps does not provide an adequate framework within which other studies of cultural memory might be securely couched: it offers no explicit and transposable theory, and few in-depth, original case studies from which observations of a theoretical, generally applicable kind might be extrapolated. Equally importantly, Halbwachs devotes very little space to considering how memories are maintained and disseminated. This is a significant omission, for if collective memory is by definition drawn from the past, then the social and material means of its transmission through time, between individuals, must be of central concern to sociologists and, of course, scholars of that emphatically material enterprise, performance.

There is no such omission in the work of sociologist Paul Connerton. In his concise *How Societies Remember* (1989) he certainly considers the nature of memory *per se*, juxtaposing a range of broad traditions within which it has been conceptualised.[15] A main focus of the book, however, is the collective and material mechanisms by which memory is passed on. Under the rubric of what he calls "commemorative ceremonies," he explores "official" enactments, the kind of national or society-wide means of transmission that have been the subject of numerous studies in the past. More intriguingly, he also considers less formal bodily practices, the way apparently casual, even doxic behaviours may in fact embody inherited dispositions of a conceptually dense kind. Discussing fashion in France after the Revolution, for example, he notes:

> Styles of clothing in Paris passed through two phases during the revolutionary period. During the first, which dominated the years 1791-4, clothes became uniforms. The culotte of simple cut and the absence of adornments were emblematic of the desire to eliminate social barriers in the striving for equality: by making the body neutral, citizens were free to deal with one another without the intrusion of differences of social status. During the second phase, which dominated the years of Thermidor beginning in 1795, liberty of dress came to mean free bodily movement. People now began to dress in such a way as to expose their bodies to one another on the street and to display the motions of the body… This was a

moment in the history of Paris when inhibitory rules were suspended: when, as in all carnival, the people acted out their awareness that established authority was, in reality, a matter of local prescription.[16]

For Connerton, then, even ephemeral codes of fashion can function as vehicles for cultural remembering. Apparently unregulated, born of informal social interaction, they are nevertheless capable of conveying highly nuanced conceptions of a common history. Yet the above example also makes evident another quality of embodied memory. For the fashions described do not simply reflect the past, they recreate it, and effectively re-narrativise events individuals might actually have experienced. Cultural memory is not simply passed on in Connerton's account, it is made afresh, bodies enacting new visions of a collective past.

This points the way towards a significant issue. It is perhaps easy to imagine the embodiment of memory as an essentially static process, for, drawing from and deferring to the past, imprinted on the bodies of the present, it can appear exclusively reiterative. This impression has been countered in a number of studies, but nowhere more cogently than in the work of anthropologist Margaret Thompson Drewal. In her *Yoruba Ritual: Performers, Play, Agency* (1992), Drewal makes the point that even "traditional," apparently fixed somatic practices in fact respond to historical circumstance, and so are always in the process of change, are formed of "repetition with revision."[17] This can be extended to include our understanding of embodied memory. Eric Hobsbawm and Terence Ranger demonstrated that traditions may be invented – that cultural enactments of the past are always conceived in a present, and necessarily serve present interests.[18] Similarly, culture of necessity constructs its memories, if only because their reproduction in concrete practices is always shaped by the aesthetic and ideational dispositions of the society that remembers. As Raymond Williams pointed out, "no generation speaks quite the same language as its predecessors,"[19] with the consequence that each models its memories in a different way.

This conception of cultural acts as essentially constructive, *making* meaning, is central to the third and newest body of writing I want to consider, that deriving from the discipline of Performance Studies. As a distinct discipline, Performance Studies emerged in the late 1960s and early '70s, building upon discussions between sociologist Erving Goffman, anthropologists Victor Turner and Dwight Conquergood, and director and performance theorist Richard Schechner.[20] Having written on the presentation of self in everyday life, Goffman had already demonstrated an interest in the theatricality of the quotidian,[21] while Conquergood addressed performativity as a tool for real-world activism. In his numerous studies of rituals, Turner construed them as mechanisms for socio-cultural renewal and transformation, and Schechner's experimental theatre productions worked to question given distinctions between social and performance space.

It was not insignificant, then, that the new discipline proved fundamentally interdisciplinary, admitting no absolute distinction between activities traditionally ring-fenced as "performance" and other kinds of enacted event. Football games, political protests and productions of *Hamlet*, the hawker's calling of his wares and the TV personality's careful manufacture of his public persona – all are arguably species of what Schechner famously termed "restored" or "twice-behaved behaviour," activities that are neither purely functional nor entirely spontaneous but defer to prior actions or models for action, and so are in some sense reiterations.[22] At a time when structuralist writing most often focused on language, Performance Studies turned its attention to the body as the principal medium of memory's transmission.

Of the many works to emerge from the discipline, two stand out as especially apposite to the essays in this volume. Considering what he calls the "geohistorical matrix of the circum-Atlantic world," in *Cities of the Dead* (1996) Joseph Roach examines the modes of performance that emerged from economic and cultural exchange between Europe, Africa and the Americas (emblematised in the examples of London and New Orleans) in the seventeenth and eighteenth centuries.[23] No performance or model for performance is beyond the scope of Roach's consideration, as he ranges across events and texts as diverse as Thomas Betterton's funeral, Dryden's *The Indian Emperour*, and the work of Mardi Gras "krewes." Crucially, the study is underpinned by Roach's assertion that performance, in the global sense implied by the discipline, entails processes of remembering, forgetting and reinventing – of restating past values, dispositions and relationships via "surrogates," enacting new dispositions, and so on. For Structuralism, performance was always in some sense secondary, the *parole* to the abstract *langue* that is culture: for Halbwachs memory was separable from the material means of its transmission. But for Roach, memory and meaning are imminent in the act itself, generated and negotiated by particular bodies, specific acts. Performance thus forms the very substance of cultural life, is the *process* in which the terms of collective existence are made, remade and transformed.

Diana Taylor shares this broad assumption. At the centre of her book *The Archive and the Repertoire: Performing Cultural Memory in the Americas* (2003) is a non-dogmatic proposal: while archives typically comprise an official record, and hence lend themselves to dominant viewpoints, the repertoire, with its circulation of unofficial, apparently ephemeral materials, is the more likely repository of the histories and experiences of the marginalised.[24] It is the latter – memory not collected and written down but embodied in practice – that she explores in the form of a variety of cultural performances both modern and historical, from the "self-fashioning" of celebrity fortune tellers to the performances of indigenous peoples in fifteenth-century Mexico, and memorials to Diana Spencer. Such performances may or may not be overtly political in content, but, for Taylor, all negotiate a basic political dynamic. As an accumulation of official viewpoints, the archive comprises an ossification of hegemonic structures. It is only in the comparatively unregulated realm of the repertoire that non-hegemonic views may be postulated. The place where alternatives may be proposed, new meanings *made*, the repertoire is the domain of cultural process, and therefore the arena in which acts of resistance can take place.

***

What emerges from the interaction of these perspectives is a vision of performance as an essentially *constructive* medium, and one for which orthodox distinctions between the real and the theatrical, and the functional and conceptual, cannot be maintained. However and wherever they appear, bodies and their actions are shaped by, give form *to*, figures drawn from cultural memories. If they thus comprise a means of reproducing those memories, through time and between individuals, as articulators of an unofficial repertoire bodies also provide an arena in which they can be adapted and contested.

In their different ways, all the essays in this volume deal with this reiterative or adaptive process. As Ric Knowles notes, Canada was the first country to officially adopt a policy of multiculturalism, but the outcomes, he argues, have not been entirely positive. Implicitly taking an essentialist, exoticised view of cultural difference, the policy has resulted in a theatre dedicated to preserving immigrants' cultural heritage, one that fails to acknowledge the fluidity of the nation's diasporic identities, and their interaction in a modern *inter*cultural milieu. It is this fluidity and interaction he explores via the examples of four recent works of a different stripe, all performed in the multicultural city of Toronto. Rather than offer some nostalgic depiction of a "home" culture, each piece traces the interpenetration of past memory and present reality, dealing with the modern subject's negotiation of an identity that encompasses both. If they explore this in their themes and narratives, Knowles asserts, they also do so via bodily practices, developing somatic forms that function as mnemonics of cultural memory.

The body as an instrument for enacting cultural identity, and the possibility of that identity's reinvention, are also at the centre of Royona Mitra's chapter. With numerous individuals having transplanted from Asia, Africa and Eastern Europe to a new life in the West, migration, she observes, is a central feature of contemporary cultural experience. Having two "homes" – or, in a state of ongoing cultural "transit," effectively having none – migrants and their descendents have no obvious and given body of cultural memories in which their own identities might be anchored, and no somatic repertoire to give those identities form. It is the condition of these "diasporic agents," Mitra argues, that is addressed in Akram Kahn's dance *Bahok*. Caught in the in-betweenness of transit, its culturally diverse characters trace a postmodern state of hybridity in their very actions, are forced to negotiate a relationship to multiple cultural locations and to each other. But this is not an entirely negative situation, Mitra asserts, for in the process essentialist ideas of "home" are challenged, the dance ultimately offering the possibility of an empowering *trans*nationality in which new identities are created self-reflectively.

Approaching the question of diasporic agency from a somewhat different direction, in her chapter Roberta Mock uses the term "autotopographical" to describe the relationship between autobiography, place and the body in the work of Rachel Rosenthal. Overlapping interiority and exteriority, personal biography and global history, in a series of performances Rosenthal has offered her own body as mythic metaphor for the geographical world. Since topology is a powerfully constructive discourse, defining not just place but the subject's relationship to it, Mock argues, Rosenthal's work comprises a "writing of self," a process implicated in the creation of cultural identity. But underpinning this, often unspoken, is the structuring presence of a more literal social identity, that of the diasporic Jewish woman. For while Jewishness has often been suppressed over the last century, the terms on which Jewish identity was founded nevertheless re-emerge as a "spectral visibility" haunting modern culture. It is a similar haunting that Mock traces through Rosenthal's work, exploring how Jewishness appears not only in her choice of materials but in the themes and geo-somatic symbologies it provides.

Trauma, Bryoni Trezise notes, is no less subject to cultural embodiment. It is not simply memories of traumatic events that are transmitted across time, for such memories are themselves typically couched within given perspectives, construing those events in specific ways. Thus testaments to trauma also provide for later generations particular subject positions, embedding cultural identities in their conceptualisations of the past. It is this principle she brings to her exploration of three memorials to the Holocaust. Christian Boltanski's *Missing House*, Peter Eisenman's *Memorial to the Murdered Jews of Europe* and the Auschwitz-Birkenau Memorial and Museum certainly offer quite different kinds of testimony, but they more importantly provide different perceptual experiences, effectively requiring that participants adopt a definable position in relation to the horrors scarring mid twentieth-century Europe. In this sense they comprise embodiments of embodiment, demanding that visitors interpretively perform a specific cognitive relationship to what has gone before.

Specificity of site is also central to Cariad Astles' chapter, for its setting is Barcelona, a city whose history is marked by cycles of occupation and independence. Deliberately stripped of its Catalan identity in the post-Civil War period, it was re-presented as a Castillian Spanish city until the end of Franco's dictatorship. It is in this context of repression followed by liberation, Astles notes, that puppeteers such as Joan Biaxas worked to assert Catalan cultural identity. A traditional Catalan medium, puppetry is inherently redolent of Catalan culture, and in Biaxas's hands the bodies of its marionettes became instruments of carnivalesque assault against the prevailing political order. Equally important was the role of *matter* in Biaxas's work, however, for in incorporating materials that were visibly worked and used, he presented audiences with tangible traces of past human activity. The resulting performances thus comprised materialisations of memory, mythically asserting Barcelona's status as the place of multiple linkages, connected to the greater human world.

The embodiment of cultural identity is similarly at the heart of Ruth Hellier-Tinoco's chapter. The construction of national identity in Mexico, she notes, has since independence involved mobilisation of the objects, sites and iconographies of a prehispanic, sometimes mythical Mexican past. Performance has played a role in this, with the bodies of actors and dancers "transmuted" into symbols of myth and history. If cultural identity always involves an appeal to a remembered past, in Mexico this appeal has particular urgency, for, founded in invasion and conquest, built upon shifting borders, the question "Who am I?" has singular resonance for that country's people. It is the continuation of this process of identity formation today that Hellier-Tinoco explores via four modern performances. The pieces are very different, comprising two contemporary theatre works, one traditional, apparently authentic cultural event, and a filmed record of another such event. But in each the bodies of "performers" are deployed as icons of a Mexicanness built of the past, made to bear the weight of memory.

Michelle Liu Carriger's chapter is less concerned with the historical meaning of *Chanoyu*, the so-called "Japanese Tea ceremony," than with its character as a transposable act of embodiment, one that can be remobilised in the present. Tea certainly reflects principles basic to Zen Buddhism, implicitly favouring the negation of self in favour of the here and now of its performance. But this very refusal of an abstract meaning lying beyond the material act, she argues, renders it available to changing narrativisations. This is in part a result of Tea's position at the intersection of two temporalities, for, borne of long tradition and disciplined practice, yet contingent and ultimately unrepeatable, it both "disappears" in Peggy Phelan's sense and involves an act of reiterative "surrogacy" as described by Joseph Roach. Reaching into the past and genuinely reproducing material bodily practices, but leaving those practices semically unfixed, it comprises a canvas on which shifting significances can be projected.

Taking quite a different tack, Paul Rae begins his exploration of embodiment and memory in Singapore with an emphatically modern Asian luxury commodity, the "iDesire" massage chair. The state of Singapore, he argues, was in large part founded on the erasure of existing cultural memories, for it was only by effacing the diversity of specific histories and experiences that the modern, unified state was brought conceptually into being. While this effacement most obviously involved mechanisms for overt social control, ranging from modes of surveillance to the creation of an "official" national history, it emerged more obliquely as various "techniques of the self," practices of bodily self-monitoring for which the iDesire is a modern exemplar. If bodies thus comprise targets for socio-cultural discipline in Singapore, however, it is because they offer themselves as vehicles for collective memory, which also makes them repositories for memories of an unofficial kind. This is most of all the case with performing bodies, Rae maintains, for it is in theatre and films about theatre that he finds acknowledgement of the role played by the body in Singapore, and traces of that nation's cultural loss.

The cultural "writing" of place is equally crucial to Minty Donald's chapter, albeit that she deals with a place of a different scale. Today's "heritage industry," she notes, inherently tends towards cultural stasis, for in ascribing to objects and sites a limited number of established and orthodox meanings, it renders them expressive of a homogenised history. Hermetically sealing the past, it thereby removes them from the processes of present remembering. But performative, embodied practices have the capacity to challenge memory's ossification, Donald argues, and such was the aim of her project *Glimmers in Limbo*. Comprising a number of performances in and around the disused Britannia Panopticon Music Hall in Glasgow, it sought to destabilise the hegemonic meanings attached to the site, prompt "imaginative rememberings" that linked past to present in new and diverse ways. The ultimate goal was a multiple layering of history, making the now decrepit venue the locus of present cognitive activities, and hence of diverse and competing narratives.

The narrativisation of the material is approached from a different direction by Ross Brown. Today's preoccupation with the visual is a peculiarly modern phenomenon, he argues, and the audial played a far greater role in premodern cultures. It could do so in part because of sound's immersive quality, for, resonating within the body, refusing to not be heard, it denies any easy Cartesian distinction between self and external world. It was therefore able to function as expression of greater, holistic paradigms, make of the body "a microcosmic extension of a universe." It is this perspective that Brown brings to his account of the two-minute silence. In reality such events are experienced as anything but silent, for they serve to frame the sounds emanating from the environment and from one's own body. They thereby effect a heightened recognition of an existential situation, the individual's relationship to their surroundings, and particularly to the crowd. Communal yet solitary, free of intentional sounds but experienced as supremely noisy, they recontexualise the solipsism of the modern subject, comprise "a powerfully unifying agreement that at this moment, nothing need be said."

Works Cited

Bakhtin, M. (1993) *Rabelais and His World* [1941], trans. Hélène
    Iswolsky, Bloomington: Indiana University Press.
Bourdieu, P. (1967) *The Algerians* [1961], trans. Peter Neal, New York:
    Beacon Books.
—. (1977) *Outline of a Theory of Practice* [1972], trans. Richard Nice,
    Cambridge: Cambridge University Press.
Butler, J. (1990) *Gender Trouble: Feminism and the Subversion of
    Identity*, London & New York: Routledge.
Connerton, P. (1989) *How Societies Remember*, Cambridge: Cambridge
    University Press.
Counsell, C. and P. Stanley (2005) "Performing Impairment: Modernity
    and the Cultural Enactment of Disability," *Atenea*, 2:1 (December),
    pp.24-38.
Drewal, M. T. (1992) *Yoruba Ritual: Performers, Play, Agency*,
    Bloomington: Indiana University Press.
Durkheim, É. (1933) *The Division of Labour in Society* [1893], trans.
    George Simpson, New York: Macmillan.
—. (1995) *The Elementary Forms of Religious Life* [1912], trans. Karen E.
    Fields, New York: The Free Press.
Elias, N. (1994) *The Civilizing Process: Sociogenetic and Psychogenetic
    Investigations* [1939], trans. Edmund Jephcott, London: Blackwell.
Foucault, M. (1977) *Discipline and Punish: The Birth of the Prison*
    [1975], trans. Alan Sheridan, Harmondsworth: Penguin
Goffman, E. (1959) *The Presentation of Self in Everyday Life*, New York:
    Doubleday.
Halbwachs, M. (1992) *On Collective Memory*, trans. & ed. Lewis A.
    Coser, Chicago: University of Chicago Press.
Hobsbawm, E. and T. Ranger (Eds.) (1983) *The Invention of Tradition*,
    Cambridge: Cambridge University Press.
Lévi-Strauss, C. (1966) *The Savage Mind* [1962], London: Weidenfeld and
    Nicholson.
Mauss, M. (1974) "The Techniques of the Body" [1935], *Economy and
    Society*, 2:1 (February), pp.70-88.
Roach, J. (1996) *Cities of the Dead: Circum-Atlantic Performance*, New
    York: Columbia University Press.
Schechner, R. (2006) *Performance Studies: An Introduction* [2002], New
    York and London: Routledge.
Taylor, D. (2003) *The Archive and the Repertoire: Performing Cultural
    Memory in the Americas*, Durham & London: Duke University Press.

Williams, R. (1977) *Marxism and Literature*, Oxford: Oxford University Press.

Notes

[1] It is particularly interesting to view Durkheim's work in this light, for in attributing a "mechanical solidarity" to premodern societies and an "organic solidarity" to the modern, he implicitly proffered a conception of the latter as fundamentally rational, geared to function, and the former as based in the mere repetition of tradition. See Émile Durkheim (1933) *The Division of Labour in Society*, New York: Macmillan.

[2] Marcel Mauss (1974) "The Techniques of the Body," *Economy and Society*, 2/1 (February), pp.70-88.

[3] Although the term is probably most associated with Pierre Bourdieu today, its modern use in fact derives from the work of Mauss and Elias.

[4] Norbert Elias (1994) *The Civilizing Process: Sociogenetic and Psychogenetic Investigations*, London: Blackwell.

[5] Mikhail Bakhtin (1993) *Rabelais and His World*, Bloomington: Indiana University Press.

[6] The relatively late work, *The Savage Mind* (1966), London: Weidenfeld and Nicholson, represents Lévi-Strauss's developed thought in this respect.

[7] See, for example, Pierre Bourdieu (1961) *The Algerians*, New York: Beacon Books. Bourdieu would soon abandon what he called the "blissful structuralism" of his early work, even critiquing Lévi-Strauss for what he saw as the other's underlying essentialism. Indeed, Bourdieu's later theory was in large part built around attempts to avoid, or perhaps reconcile, the twin evils of structuralist "objectivism" and Sartrean "subjectivism." See Pierre Bourdieu (1977) *Outline of a Theory of Practice*, Cambridge: Cambridge University Press.

[8] Michel Foucault (1977) *Discipline and Punish: The Birth of the Prison*, Harmondsworth: Penguin.

[9] Judith Butler (1990) *Gender Trouble: Feminism and the Subversion of Identity*, London & New York: Routledge.

[10] See for example Colin Counsell and Peri Stanley (2005) "Performing Impairment: Modernity and the Cultural Enactment of Disability," *Atenea*, 2/1 (December), pp.24-38.

[11] This is evident in the "pessimism" of New Historicist writing, for example, its foundation in such Foucaultian assumptions leading to a propensity to find modes of oppression in materials that might otherwise appear politically ambiguous, or even neutral.

[12] In the later, "post-structuralist" phase of his work Foucault acknowledged the possibility of somatic resistance. While in *Discipline and Punish* he gives a fully theorised account of how dissident acts are enveloped within the greater episteme, in his later work he does not offer quite so thoroughgoing an explanation of why

he now viewed such resistance as potentially effective. See, for example, the three volumes (1979, 1987 and 1988) of his *The History of Sexuality*, Harmondsworth: Penguin.

[13] Émile Durkheim (1995) *The Elementary Forms of Religious Life*, New York: The Free Press.

[14] Reproduced in Maurice Halbwachs (1992) *On Collective Memory*, Chicago: University of Chicago Press.

[15] Paul Connerton (1989) *How Societies Remember*, Cambridge: Cambridge University Press.

[16] *Ibid*, p.10.

[17] Margaret Thompson Drewal (1992) *Yoruba Ritual: Performers, Play, Agency*, Bloomington: Indiana University Press.

[18] See Eric Hobsbawm and Terence Ranger (Eds.) (1983) *The Invention of Tradition*, Cambridge: Cambridge University Press.

[19] Raymond Williams (1977) *Marxism and Literature*, Oxford: Oxford University Press, p.131.

[20] See the special edition of *The Drama Review*, "Theatre and the Social Sciences," Fall 1973, which explored the interaction of these disciplinary perspectives.

[21] Erving Goffman (1959) *The Presentation of Self in Everyday Life*, New York: Doubleday.

[22] See for example Richard Schechner (2006) *Performance Studies: An Introduction*, New York and London: Routledge.

[23] Joseph Roach (1996) *Cities of the Dead: Circum-Atlantic Performance*, New York: Columbia University Press.

[24] Diana Taylor (2003) *The Archive and the Repertoire: Performing Cultural Memory in the Americas*, Durham & London: Duke University Press.

PERFORMING INTERCULTURAL MEMORY IN THE DIASPORIC PRESENT: THE CASE OF TORONTO

RIC KNOWLES

All memory bridges difference. It takes place in the present, but recalls, incorporates, or appropriates the past. All *cultural* memory is performative. It involves the transmission of culture through bodily practices such as ritual, repetition and habit. I consider here some of the ways in which communities in diaspora interact and constitute themselves as communities through the performative enactment of *inter*cultural memory. I am using the city of Toronto as my test case because it hosts one of the world's most complex intercultural performance ecologies. The city claims in its promotional literature to be at once the third most active theatre centre in the English-speaking world and the world's most multicultural city. Not only is Toronto's immigrant population approaching the 50% mark, but the minorities who will soon comprise its majority come from a genuinely global range of cultures, mingling across many generations of immigration, and co-existing in the city's core, where there are no significant "ethnic enclaves,"[1] with a diverse population from various Aboriginal communities as well as from the so-called "founding" settler-invader British and French cultures. Toronto is, too, the largest city in the first country in the world to have adopted multiculturalism, in the 1980s, as official state policy.

Official multiculturalism, often celebrated as Pierre Elliott Trudeau's "idealist dream,"[2] has nevertheless had its detractors.[3] Seen as a way of managing (containing and controlling) diversity, deflecting attention from social inequities by privileging untouchable cultural difference, and commodifying or exoticizing difference in the programming of diversity slots at the city's mainstream theatres, official multiculturalism has been something of a false friend to those grass-roots theatre practitioners who want to challenge the hegemony of whiteness on the city's stages. Chief among the policy's problems are its focus on "preserving" immigrants' "cultural heritage,"[4] its focus on "tolerance" as a marker of Canadian national identity – which posits a Canadian "us" who generously tolerate an othered, ethnic "them"[5] – and its explicit exclusion of First Nations. In terms of cultural memory, the policy problematically constructs memory in essentialist, static, and nostalgic terms in relation to dehistoricized ethnic "homelands," atomizing communities of memory into separate "ethnic" enclaves. It makes sense, then, that much of the city's grass-roots *intra*cultural performance practice works against this, performatively, to forge intersecting and fluid diasporic identities in the city.

In focusing on *inter*cultural memory, I am attempting to take into account scholarship on cultural memory as both social[6] and, as a function of social ritual and habit, embodied, performed, and, through performance, transmitted across generations.[7] Taking into account the performative nature of social identities – gendered, classed, and raced – as constituted through ritual repetition,[8] I accept Joseph Roach's concept of "performance genealogies," which he sees as drawing upon "the idea of expressive movements as *mnemonic reserves*, including patterned movements made and remembered by bodies, residual movements retained implicitly in images or words… and imaginary movements dreamed in minds not prior to language but constitutive of it."[9] I also find useful Roach's concept of "surrogation" as a mode of cultural transmission-by-replacement ("the king is dead, long live the king"), together with Diana Taylor's elaboration that sometimes, particularly in postcolonial cultures, the doubling repressed by surrogation *preserves*, rather than erases, its antecedents.[10] In introducing the concept of *inter*cultural memory I am attempting to understand the transmission and transformation of cultural memory in diaspora across various kinds of difference.

If it is true that all memory bridges difference, it is equally true that all cultural memory involves transference, in which the individual subject remembers events that s/he did not, in fact, experience, practices that s/he did not perform. Ross Chambers has examined the phenomenon of "orphaned memory" to explain the ways in which the memories of a dead generation of Holocaust children survive in a body to whom they do not, in any experiential sense, "belong."[11] They are "fostered" – technically "false" as individual memory, but as cultural memory embodying profound and otherwise inaccessible truth: the memories of the dead. Similarly, Marita Sturken suggests that so-called "false memory syndrome," in which individual subjects recall the experience of sexual abuse that did not happen to them, can be considered to *be* cultural memory. She argues that events that may not have happened to the person who "remembers" them are nevertheless culturally "true" insofar as they rightly characterize a lived, embodied culture of systemic sexual violence.[12]

How are these transferences affected? Marianne Hirsch puts considerable faith in the power of art to produce empathy among audiences who do not simply witness representations, but undergo "emotional and bodily experience" that is incorporated and felt as embodied memory.[13] Alison Landsberg, considering the transcultural power of mass culture to "suture" to spectators memories of events through which they have not lived, labels this process "prosthetic memory."[14] Empathy can be a double-edged sword, its effects ranging from the easy catharsis of the "good cry" to the appropriation, without cost or context, of others' experiences. But in specific performance contexts certain forms of non-appropriative empathy can also provoke the genuine transference of embodied, practiced memory across difference. When, in Roach's terms, "patterned movements made and remembered by bodies, residual movements retained implicitly in images or words… and imaginary [or imagined] movements" come to inhabit the muscles and socialization of the body, the possibility exists of the transference, across difference, of embodied "mnemonic reserves."

Addressing the question of transference, Paul Connerton claims that "if there is such a thing as social memory" it is performative, operating through commemorative ceremonies, bodily practices, and habit.[15] It is, consciously or not, *taught*, as when young girls learn with their mother's milk, as it were, to cross their legs when sitting, young boys to take up space in ways denied their sisters. If this is so, then cultural memories can be transferred, not only generationally within a family or community, as in Hirsch's concept of "postmemory,"[16] but also across other kinds of difference.

In diaspora this transference crosses both generations and geographies, and it involves the intercultural transformation of the very performance practices it employs. There are various kinds of theatrical practice in Toronto that use the performance forms of "home" communities, invoking embodied cultural memories to (re-)constitute different kinds of diasporic community. Some companies, such as Carlos Bulosan (Filipino) Theatre Company, are dedicated to supporting and reflecting specific communities of memory. Others, such as the AfriCan Theatre Ensemble, Theatre Archipelago, and Rasik Arts, primarily perform work from cultural "homelands" – Africa, the Caribbean, and South Asia – evoking, sometimes nostalgically, cultural memory in diaspora. Others, such as Obsidian Theatre, b-current, fu-GEN Asian Canadian Theatre, Red Sky Performance, and Native Earth Performing Arts, constitute internally diverse or even historically conflicted communities as "African Canadian," "Asian Canadian" and "Aboriginal," developing new work that speaks across such differences, and producing intercultural memory among potentially affiliated communities of interest. Finally, companies such as Cahoots Theatre Projects, Modern Times Stage Company, and the feminist Nightwood Theatre, are more broadly intercultural, creating performance forms that bridge explicit and acknowledged differences. These companies and others actively intersect, establishing coalitions of difference among what Yvette Nolan, Managing Artistic Director of Native Earth Performing Arts, calls the city's "brown caucus," working together in what Ella Shohat and Robert Stam call "*mutual and reciprocal relativization.*"[17]

I look elsewhere at what this activity means for the constitution of Toronto as a multicultural city and the (re-)constitution of its broadly diasporic subjectivities.[18] Here I want to consider four recent performances that employ the performance forms of minoritized cultures to "build memory."[19] At the level of representation, the memories these shows address and suture are increasingly traumatic in terms of the levels of displacement they portray, moving from voluntary immigration (and voluntary memory), through harrowing refugee experience, to involuntary trauma memories of enforced immigration, colonization and genocide. My case studies also move from the individual effort to suture a divided cultural identity to the communal building of shared cultural memory, to the actual *constitution* of new forms of community through "prosthetic" memory-making that works to reconstitute diasporic subjectivities through the embodied practices of intercultural memory.

Fish Eyes

Fish Eyes, a solo show written and performed by South Asian Canadian Anita Majumdar, began when Majumdar was a theatre student at University of British Columbia (UBC). Having grown up an only child in the Vancouver suburb of Port Moody, where she was "one of maybe three South Asians in my school, from elementary school to graduating in grade twelve," Majumdar says that when she went to UBC, "it was important to me to own my culture and investigate what this other side of me was."[20] Although she had taken and quit classes in ballet, piano and figure skating as a child, her father wouldn't allow her to take Indian dance, so she set out at UBC to construct a set of embodied memories – "patterned movements [as] mnemonic reserves" – of her South Asian self. These were not specific to her own Bengali heritage, but were both diasporic and pan-Indian. As a theatre student at UBC she enrolled, outside the program, in classes in Kathak, a narrative dance form from Northern India that fuses Hindu and Muslim cultures. She also took language classes in Hindi – ironically, from a white American, Ken Bryant – where she was exposed for the first time to "a sea of brown faces." Majumdar performed with a dance troupe in Vancouver but kept her dancing separate from her theatre training, which at UBC was overwhelmingly western. Only later, in her final years at the National Theatre School, was she encouraged by faculty and fellow students to integrate her dance life into her acting – which meant merging her cultural identities.

Fish Eyes developed over several years from a 15-minute in-school exercise to a full-length professional production. But it retained its interdisciplinarity as dance and theatre, as well as its interculturalism as both Canadian and "pan-Indian." Majumdar describes being in India when *Fish Eyes* was first conceived:

> We were on a … 12-hour trip back from the Taj Mahal to where I was staying in Lucknow [in Northern India]. We were stuck on the national highway … and I was looking through these fields, this vast land, and I suddenly felt this great need to be able to fuse the two countries that I come from…. And when I got back to Calcutta [in West Bengal] I had a blue costume stitched for what my idea of what the play was going to be.[21]

At first, *Fish Eyes* seems to be a simple sketch about Meena – short for Meenakshi, meaning "Fish Eyes" – a teenage Canadian born to South Asian immigrant parents, caught between the pressures and pleasures of her last year in a very white high school and her parents' requirement that she take classes in Indian classical dance. Meanwhile, her friends "are going to parties…and making out in closets with hot, popular boys like Buddy Cain, and drinking lots of beer and making best friends with popular girls like Candace Paskas because she holds your head back while you throw up."[22]

The play is autobiographical in form, not content. Where Majumdar chose at the age of 18 to take dance and language classes as performative entrées into the South Asian side of her culture, Meena grows up under the wing of Kalyani Aunty ("happy cow"[23]), an exuberant if lovelorn woman who "lactate[s] butter chicken,"[24] readies Meena for the Lord Ganesh festival and the All India Dance Competition (where she will perform "Extreme Nimbooda") – and accompanies her in her pink Volvo to Toronto's "Little India"[25] where they purchase Indian foods, Thumbs Up, henna, and other trappings of the homeland.

Kalyani Aunty provides the play's most trenchant, if comic, postcolonial critiques –"you know how many places British colonize? 77! 77 in whole of the world, Meena! They have so much land, SO MUCH LAND, then be giving us generous gift: two blocks of East Gerrard Street?! Oh thank you, *thank you* British Raj!"[26] And she speaks in the play for the immigrant community's compensatory nostalgia for all things Indian, while at the same time aspiring to take her students' work back to the old country to demonstrate its quality. But her most significant role is as one dance teacher in an intergenerational chain, making regular calls to her own teacher in India to report her students' progress. As such, she serves as the agent for the transmission of embodied, if transformed, cultural memory through dance.

For of course the play is not reverent about India, nor is it purist in its treatment of the traditions of Indian dance. "I don't like purist work," Majumdar says. "I get bored with it.... What I really like is seeing the invention of new forms."[27] In fact, the play includes elements of the South Indian Bharata Natyam, the northern Kathak, and the North-eastern Odissi dances, sometimes combined within a single movement sequence. It also includes one parodic, cross-dressed Punjabi dance and a comic toothbrush dance, conceived early on as a way of imagining how a Canadian might find her symbolic Indian mudras – hand gestures – informing her work as a dental hygienist. These various positions and mudras function in the play in clear and uncomplicated ways as Roach's "mnemonic reserves … made and remembered by bodies" in which they can be combined, complicated, and clustered. But, as Majumdar says, "we never said 'Meena studies Kathak, or Meena studies Odissi.' It's a mix of all those." And of course the play is not Indian classical dance, but South Asian Canadian dance theatre – itself a newly minted form.

Figure 1: Anita Majumdar in *Fish Eyes* using the "Katakamukha" mudra indicating the lotus of purity, from the Bharata Natham dance tradition. Photo: Rob Daly.

Nevertheless, the play *is* structured around Indian classical dance. Meena's narrative and Majumdar's character transitions are signalled by specific mudras – "Kartarimukha" (scissors), from the Bharata Natyam dance tradition; "Katakamukha," the gesture usually used across the chest and indicating the lotus of purity; and so on (See *Figure 1*). And the play incorporates a mixture of forms that bring together within Toronto a "South Asian" community, a kind of "pan-Indian" experience that can only happen in diaspora. As such it helps to constitute a performative reinvention of embodied, intercultural memory, and along with it community identities and individual subjectivities that have not previously existed.

Fish Eyes was first intended for a broad, non-South Asian theatre audience. It was directed by Gregory Prest, a white male classmate of Majumdar's from NTS and, together with other work by Majumdar and others, it is contributing to the performative reconstitution of the intercultural performance ecology of Toronto. But the play has also reached a more specific South Asian Canadian community, partly because it has *not* been folkloric, targeted to the ghettoized community centres of official multiculturalism. It has reached its South Asian Canadian audience partly because Majumdar developed and performed it at established theatres, refusing to play multicultural venues in suburban Mississauga, Scarborough, or Brampton.

In spite of some early criticism in the South Asian press of the show's perceived critique of India,[28] *Fish Eyes* proved itself downtown, where its success validated the show within its home community and began to play its role in reconstituting that community as pan-Indian. Majumdar talks about how the show serves South Asian audiences as a site of memory-making, where they come together to compare traditions, cross classes, castes, and South Asian cultures, and negotiate new, crossover identities in diaspora. The show's success also led to a well received production in late 2006 at the prestigious diasporic "Other Festival" in India itself, where (who knows?) it may have contributed to the reconfiguration of inter- and intranational subjectivities *within* the subcontinent through the transformative injection of embodied, performative and diasporic, intercultural memories.

Singkil

Singkil, written by Catherine Hernandez and produced in 2007 by fu-GEN Asian Canadian Theatre Company, directed by Nina Lee Aquino, also centres on dance: in this case Filipino folk dance, the "Singkil" of the play's title. And like *Fish Eyes,* the play is concerned crucially with the intergenerational teaching, learning and transformation of cultures in diaspora through embodied performance. But both as process and product, *Singkil* moves from the individual reinvention of self through performative memory-making more directly into the knitting together of a larger community, and the displacement the play represents at its heart – a mother-daughter rift – is more traumatic.

Singkil began with an event that is represented in the finished play: Filipina playwright Catherine Hernandez, rifling through family photos on her 18th birthday in an effort of conscious memory-making, discovered an image of her mother, Cecille Hernandez, dancing the Singkil. Looking at the date on the back, Hernandez discovered herself in the picture: her mother had been pregnant with her when the photo was taken. An accomplished dancer herself, Hernandez had not realized she had been "dancing this dance [my] entire life."[29]

As both process and product, deliberately and inadvertently, *Singkil* was very much about mothers, daughters, and the transmission of cultural memory through performance. The play deals with the struggles of the partly autobiographical Mimi, played by Nadine Villasin, to come to terms with the memory, and loss, of her mother Maria. She does so in part by learning the Singkil, the dance that her mother had abandoned – and along with it her sense of self – when she came to Canada. Two weeks into rehearsal for the show, the company learned that Nadine's own mother, Fely Villasin, who founded Carlos Bulosan, the Filipino Theatre Company Nadine had inherited as Artistic Director, had died suddenly from cancer. Nadine, playing a woman coming to terms with her mother's death by learning her performance traditions, missed only one rehearsal, and the company, for whom her mother was an icon, rallied around her. Less than two weeks later, a week before opening night, director Nina Lee Aquino's water broke while she was setting cues. She finished the cue she was working on, made notes for the next day's scheduling, and went into labour with her own daughter, Eponine, whom she speaks of only partly in jest as the inheritor of fu-GEN. Hernandez, a prenatal educator, was present at the birth.

But it had been all about mothers and daughters from the beginning. In the workshop production at Factory Theatre in 2005, the mother-daughter team of Cecille and Catherine Hernandez attended rehearsals to teach the cast the Singkil, the latter carrying her own 1½-year-old daughter Arden on her hip. "[It was] three generations of us doing this dance," says Hernandez, "and it was wonderful…. I don't know if Arden will ever get into it, but she loves watching it."

In a very real sense, teaching and learning the dance across generational and cultural differences internal to the Filipino community, teaching one another Tagalog (one of the major languages of the Philippines, used in the play), teaching the use of the traditional kulintang gongs (see *Figure 2*), and exploring informally, in breaks, the respective foods, traditions, and behaviours – the embodied memories – of the largely Filipino company, constituted not simply the rehearsal of a play, but the rehearsal of a community in diaspora. Not everyone spoke Tagalog, and the best versed in the language was the youngest cast member and most recent immigrant, Rose Cortez. Not everyone knew the Singkil, in spite of the dance's being a major archetype of Filipino identity, a traditional Muslim dance that nevertheless cuts across the different religious and geographical communities in the country's dispersed northern and southern islands. Hernandez talks about the central importance of teaching the dance to Karen Ancheta (Maria), who was raised in Hamilton, Ontario, "totally, you know, a steel-town girl, who doesn't speak Tagalog."

Figure 2: Playwright Catherine Hernandez in rehearsal for *Singkil*, teaching cast member Rose Cortez the kulintang. Photo: Ric Knowles.

Rehearsals began with the actors creating, with choreographer Clare Preuss, movement vocabularies associated with motifs in the play and aspects of their characters, movements that were then invested with the gestural vocabulary and physical embodiment – the mnemonic reserves – of the Singkil. Hernandez taught the cast the rhythms, the walk, the way the body is carried, explaining all of this in culturally specific ways, invoking cultural memory: "you're regal, with the half smile of a Buddha"; "it's a patriarchal society, so the men move differently"; "the hands (and fans) go in opposite directions, because this is the east, and we move in opposite ways"; "older Filipino men have a rhythm when they walk, or even stand: you could put a song to it"; and so on. The music, too, was adapted from Filipino Muslim chants, folk songs, and the Singkil rhythms by the also Filipino composer, Romeo Candido, using, among other things, the traditional kulintang gongs live amidst the electronic soundscape. In a very real sense the company was learning embodied memory from one another, embodied ways of being Filipino in diaspora.

This learning process was also represented in the action of the play, as Mimi's "Tita" (loosely "Auntie") Norma, who has danced the Singkil with Mimi's mother in the Philippines, arrives in Toronto, and after considerable struggle begins to teach Mimi the movements, rhythms, modes of embodiment, and cultural significance of the Singkil – a dance based on the story of a Muslim princess who dances gracefully through the crashing forest of an earthquake and emerges unscathed. This was not simply folkloric, nor was it the nostalgic reproduction in diaspora of a slice of the homeland. Even as rehearsals negotiated and the show represented invented rituals of birthing and bereavement, so the dance that Mimi learns and finally performs in reconciling with her mother's ghost (who we see perform the traditional Singkil early in the play) is one of continuity, homage, and transformation. Mimi entered at the end carrying the Singkil fans she had inherited from her mother, assuming a traditional pose, but early on she threw down her fans, and performed a dance that combined elements of the dances of the Asik girl (the traditional supporting role that had been danced by her Tita Norma) and the Princess (that had been performed by her mother). But, without the fans or the traditional "Sari Manok" head gear, she constituted her own independent mode of expression on a stage without even the bamboo poles (and symbolic dangers) of the traditional dance.[30]

The production finally offered its own model of contemporary, transformative, and interdisciplinary interculturalism both within and beyond the Filipino community, and built its own performative memory. Because of course, like *Fish Eyes*, this was not dance, but movement-based theatre, transforming a traditional performance form while using its modes of embodiment to inform an innovative theatrical practice within Canada. The production was intercultural, moreover, in the constitution of the company and its audience address. The playwright, director, composer, and four of the five actors were from various Filipino backgrounds and generations of immigration, and much of the rehearsal process explored those relationships and identities, cultivating a shared intracultural memory. But it was important to the playwright that the show was staged, *not* by the specifically Filipino Carlos Bulosan Theatre Company, but by fu-GEN Asian Canadian Theatre – "it's a work for fu-GEN," she says – and no small part of the cultural work it performed had to do with fu-GEN's ongoing project of constituting diasporic pan-Asian subjectivities in Toronto through shared intercultural memory. The set and costume designers were both Chinese Canadian, the fifth cast member Chinese/Scottish Canadian, and the stage manager Korean Canadian. The only people involved in rehearsals who were not of Asian descent were South Asian Canadian lighting designer Arun Srinivasan, Swiss Canadian choreographer Clare Preuss, and myself, a third generation Canadian of Anglo/Scottish descent.[31] And the production's intended audience constituted a series of concentric circles: the Filipino community, expanding outward to the Asian Canadian community, beyond that to a burgeoning arts and culture audience from non-dominant cultures collaborating in various kinds of solidarity – the "brown caucus" – and finally, least importantly to the creators, to a dominant-culture audience – all united in a kind of embodied but "prosthetic" memory functioning to shift and complicate dominant understandings of the city as imagined community.

The Sheep and the Whale

In Africa, when a young man begins to think and ask questions, they give him a potion. When he takes it, he loses his memory, he doesn't know where he's from or what his name is anymore, and his body only knows how to do one thing: walk North, always North without ever looking back…. Then, they take out the young man's heart, bury it in the sand and say, 'Now, leave your heart in the South, and go find your memory in the North.' I can't stay in the South, because I won't have a memory, and I can't stay in the North because I won't have a heart…. Here, halfway between North and South, I'm more fragile than a spider web, because I don't have either a heart or a memory.[32]

These lines are spoken by the African Stowaway, who is ultimately thrown overboard, "here, halfway between North and South," by the crew of the ship that constitutes the set of *The Sheep and the Whale*. The play was written in French by Moroccan Canadian Ahmed Ghazali, translated into English by Quebecker Bobby Theodore, and directed at Theatre Passe Muraille by Iranian Canadian Soheil Parsa in a coproduction by Parsa's Modern Times Stage Company and Cahoots Theatre Projects in February 2007. The play presents a very different relationship between intercultural memory and ritual performance than those I've been looking at, a differently gendered setting from the women-centered spaces of *Fish Eyes* and *Singkil*, and a very different vision of diaspora. The immigrants here are illegal, desperate refugees and the stakes are literally life and death. And cultural memory, as represented here, is traumatic and involuntary.

The Sheep and the Whale is set in the Strait of Gibraltar onboard a dilapidated, once Russian, now multinational "Oceans International" freighter.[33] The ship has just come upon a storm-ravaged boat that has sunk smuggling Morrocan refugees into Europe. As the play opens, the crew is fishing ten dead bodies, plus the surviving smuggler, out of the sea, and the subsequent action occurs as the Russian Captain requests permission to take the bodies into port – somewhere. Gibraltar won't take them because it's not their problem; Algeciras won't take them because "it happens all the time"[34]; and Tangiers isn't responding because they are celebrating Aïd El-Kebir, the Festival of Sacrifice at which each family slaughters a sheep in memory of the prophet Ibrahim.

Ghazali's stage directions articulate the setting allegorically as the ship of the world: its containers, corridors and dark places represent "The South, Africa, the jungle, the north of Paris, the ghetto, housing projects, shantytowns of Bombay, Harlem, the cemetary, a mess, the 3rd World, the tribe, the medina of Fez"; its cabins represent "Europe, the Western World, the modern city, the rich North, the skyscrapers, the bourgeois neighborhoods"; and its deck "the gulf between North and South, between Europe and Africa, between the West and the East, between Blacks and Whites, rich and poor, modern and primitive."[35] The characters also function in part allegorically, the stowaways, the survivor and the dead representing the dark places of the ship and the world, the crew the liminal space between that is also the Strait of Gibraltar, and the passengers, Europe.

But those passengers consist of an interracial couple, the French Hélène, metonymic of Europe, and her partner Hassan, who, we discover at the same time she does, arrived in France illegally, "snuck across the Strait […] like them" – that is, the dead refugees.[36] It is Hassan's crisis of involuntary memory on which the action hinges. The couple is returning to Paris from a holiday on the Canary Islands, which Hassan has unconsciously chosen because of its proximity to his native Morocco. He has spent his time in Europe, like the Stowaway, acquiring a new memory, suppressing his heart and his memories of Africa. But confronted with the fate of his compatriots, his European identity begins to crumble. He begins involuntarily to speak with an accent, and later in Arabic, as he becomes increasingly disoriented. He dredges up memories of his failures as a child to perform the sacrifice required at Aïd El-Kebir, failure that he associates with his repression of memory: his refusal to allow Hélène to learn Arabic, his refusal to entertain the idea of a holiday in Morocco, his refusal of a Moroccan identity in diaspora. But as the action proceeds he comes increasingly to identify with the drowned Moroccans, his "brothers,"[37] as his embodied cultural memories return with a vengeance. He catches himself "humming Moroccan songs. Then words started slipping off my tongue like pieces of wood coming off a wreck..."[38] He chooses, finally, to join the corpses on the deck as a "museum of humanity,"[39] and ultimately the play stages his nightmarish re-enactment of Aïd El-Kebir – this play's performative equivalent of the dances in *Fish Eyes* and *Singkil* – in which he is stripped to the waist and forced to perform the ritual of sacrifice. He emerges from the dream letting out "great screams of rage, like someone undergoing an exorcism" (see *Figure 3*).[40]

Figure 3: Andy Valasquez (centre) as Hassan, with Debbie Y. Nichols and David Collins performing Hassan's nightmarish re-enactment of Aïd El-Kebir, the ritual of sacrifice in Ahmed Ghazali's *The Sheep and the Whale*. Photo: Guy Bertrand.

What issues from this is Hassan's brutal offstage sex with – rape of? – Hélène-as-Europe,[41] and his equally nightmarish, prophetic vision of Europe overcome by its "others" literally walking across the accumulation of corpses filling the Strait.[42] He and Hélène finally separate, each returning to her or his native culture, their embodiment of any kind of utopion intercultural vision a dismal failure. It is this pessimistic vision that Jean Yoon lamented in her keynote address to the "Shipping of Souls" conference held at Passe Muraille in association with the run of the play.[43] It would seem that both Hassan's and Hélène's cultural memories are intransigent, determinate, and militate against any final form of intercultural exchange.

In terms of what is *represented* in the play, in the Strait of Gibraltar, Yoon's reading is correct. But the rehearsal process in Toronto, the production's embodiment of that process and its reception represent something different. Parsa cast the show, as he does most Modern Times' productions, broadly interculturally, and with the exception of roles that require specific racial identification – the Black Stowaway, the white European woman, the Russian Captain – across racial lines. Parsa trained in Western acting methods in Tehran, ironically, and after fleeing Iran in the wake of the Islamic revolution educated himself in Persian/Iranian performance forms – acquiring "mnemonic reserves" as Majumdar had done at the University of British Columbia – studying theatre at Toronto's York University. His company is dedicated to working interculturally across Eastern and Western performance forms, and he casts actors from different traditions and styles of theatre in his shows, which rely heavily on a kind of neo-modernist stylization, including stylized movement.

Parsa's staging of Hassan's nightmare vision of the Aïd El-Kebir ritual is a case in point. The production process modelled communal ways of dealing with trauma memory through ethical witnessing, performance and testimony, the multicultural cast and audience engaging in what Roger Simon (with Mario Di Paolantonio and Mark Clamen) calls "remembrance as praxis," where "public practices of memory can have a transitive function … as actions that 'pass over' and take effect on another person or persons."[44] Parsa describes early rehearsals of the scene:

> The actors read the piece, and at the end they started dancing. Some people tried to please me and do some Sufi dance, turning around. And I said, 'Oh my god, this is so deadly. It's so folkloric….' I stopped everybody and said, 'Look, the worst thing in theatre, especially in terms of movement – if you don't know the dance, if you don't know the culture – is to start imitating…. Let's simplify it. What is the essence of this scene?'

What the actors finally performed was less imitation than homage and witnessing, as their bodies assumed the truth of traumatic events that, through performing the play, they and the audience were witnessing (that is, "bearing witness to"). Like the bearers of Ross Chambers' "orphaned memory," the players and the play in *The Sheep and the Whale* became the bearers and transmitters of the memories of the dead – "their bodies strewn across the bottoms of the oceans and the seas" – to whom the play was dedicated.[45]

If in its *representation* of interculturalism, then, *The Sheep and the Whale* was pessimistic, as process and production the show embodied intercultural solidarities in Toronto, and enacted a transference of embodied performative forms of cultural memory – in this case, trauma memory – through transformative movement. The cast member who came closest in performance to the Sufi dance tradition was an African Canadian dancer with no cultural links to Morocco or to Islam.

The Scrubbing Project

I will carry you. I will care for you, I will feed you, and I will sing you songs of comfort.
I will wash away the dirt, and the ragged flecks of flesh and skin
And you will be warm
And you will be loved
       And I will build memory.[46]

These lines are spoken by Esperanza, "the massacre collector" played by Monique Mojica in Turtle Gals Performance Ensemble's 2005-06 production of *The Scrubbing Project*. She says this as she gathers up the bones of her ancestors that she carries with her always, along with, as Mojica says, "the history of Native women on this continent."[47] *The Scrubbing Project*, collectively written and performed by Turtle Gals Performance Ensemble (consisting at that time of founders Jani Lauzon, Monique Mojica and Michelle St. John[48]), is entirely about, as the flyer for the 2002 production said, "Identity, Tradition, and Memory." It extends still further the role of the audience as participant-witnesses of involuntary trauma memory, while also consciously attempting to reconnect with, rebuild, and reinvent pre-contact cultural memories and communities as a "project" in healing.

The play moves between the celestial, Broadway-inflected "Star World" realm of three "angels" – Winged Victory, Dove and Valkyrie (see *Figure*

4) – and the abject human world of "three raggedy-assed half-breeds at the turn of the 21st Century"[49] – Esperanza, Blessed Ophelia and Branda X – whom the starworld characters are sent by an ethereal, voice-over "Lydia" to help. Branda's daughter has been taken away and is lost to her; Esperanza can't get beyond the victim position, bury the bones of her dead and move to recovery; and Ophelia is trapped at age 13 in her self image as a Catholic Saint. All, in the words of the play's darkly comic "support group," are "living with genocide": "My name is Blessed Ophelia, and I am living with genocide. / Hello, Blessed Ophelia."[50]

Figure 4: The "Star World" of The Turtle Gals' *The Scrubbing Project* with (left to right) Monique Mojica, Michelle St. John and Jani Lauzon. Photo: Nir Bareket.

This is is not a play about diaspora in the same sense as the others I've been dealing with, nor is it about immigration, although immigration plays a role. These Aboriginal women, *as* Aboriginal, are displaced, spiritually and materially, *within* the land of their ancestors and, as mixed race women, within their own bodies. The scale of the rupture effected in cultural memory by colonization, moreover, is monumental, defeating any of the pieties or potential nostalgias of the official muliticultural policies from which Native peoples were excluded. But *The Scrubbing Project* is nevertheless deeply, personally intercultural, dealing as it does with the mixed races of its creators, and indeed, through the sexual technologies of colonization, of most Aboriginal peoples throughout Turtle Island (the name used among many First Nations for North America). Lauzon, Mojica and St. John are from diverse heritages: the Métis Lauzon, as she says, is "Finndian"[51]; Mojica is Kuna-Rappahonnock and Ashknazi, her father being a European Holocaust survivor; and St. John is Wampanoag and Ashkenazi, her immediate Jewish roots being in Brooklyn. But their cultural memory is no less real or material for being mixed:

> We build memory ...
> A *wailing wall* that will stretch across this *grandmother turtle.*[52]

The mandate of Turtle Gals is to explore "a continuum of past, present, and future expressed as stories using our bodies and voices. We draw on traditional forms of story telling, oratory, song and dance integrating them with current technology and popular culture to develop non-linear multi-disciplinary theatre forms,"[53] including, in the case of *The Scrubbing Project,* Broadway musicals, vaudeville, Marx Brothers' and other slapstick routines, Medicine Shows, and a ritual of remembrance invented before our eyes, in which the performers' different backgrounds, memories, and traditions come to the fore – as when Ophelia brings gefilte fish and Branda Kentucky Fried Chicken to the Native ceremony, or when Esperanza finds death camps in her "bundle" and genocide on both sides of the family.[54]

The hybrid form of *The Scrubbing Project* grows out of the writer/performers' own hybridized identities and their own internalized racism as a manifestation of trauma. But the play also centrally deals, as Anishnaabe scholar Jill Carter points out, with "recovery, remembrance, revitalization and reintegration of *all* Aboriginal peoples"[55]:

> With *The Scrubbing Project* Turtle Gals has invented a container – and imagined a ceremony in which to frame it – that unabashedly celebrates our dualities, that suggests a methodology for their integration and balance, and that locates (and locates us around) an essential centre.[56]

The Scrubbing Project, then, draws upon traditional performance forms re-mixed and reconstituted as it re-members the dismemberment that was colonization, and *assumes* and *heals* the trauma memories of that history. It attempts to perform into being new intercultural memories and new ways of living in the world through new rituals that are nevertheless rooted in the blood memories of the indigenous and mixed-race first peoples of Turtle Island.

Conclusion

The Scrubbing Project ends with the unfurling out into the audience of three very long birchbark scrolls listing the names of the intercultural dead, which spectators pass back through the house, linking those onstage and off as participants in a powerful ritual of testimony, witnessing and remembrance. As Carter argues, "this *Project* does not simply evoke mood, invite identification, or solicit sympathy. The performers demand my participation in the conversation: They remember that *we might remember together* – 'I add my breath to your breath.'"[57]

> It is a *project* that demands our utter engagement and active participation.... *The Scrubbing Project*, as a contemporary rite of re-membering and healing, does not merely *show* us the way: It moves our feet along the path, and transforms us from passive receptors into acitve agents in the ongoing *project* of creation and re-creation.[58]

Carter is writing as a Native woman, albeit from a different First Nation than Lauzon, Mojica, or St. John. But she is describing an experience and a project that reaches across greater differences than this, to which each of the shows I have been discussing contributes. Each of these shows at its best creates, and contributes to, the constitution of Toronto as a genuinely heterotopic space "of alternate ordering"[59] in which the troublesome doubling of Roach's surrogation becomes a prosthetic suturing together of new, re-membered forms with the traditional performance forms that haunt them. Rejecting the atomizing nostalgias of official multiculturalism, each of these shows represents, enacts, and transmits to diverse Toronto participant-audiences a genuinely transformative, border-crossing, intercultural memory, the visceral stitching together from below of a larger intercultural community in the city through performative acts of re-membering across real, acknowledged and respected difference.[60]

Works Cited

Bannerji, H. (2000) *The Dark Side of the Nation: Essays on Multiculturalism, Nationalism, and Gender*, Toronto: Canadian Scholars Press.

Bissoondath, N. (1994) *Selling Illusions: The Cult of Multiculturalism in Canada*, Toronto: Penguin.

Butler, J. (1990) "Performative Acts and Gender Constitution: An Essay on Phenomenology and Feminist Theory," in Case, S.-E. (Ed.) *Performing Feminisms*, Baltimore: Johns Hopkins UP, pp.270-82.

Carter, J. (2006) "Writing, Righting, 'Riting': *The Scrubbing Project* Remembers a New 'Nation' and Reconfigures Ancient Ties," *alt.theatre* 4, pp.13-17.

Chambers, R. (2002) "Orphaned Memories, Foster Writing, Phantom Pain: The *Fragments* Affair," in Miller and Tougaw (Eds.) *Extremities: Trauma, Testimony, and Community*, Urbana: University of Illinois Press, pp.92-111.

Connerton, P. (1989) *How Societies Remember*, Cambridge: Cambridge University Press.

Foster, C. (2005) *Where Race Does Not Matter: The New Spirit of Modernity*, Toronto: Penguin.

Foucault, M. (1986) "Of Other Spaces," *Diacritics*, 16.1, pp.22-27.

Ghazali, A. (2006) *The Sheep and the Whale*, trans. Bobby Theodore. Unpublished production script.

Gunew, S. (2004) *Haunted Nations: The Colonial Dimensions of Multiculturalisms*, London: Routledge.

Halbwachs, M. (1992) *On Collective Memory*, ed. and trans. Lewis A. Cosner, Chicago: University of Chicago Press.

Hernandez, C. (2006) *Singkil*. Unpublished production script.

—. (2007) Personal Interview, Factory Theatre, Toronto, 29 January.

Hetherington, K. (1997) *The Badlands of Modernity: Heterotopia and Social Ordering*, London: Routledge.

Hirsch, M. (1997) *Family Frames: Photography, Narrative, and Postmemory*, Cambridge, Mass: Harvard University Press.

—. (2002) "Marked by Memory: Feminist Reflections on Trauma and Transmission," in Miller and Tougaw (Eds.) *Extremities: Trauma, Testimony, and Community*, Urbana: Univeristy of Illinois Press, pp.71-91.

Kamboureli, S. (2000) *Scandalous Bodies: Diasporic Literature in English Canada*, Toronto: Oxford University Press.

Knowles, R. (2009) "Multicultural Text, Intercultural Performance: The Performance Ecology of Contemporary Toronto," in Hopkins, D. J., S. Orr and K. Solga (Eds.) *Performance and the City*, Basingstoke: Palgrave Macmillan.

Landsberg, A. (2004) *Prosthetic Memory: The Transformation of American Remembrance in the Age of Mass Culture*, New York: Columbia University Press.

Majumdar, A. (2006) *Fish Eyes*. Unpublished manuscript.

—. (2007) Personal Interview, Epicure Café, Toronto.

Miller, N. K. and J. Tougaw (Eds.) (2002) *Extremities: Trauma, Testimony, and Community*, Urbana: University of Illinois Press.

Mojica, M. (2006) "Chocolate Woman Dreams the Milky Way," Distinguished Lecture Series (Aboriginal Studies Program and First Nations House), University of Toronto, 30 January.

Multiculturalism and Citizenship Canada (1991) *The Canadian Multiculturalism Act: A Guide for Canadians*, Ottawa: Minister of Supply and Services Canada.

Nolan, Y. (2006) Personal Interview, Native Earth Performing Arts Office, Distillery District, Toronto, 29 June.

Parsa, S. (2007) Personal Interview, Balzac's, Distillery District, Toronto, 6 March.

Qadeer, M. and S. Kumar (2006) "Ethnic Enclaves and Social Cohesion," in *Our Diverse Cities: Challenges and Opportunities*, *Canadian Journal of Urban Research* 15.2, Supplement, pp.1-17.

Roach, J. (1996) *Cities of the Dead: Circum-Atlantic Performance*, New York: Columbia University Press.

Shohat, E. and R. Stam (1994) *Unthinking Eurocentrism: Multiculturalism and the Media*. London: Routledge.

Simon, R. with M. Di Paolantonio and M. Clamen (2005) "Remembrance as Praxis and the Ethics of the Interhuman," in Simon, R. (Ed.) *The Touch of the Past: Remembrance, Learning, and Ethics*, New York: Palgrave Macmillan, pp.132-55.

Sturken, M. (1999) "Narratives of Recovery: Repressed Memory as Cultural Memory," in Bal, M., J. Crewe, and L. Spitzer (Eds.) *Acts of Memory: Cultural Recall in the Present*, Hanover: University Press of New England, pp.231-48.

Syerah. "Summerworks Theatre Festival: Fish Eyes," *Mybindi.com* 2000, at: http://mybindi.com/arts-entertainment/WHATSON/fisheyes.cfm (accessed 5 June 2007).

Taylor, D. (2003) *The Archive and the Repertoire: Performing Cultural Memory in the Americas*. Durham: Duke UP.

Turtle Gals Performance Ensemble, Information Sheet, Turtle Gals Performance Ensemble office files.

—. *The Scrubbing Project* (2005) Unpublished touring script.

—. *The Scrubbing Project* (2002) co-produced by Turtle Gals Performance Ensemble, Native Earth Performing Arts, and Factory Theatre at Factory Theatre, Promotional Flyer.

Yoon, J. (2007) Keynote Address, The Shipping of Souls Conference, Theatre Passe Muraille, Toronto, 26 February.

Notes

[1] Mohammed Qadeer, and Sandeep Kumar (2006) "Ethnic Enclaves and Social Cohesion," *Our Diverse Cities: Challenges and Opportunities*, *Canadian Journal of Urban Research*, 15.2, Supplement, pp.1-17.

[2] Cecil Foster (2005) *Where Race Does Not Matter: The New Spirit of Modernity*, Toronto: Penguin.

[3] For critiques of Canadian multiculturalism see Neil Bissoondath (1994) *Selling Illusions: The Cult of Multiculturalism in Canada*, Toronto: Penguin; Himani Bannerji (2000) *The Dark Side of the Nation: Essays on Multiculturalism, Nationalism, and Gender*, Toronto: Canadian Scholars Press; Sneja Gunew (2004) *Haunted Nations: The Colonial Dimensions of Multiculturalisms*, London: Routledge; Smaro Kamboureli (2000) *Scandalous Bodies: Diasporic Literature in English Canada*, Toronto: Oxford University Press; Ric Knowles (2009) "Multicultural Text, Intercultural Performance: The Performance Ecology of Contemporary Toronto," in Hopkins, Orr and Solga (Eds.) *Performance and the City*, Basingstoke: Palgrave Macmillan.

[4] Multiculturalism and Citizenship Canada (1991) *The Canadian Multiculturalism Act: A Guide for Canadians*, Ottawa: Minister of Supply and Services Canada.

[5] Bannerji (2000), pp.215-50.

[6] Maurice Halbwachs (1992) *On Collective Memory*, Chicago: University of Chicago Press.

[7] Paul Connerton (1989) *How Societies Remember*, Cambridge: Cambridge University Press.

[8] Judith Butler (1990) "Performative Acts and Gender Constitution: An Essay on Phenomenology and Feminist Theory," in Case, S.E. (Ed.) *Performing Feminisms*, Baltimore: Johns Hopkins University Press.

[9] Joseph Roach (1996) *Cities of the Dead: Circum-Atlantic Performance*, New York: Columbia University Press, p.26; my emphasis.

[10] Diana Taylor (2003) *The Archive and the Repertoire: Performing Cultural Memory in the Americas*. Durham: Duke University Press, pp.174-5.

[11] See Ross Chambers (2002) "Orphaned Memories, Foster Writing, Phantom Pain: The *Fragments* Affair," in Miller and Tougaw (Eds.) *Extremities: Trauma, Testimony, and Community*, Urbana: University of Illinois Press, pp.92-111.

[12] Marita Sturken (1999) "Narratives of Recovery: Repressed Memory as Cultural Memory," in Bal, Crewe and Spitzer (Eds.) *Acts of Memory: Cultural Recall in the Present*, Hanover: University Press of New England, pp.231-48.

[13] Marianne Hirsch (2002) "Marked by Memory: Feminist Reflections on Trauma and Transmission," in Miller and Tougaw, pp.71-91

[14] See Alison Landsberg (2004) *Prosthetic Memory: The Transformation of American Remembrance in the Age of Mass Culture*, New York: Columbia UP, p.14 and *passim*. Landsberg's concept of prosthetic memory is compelling, but her work is worrisomely indifferent about the distinction between the memory of actual events that did not happen to the remembering subject and the inculcation of manufactured cultural memories through the use of powerful mass media.

[15] Paul Connerton (1989) *How Societies Remember*, Cambridge: Cambridge University Press, pp.4-5.

[16] Marianne Hirsch (1997) *Family Frames: Photography, Narrative, and Postmemory*, Cambridge, Mass: Harvard University Press.

[17] Ella Shohat and Robert Stam (1994) *Unthinking Eurocentrism: Multiculturalism and the Media*. London: Routledge, p.359.

[18] Knowles (2009).

[19] Turtle Gals (2005) *The Scrubbing Project*. Unpublished touring script, p.37.

[20] Anita Majumdar (2007) Personal Interview with the author, Epicure Café, Toronto.

[21] *Ibid.*

[22] Anita Majumdar (2006) *Fish Eyes*. Unpublished manuscript, pp.2-3.

[23] *Ibid.*, p.1.

[24] *Ibid.*, p.2.

[25] *Ibid.*, p.3.

[26] *Ibid.*, p.9.

[27] Majumdar (2007).

[28] Syerah. "Summerworks Theatre Festival: Fish Eyes," *Mybindi.com*, at: http://mybindi.com/arts-entertainment/WHATSON/fisheyes.cfm (accessed 5 June 2007).

[29] Catherine Hernandez (2007) Personal Interview, Factory Theatre, Toronto, 29 January. In the play itself, Norma twice tells Mimi "you've been dancing the Singkil your entire life" (p.19 & p.60), the second time giving her the dated photograph.

[30] These transformations were more a function of Aquino's production than of Hernandez's script, which had originally called for a much more traditional version of the Singkil at the end – another example of the negotiation of subjectivities in diaspora.

[31] I worked on the show with Nina Lee Aquino as an Associate Dramaturg; pre-production dramaturgy was by Yvette Nolan, the Algonquin artistic director of Native Earth Performing Arts.

[32] Ahmed Ghazali (2006) *The Sheep and the Whale*, trans. Bobby Theodore. Unpublished production script, p.23.

[33] The play mounts a searing critique of economic globalization as productive of the kinds of human displacement that it represents, the details of which are beyond the scope of this essay. The production itself, however, represents a grass-roots transcultural collaboration that speaks back to corporate globalization.

[34] Ghazali (2006), p.9.

[35] *Ibid.*, pp.2-3.

[36] *Ibid.*, pp.46-7.

[37] *Ibid.*, p.49.

[38] *Ibid.*, p.44.

[39] *Ibid.*, p.48.

[40] *Ibid.*, p.42.

[41] The gendered fact of Hassan's occupying the central subjectivity while Hélène plays a largely symbolic role is disturbing, and leads almost inevitably to a rape that may be emblematic, but is nevertheless played out on the body of a woman – though in production it happened offstage. The relative bleakness of this production as opposed to *Fish Eyes*, *Singkil*, or *The Scrubbing Project* is related to its being gendered male and taking place in an overwhelmingly masculine shipboard setting.

[42] Ghazali (2006), pp.47-8.

[43] Jean Yoon (2007) Keynote Address, The Shipping of Souls Conference, Theatre Passe Muraille, Toronto, 26 February.

[44] Roger Simon, with Mario Di Paolantonio and Mark Clamen, (2005) "Remembrance as Praxis and the Ethics of the Interhuman," in Roger Simon (Ed.) *The Touch of the Past: Remembrance, Learning, and Ethics*, New York: Palgrave Macmillan, pp.132-3.

[45] Ghazali (2006), p.2.

[46] Turtle Gals (2005), p.37.

[47] Monique Mojica (2006) "Chocolate Woman Dreams the Milky Way," Distinguished Lecture Series (Aboriginal Studies Program and First Nations House), University of Toronto, 30 January, p.8.

[48] Monique Mojica left the ensemble in the summer of 2006, and has since been replaced by Falen Johnson and Cheri Maracle.

[49] Turtle Gals (2005), p.4.

[50] *Ibid.*, p.14.

[51] *Ibid.*, p.24.

[52] *Ibid.*, p.44; my emphasis.

[53] Turtle Gals, Information Sheet.

[54] The complexities of *The Scrubbing Project*, of the vast body of scholarship on Holocaust memory, and of the burgeoning field of mixed-race studies make a thorough exploration of this moment beyond the scope of this essay.

[55] Jill Carter (2006) "Writing, Righting, 'Riting': *The Scrubbing Project* Remembers a New 'Nation' and Reconfigures Ancient Ties," *alt.theatre* 4, pp.1-2; emphasis in the original.

[56] *Ibid.*, p.14.

[57] *Ibid.*, quoting *The Srubbing Project*, p.33.

[58] *Ibid.*, p.17; emphasis in the original.

[59] See Michel Foucault (1986) "Of Other Spaces," *Diacritics*, 16.1, pp.22-27; and Kevin Hetherington (1997) *The Badlands of Modernity: Heterotopia and Social Ordering*, London: Routledge, p.viii.

[60] This chapter was previously published in Marc Maufort & Caroline De Wagter (Eds.) (2008) *Signatures of the Past: Cultural Memory in Contemporary Anglophone North American Drama*, Bruxelles: P.I.E. Peter Lang. We thank the publishers and editors for their kind permission to reprint it here.

EMBODIMENT OF MEMORY
AND THE DIASPORIC AGENT
IN AKRAM KHAN COMPANY'S *BAHOK*

ROYONA MITRA

The recent proliferation of conceptual writings on "the body" and "embodiment" within dance studies suggests that the lived body, with its embodied intellect, feelings and experiences, has come to occupy the heart of contemporary performance practice. Critical enquiry of current dance practice has shifted from analysing the body as an object through which form and choreographic structures are played out, to recognising the body as belonging to a subject, thereby acknowledging its historicity and all its contextual relations as embodied within it. Ian Burkitt substantiates that embodiment shifts bodies from being mere passive constructs to becoming "productive" (capable of transformation through acts), "communicative" (activating power through generating/deconstructing meaning), "powerful" (by using the ability to transform ideology) and "thinking" (by exercising agency).[1]

An equally prevalent concept has been the theorising of the body as a storehouse of "cultural memory." Jan Assmann has articulated the need for human beings to find a means through which to sustain the practice of social customs and ideological behaviour patterns through generations.[2] Assmann suggests that cultural memory enables the transmission of such socialised knowledge through time. Cultural Studies' recent postulations on the relationships between nation, culture, community and individual have once again placed the body at the centre of these negotiations. Through the modernist project, the body has been constructed as an ideological apparatus via which ritualised social customs, shared histories and institutionalised cultural memories are carried and transmitted through generations. The body houses a shared, collective and communal history that is referred to as "cultural memory." Confined to a specific group of people contained within an artificial border like that of a nation, cultural memory functions as a strategic mechanism of belonging and inclusion. It is vital to note however that this body's security lies in its ability to activate and exercise its cultural memory only within the confines or contexts of the nation that lends it an identity.

Outside the borders of its own nation, however, having to live alongside bodies with competing cultural memories and unable to find other bodies sharing its own history, the body's cultural memory ceases to remain a common reference point of shared existence. To this end, I propose that within a transnational context, having to survive alongside bodies with parallel cultural memories, the distinct cultural memory stored within a singular body can be dismantled. In its place, over time, a new shared experience and language emerges in the bodies of those who occupy this transitory space. This new language is not permanent and consequently not institutionalised into becoming a cultural memory but becomes a part of the growth of one's transnational identity. I further propose that the dismantling of cultural memory and the growth of new shared experiences fortify the embodiment of simultaneous and multiple reference points within singular nomadic bodies. It is the potential for ideological resistance that lies latent within this transnational body that appeals to me; the body that is not governed by any singular and shared system of belonging and whose powers of expression are not monitored via the ideological control of "cultural memory."

This chapter is dedicated to the study of the corporealities of such transnational "diasporic agents" and their evocation of memory, home and hybridity in *Bahok* (2008), the result of a recent collaboration between Akram Khan Company[3] and the National Ballet of China.[4] My analysis will rest on two inter-related frameworks that characterise diasporic existence: the contested relationship with the notion of "home" and the inherent condition of "hybridity." In recent years, postcolonial studies have attacked essentialist ideas of "home" by acknowledging multiple narratives of migration from "homelands" to the creation of multiple homes in transnational spaces. Many have further argued that a migrant's associations with dual (if not multiple) homes can give rise to hybrid identity constructions.[5] Embedded within the contested and romanticised imaginings of "home" is the diasporic agent's embodiment of cultural memory, and, I propose, its gradual dismantling into the folds of a transnational existence.

Bahok, an artistic commentary on the postmodern realities of globalisation and travel, is an exposé of the experiences of eight distinct individuals who find themselves stuck in an unidentified global transit zone. Each of these individuals is a *bahok*, a carrier (in Bengali) of their embodied history, thoughts, experiences and intellect, and this liminal transit zone makes space for them to shed their literal and metaphoric load before, and instigated by, each other. *Bahok* exploits the emotional and physical space that opens up between the individuals' past rootedness and their present and shared uprootedness and makes them confront their nomadic reality. It further demonstrates that for these eight individuals in search of belonging, their distinct and embodied cultural memory becomes irrelevant outside the borders of their national identities. As a commentary on embodiment, memory and identity, *Bahok* is therefore an ideal subject of analysis and theorisation.

Bahok and Home

An urban, cold and grey environment washed by a very stark white light defines the space where *Bahok* unfolds. Several wooden chairs, equally utilitarian, strategically create the atmosphere of a waiting room. A huge digital message board hangs from centre stage and displays messages reminiscent of airport announcement screens. Through the course of the performance, at strategic points, it reads, "Please Wait," "Delayed," "Cancelled" and other, similar messages to draw out the waiting game for the performers. Gradually we encounter eight travellers, with their distinct and idiosyncratic bodies, characteristics and baggage. They have all clearly arrived from somewhere but cannot find a way out. They seem unsure of their destinations while simultaneously searching for their places of origin. Each of their bodies has been altered by journeying and bears the marks of the emotional and physical condition of transience and rupture. We witness volatile bodies, agile bodies, grounded bodies, tired bodies, frivolous bodies, playful bodies, fragmented bodies and distorted bodies, all in this one liminal space.

Helen Grehan postulates on the impact that dislocation and relocation has on the body of the diasporic subject and asks,

> [...] how is the body marked or inscribed by this journeying and how does the diasporic subject inscribe him/herself within/on the landscapes s/he traverses?[6]

Additionally I question how the diasporic space shapes the body that moves in and through it. Dance's reliance on the body as its primary means of communication therefore makes it an ideal discipline through which the transnational bodies in *Bahok* can be unpacked and examined. These bodies strongly insinuate through their distinctive patterns of physicality how diaspora impacts on one's embodied corporeality and lived experience. But a distinction must be drawn here between the bodies marked by the experience of *dislocation* and the bodies shaped by the experience of *relocation*.

At this stage it is vital to theorise these eight *bahoks*, these transnational subjects, as "diasporic agents." I wish to distinguish this "agent" from earlier generations of migrants whose reasons for dislocation must be acknowledged as significantly different to the migratory patterns of the more privileged future generations. So while *dislocation* was often enforced upon early generations of migrants, *relocation* has become a matter of choice and empowerment for future generations. The latter category of migrants are diasporic agents: those who are empowered by mobility and flow of capital to make a choice to relocate, privileged with the agency that arises from their global positioning, and enabled to comment upon local and global issues with equal impact.

In a 1996 study on literature of the Indian diaspora, Vijay Mishra makes a similar point of distinction between the "Old Indian Diaspora" and the "New Indian Diaspora." He claims that while the Old Indian Diaspora is a product of colonial and classic capitalism, the New Indian Diaspora is backed by mid to late twentieth-century advanced and global capitalism and its consequent by-product of cosmopolitanism.[7] Nikos Papastergiadis considers the potential agency residing in the new cosmopolitan migrant and its impact on a host country.[8] He argues that migrants in metropolitan spaces become agents of cultural and social changes, empowered to transform the host country at many different dimensions. The subject of Mishra's New Indian Diaspora is my diasporic agent, and a product of globalisation. But there is a key distinction between the two concepts. While Mishra focuses on the Indian diaspora in literature, my focus is global and extends beyond literature into multiple disciplines. In this sense it mirrors more closely Papastergiadis' cosmopolitan migrants who become agents of social and cultural change in a host country at multiple dimensions.

In dance, Akram Khan Company is one such diasporic and cosmopolitan agent. Its Artistic Director, Akram Khan, is a second generation British-Bangladeshi, who has positioned himself as a global and cosmopolitan artist through transnational collaborations. The mobility offered by global finance of advanced capitalism supports Khan's transnational operation. Farooq Chaudhry, the company's producer, echoes Khan's desire to explore the nature of diasporic existences. A second generation British-Pakistani, Chaudhry grew up through years of strategic identity negotiation, and realised the importance of mobility. Khan's and Chaudhry's unique creative partnership and their shared desire to explore corporeal expressions of diasporic reality are enabled by the mobility they can access as transnational diasporic agents. *Bahok* is a manifestation of their shared understanding of nomadic lives. The agency articulated within the performance is therefore the agency of Khan as the Artistic Director, mediated through the corporeal voice and agency of the eight artists whose personal narratives penetrate *Bahok*. These eight artists come from Spain, India, South Africa, China, Korea and Slovakia. Additionally the agency in this analysis is my agency as a diasporic agent, a first generation British-Indian, living and working as an academic in the UK, empowered by the privilege and mobility of both finance and knowledge that support me.

To understand the experience of our *bahoks* we therefore need to understand their journeying as *relocations*, enabled through choice and mobility and harbouring interventionist agency. These *bahoks* are thus embodied subjects, and in Burkitt's terms their bodies are productive, communicative, powerful and thinking agents. We also need to understand that as a result of their multiple relocations, our *bahoks* embody multiple registers of identity and their affiliations to "home" are thus always shifting. If, for the global transnational subject, "travelling is foregrounded as a cultural practice then dwelling, too, needs to be reconceived – no longer simply the ground from which travelling departs, and to which it returns."[9] Instead home exists in multiple dimensions for the diasporic agent and is "a desire that is fulfilled or denied in varying measure to the subject… usually represented as fixed, rooted, stable – the very antithesis of travel."[10]

In *Bahok* we experience this pluralistic embodiment of homes and different individuals connect with homes at different levels. For the Spanish Lali, the search for "home" as place of origin and "home" as destination signify multiple affiliations to the concept. She is a near psychotic woman whose highly volatile and restless body represents the extent to which her nomadic existence has been embodied within her corporeality. Her inability to remain still or contained in one place, the sharp angularity of her movements, the simultaneous forward and upward leaps and her perpetually forward leaning spine suggest a body that occupies the future and is always relocating. Lali does not know where she comes from and does not know where she is heading and she has truly forgotten everything about herself. She tries to piece together her past from the facts written on torn bits of paper which she carries on her at all times. But the truth is that Lali's embodied identity is enmeshed upon and into her body as she transposes her emotional fragility into a highly volatile physicality that perpetually lacks calm. She is incapable of sharing any memory of the past as her body constantly occupies a temporality ahead of herself and her present becomes ephemeral as soon it is played out. She also functions as a confessional catalyst in *Bahok* destabilising the apparently more grounded individuals with her volatility into expressing distant memories of home.

One such individual is a South African woman who on the surface appears calm and collected. While recalling an interrogation scene at UK immigration, where she helps her Korean friend as a translator, she suddenly gets defensive when asked what she carries in her bag. She takes out a pair of shoes which are clearly not her own and identifies them as belonging to her father. The significance of carrying her father's shoes into her present and the act of stepping into the space his feet occupied in the past is an embodiment of her memory of both home and culture at once. What follows is a sequence where we see her painfully putting on her father's shoes and with them a weight of her past. She grudgingly steps into them and relives the memory of home.

Through a fractured painful dance that separates her upper body from her lower body, her legs remain rooted to her past while her upper body attempts to move forward and beyond through jolted fragmented gestures. This sequence at once captures disjuncture and movement away from home and a simultaneous and painful connection to home which she carries deep in her sinews. The very act of putting on her father's shoes thus homes and destabilises her simultaneously. George suggests that the "word 'home' immediately connotes the private sphere of patriarchal hierarchy, gendered self-identity, shelter, comfort, nurture and protection,"[11] and the body of the South African woman urgently expresses a need to escape to the comfort and shelter of home while simultaneously escaping from its patriarchal clasps.

We also encounter an Indian man from Kerala whose connection to home exists on the end of a mobile phone call to his "amma," his mother. His need to speak in Malayalam suggests that home for him is partially a memory that can be recalled through linguistic affiliations and speaking in his "mother tongue" to his mother connects him to his sense of identity. In him we see an attempt to trace his cultural memory through his own language, a tool of communication that does not help him connect to this fellow *bahoks* but one that keeps him rooted to his past and to people outside and distant from his immediate present environment. The endless mobile phone calls eventually stop connecting as the performance develops, suggesting that holding on to his cultural memory will not move him forward in his transient state. His grounded physicality of *kalaripayatu*, a Keralite martial art form, may trick us into perceiving him as secure and rooted, but the act of calling home endlessly reveals a clear sense of uprootedness and a constant attempt to secure his roots through clinging on to the past.

Salman Rushdie writes on the human need to secure connection to our birthplace:

> To explain why we become attached to our birthplaces, we pretend that we are trees and speak of 'roots.' Look under your feet. You will not find gnarled growths sprouting through the soles. Roots, I sometimes think, are a conservative myth, designed to keep us in our places.[12]

The three *bahoks* discussed above embody Rushdie's words in completely different ways. Some are so uprooted that they are unable to occupy the present moment in favour of always dwelling in the future. Others root themselves to the past and the present simultaneously through painful negotiations, and this makes their future difficult to negotiate. Still others are so linked to their past that they have no awareness of their present, let alone their future ahead. In each instance, however, "home" becomes a politicised entity that the individual's body must negotiate as part of their transnational existence.

George suggests that beyond the geographical location that it evokes, "home" is a political concept that relies on patterns of inclusion and exclusion of different groups.[13] It is an isolationist trope that engenders difference by creating notions of belonging for subjects. In *Bahok* this becomes apparent in the linguistic trope of the Keralite man that excludes his fellow travellers from sharing his experience. George further suggests that "home" is a community that is never neutral. It is instead a politically charged space where ideological control is exercised. The South African woman's fractured body suggests its urgency to break away from the ideological control of her home's patriarchal environment while simultaneously being controlled by it. Spanish Lali embodies a nomadic transnational existence in her inability to be homed at any given point, because her volatile and fragile body *is* her home.

These multiple physical narratives are carried in individual bodies that are not contained within the borders of singular nations and singular homes. Travelling through multiple borders and setting up multiple homes calls upon the individual's body to become the vehicle through which an individual is "homed" at any given point. Thus the political act of imagining home is enmeshed with and shifted onto the corporeality of the individual's physical existence. The imaginary becomes the real and the tangible. In an interview intended to elucidate the making of *Bahok,* Akram Khan comments upon the need to disassociate a singular physical location with the notion of home and to acknowledge the body's ability to home and become homed at any given point:

> When I started my own place, the first thing I did was... to throw away, simplify, no memory. We start new and never collect anything. The memory's in the body. It doesn't have to be in material things.[14]

"Home" then becomes a multiple register and embodiment of unique experiences exclusive to what Chaudhry has called "individual systems of DNA."[15]

In *Bahok* we thus encounter eight different evocations of home to counter eight different experiences of "homelessness." The need to find communal belonging through the act of collective imagination by communities is thrown into question.[16] Instead the body of the diasporic agent becomes home and this conceptually intangible notion finds a bodily reality. And since each individual's lived experience is unique, the concept of home as a singular, geographical and homogeneous entity becomes redundant and is replaced by pluralistic expressions of corporealities. Thus, as Chaudhry's words vividly capture, a generalised and flattened concept of "home," despite the common uprootedness which we witness in our *bahoks,* is a myth in itself. It needs dismantling to acknowledge the significance of subjectivity in identity construction and its relationship to belonging within transnational contexts.

Consequently the cultural memory pertaining to national borders and essentialist notions of home disintegrates gradually, and is replaced by individual and idiosyncratic modes of behaviour that avoid any form of institutionalisation or archiving. In her influential study entitled *The Archive and the Repertoire*, Diana Taylor distinguishes between two modes of cultural memory transmission. The first is "archival memory," which includes factual memory, drawn from documents, maps, textual sources, archaeological finds and other such items that are associated with permanence and can translate across time and space. "Archival memory" separates the source of knowledge from the person acquiring the knowledge, and is unchangeable. The second is what Taylor calls "repertoire" and is that form of memory which is embodied through non-verbal, gestural, oral and corporeal means. It does not rely on the written word and is thus ephemeral and non-reproducible, since it cannot be documented via conventional archival means. Taylor advocates the value of the "repertoire" as an embodied system of knowledge to rectify the historical tendency to give value to memory in the form of the written word. Using Taylor's premise that the presence of live performance cannot be captured or transmitted through the archive, I propose that the idiosyncrasies cultivated in the individual bodies in *Bahok*, dismantling notions of collective behaviour and cultural memory, create systems of "repertoire" pertinent and ephemeral to the eight individuals who occupy the liminal transit zone. There are no collective archival behaviour patterns that dominate their interactions since they do not share cultural memory from singular national boundaries.

Despite their shared sense of uprootedness, the eight individuals in *Bahok* find it impossible to communicate with each other. Every attempt at interaction is a failure. As long as they remain confined within their own movement methodologies and refuse to negotiate a collective understanding of their situation, the *bahoks* remain dysfunctional within the liminal space. In an instance when the two Chinese women perform a ballet routine on their own, they only manage to communicate with each other while the others look on in awe of their "otherness." A physical interjection into the ballet sequence from the Keralite man with his *kalaripayatu* gestures causes a breakdown of communication and the bodies literally nearly clash as tensions seem to rise within the group.

This is heightened further when the Slovakian man expresses his annoyance at the Chinese man's insistence on documenting every fleeting moment of this liminal space on his digital camera through a beautifully crafted and highly energetic choreography of dodging being photographed. They almost get into a physical fight and are kept apart by the Korean man, who attempts to ease the tension in the group. In his anxiety he freezes into a momentary fragmented gesture which he keeps repeating like a broken record. His spinal column repeatedly leans slightly forward and then is jerked back into the centre, and his head and right arm follows this pattern endlessly. As his friend comforts him, he finally blurts out, "I'm stuck!" Linguistically, physically, spatially, temporally, emotionally, he is frozen in time between his (and their) collective points of disjuncture and inability to assimilate into this transnational zone, and this dysfunctionality is played out in and on his body.

Acknowledging a collective need to regenerate, in order to free themselves from becoming permanently "stuck" in this limbo, the individuals gradually assimilate into an ensemble group hug. In considered and carefully crafted ways, they break into a final collective and explosive expression of mutation and re-growth. The ensemble moves as one, taking time to achieve this vision of synchronicity that has grown from their liminal condition. Sometimes some individuals break free of the routine and others continue, only to be drawn back into the power of the ensemble again. Their limbs slice through the air and the bodies symbolise transience and dynamism as the rhythm and pace of the section builds to a crescendo. The speed of the bodies at times makes it difficult to distinguish between the eight bodies and their individual limbs, and the ensemble collapses into a communal mass. Akram Khan comments on this key choreographic temporality:

> Concept of carrying means you have to keep moving, you have to shift. You get stopped if you dwell in the past. [But] if you're in the present then you are constantly moving and must keep moving.[17]

In this penultimate sequence their bodies simultaneously occupy their shared present, look into their distinct futures and carry with them their individual pasts. However, because they occupy the present, their bodies are ephemeral and non-archival. Based on their shared experience of liminality, the *bahoks* create their own "repertoire" and through it a system of knowledge of the present moment.

Bahok and Hybridity

Inherent in their shared repertoire is a characteristic hybridity. "Hybridity" has been theorised as both a diasporic condition and a postmodern aesthetic. The inter-disciplinarity of the dance-theatre genre of *Bahok* is born from an intersection of theatre's search for emotive narrative and dance's reliance on the body for expression of such narrative. Dance-theatre as a genre therefore negotiates a hybrid aesthetic; but in *Bahok* this genre simultaneously embodies the condition of hybridity pertinent to diasporic agents. Hybridity too appears at multiple dimensions within the piece. In a study dedicated to tracing the role of hybridity in contemporary art and culture, Nikos Papastergiadis provides a helpful overview of existing discourses on hybridity as a condition of diasporic migration:

> Hybridity has been a much abused term. It has been both trapped in the stigmatic associations of biological essentialism and elevated to promote a form of cultural nomadology.[18]

Theorists like Homi Bhabha, Stuart Hall, Paul Gilroy and others have celebrated hybridity and its anti-essentialist critique of cultural identity.[19] They have advocated hybridity as a powerful interventionist tool that harbours agency for the diasporic subject. They further argue that it lends its subjects self-critical distancing from a singular source of identity. This can enable them to reflect simultaneously upon their place of origin and their place of settlement. This would be in line with Ian Burkitt's thoughts on the embodied subject as capable of ideological resistance as already discussed.

However, the concept of hybridity has been criticised for becoming an elitist trope that empowers a small section of an already privileged and mobile global diaspora. Alberto Moreiras critiques hybridity as a "conceptual reification" of flattened identities, and "a sort of ideological cover for capitalist reterritorialization."[20] My construct of the diasporic agent as the migrant who relocates from choice backed by finance and mobility supports Moreiras' view. Additionally, Floya Anthias believes that while "hybridity" deconstructs homogenous associations of cultural identity, in part it ironically relies on an essentialist definition of cultures to define itself.[21] Kobena Mercer writes that hybridity has become a tool for the commodification of cultural difference through the "hypervisibility" of ethnicity.[22]

Papastergiadis argues that the term now suffers from a connotation that is limiting and unproductive, and calls for a new model of understanding "hybridity" that will address the current postmodern condition of ambivalence towards both fixity and mobility in contemporary culture:

> The debate should... move from a dispute over whether purity has priority over hybridity to an examination as to whether hybridity can either provide

a critical perspective on aesthetic, moral and political questions, or simply describe the general conditions of mixture in cultural identity.[23]

It is precisely this critical capacity of hybridity that *can* empower the diasporic agent to critique the socio-political conditions of contemporary life. Alongside confusion that accompanies migration and relocation comes critical insight. And it is this insight that harbours the potential to not only create interventionist art but to acknowledge the emergence of newness in the first place. This transforms the diasporic agent into an interpreter through whom new perspectives can be disseminated. *Bahok* is the vision of one such agent, Akram Khan, whose position as an artist of global reputation and influence lends the piece mobility and flow. It also becomes the vehicle through which Khan's own second generation experiences of diaspora fructify into an artistic enquiry, which is projected and mediated through the bodies of eight transnational artists. Through *Bahok*, Khan's artistic quest for a bodily articulation of diaspora continues to mature and manifest outside his own body.[24]

It is not my intention to provide an additional perspective on this already extensively debated concept. Given the elitist nature of academic discourse, and the privileged positioning of the diasporic agent, I agree that the condition of hybridity as a catalyst for art can become a trope for political and economic agency for a small section of the diaspora. I also agree that it has the potential to enhance "visibility" of ethnicity as a commodity. However, in its ability to forge new texts and enable agency, we cannot ignore the impact hybridity *can* have on contemporary arts. To judge the influential capacity of the hybrid voice, I believe it is the "intention" of each authorial vision that needs scrutiny.

My use of the word "intention" is deliberate. Mikhail Bakhtin distinguishes between unconscious, organic hybridity and conscious, intentional hybridity. In the first instance, Bakhtin believes that the amalgamation creates a mixture that is "mute and opaque."[25] It lacks self reflexivity and does not disrupt hegemonic flow. In contrast, Jacqueline Lo asserts, "conscious intentional hybridity" requires "artists to produce an internal dialogism characterised by contestation and politicisation."[26] The process is therefore inherently disruptive in its agenda, negotiating and reconciling between pioneering change and countering resistance. Bakhtin's conscious intentional hybridity coincides with Papastergiadis' emphasis on hybridity as a critical commentary that challenges hegemonic norms.

The hybridity in *Bahok* is of the conscious intentional kind, depicting the embodied subjects within *Bahok* as possessing productive, communicative, powerful and thinking bodies. At every level of the performance – spatial, cultural, linguistic, aesthetic, disciplinary and corporeal – the eight bodies on stage are hybrid products constantly forging bridges between the familiar and unfamiliar to communicate with each other. Their liminality is far more complex than the in-betweenness we associate with diasporic identity crisis. On the surface the hybridity may appear to revolve around the subjects' cultural memories, homes and notions of belonging, making it resemble an exploration of the cultural displacement associated with diasporic identity constructions. But this is only part of the hybridity that consolidates *Bahok*, not least because these *bahoks* do not have dual cultural reference points but carry the experience of multiple reference points through their transnational existences.

This distinction between duality and plurality is vital to take into consideration. Furthermore, the layers at which hybridity functions in *Bahok* are incredibly complex and can be traced within their corporeal languages. It moves the debate of hybridity from the realms of postcolonial studies and migration studies to the arena of interdisciplinary artistic enquiry. This makes *Bahok* a postmodern piece that postulates on pluralistic visions of corporealities without ever attempting to reduce them to any kind of homogeneous trope. The inter-disciplinarity of the piece embraces fragmentation and intertextuality, and creates a hybrid performance experience. And it is the intention and vision of Akram Khan as Artistic Director that simultaneously uses the performers' transnationality and their locality to contest the premise that hybridity can only be a product of migration. For just as we encounter many versions of home in *Bahok*, we experience complex and varied hybridities that coexist in this global transit zone to interrupt hegemonic conceptions of the diasporic agent.

I turn to a moment in the piece which emphasises this intervention in a subtle and sensual way, demonstrating that speed and relocation are not all that governs the life of a *bahok*, that the past and the future and the transnational spaces are not the only reference points for diasporic living. It suggests that to live in the present and the local space is just as vital. A beautiful tired woman keeps falling asleep on her co-traveller's shoulder. He politely and repeatedly tries to make her sit up in vain. He is clearly taken by her beauty and her unconscious sharing of intimacy. To cope with his embarrassment, he fantasises a sensual encounter between them.

In his fantasy their bodies and limbs become inseparable and create an illusion of becoming one and the same person in perfect unison, controlled, at ease and with no trace of fragmentation. Their limbs entwine in such perfect synchronicity that it truly becomes impossible to identify one body as distinct from the other. Their bodies are so in-tuned that they each control the other, and each give in to the other with mutual trust and understanding.

Here we see a hybrid entity emerge in totality, a newly forged creation through the body of two pre-existing *bahoks*. It is significant that this new forged entity embodies hope and calm and presence. But it is equally vital to note that it only exists in the *bahok's* imagination, perhaps indicating the hope and calm that every transnational subject has within to home their ever-transient bodies. The semantic of their dance is entirely specific to their intimate and lyrical bodily encounter. It indicates the serenity and pleasure that lies dormant in these apparently agitated bodies. It suggests that hybridity is ascertained by the disciplinary and somatic exchange that takes place between a Chinese ballet dancer and a Slovakian contemporary dancer as they indulge in this fantasy. But most importantly, it denotes that just in that moment of exchange between the two bodies, "home" is evoked as a space of familiar intimacy, traced in the intimate encounter between them. And in that present moment, their bodies are homed and are "at home" within themselves, with each other and in the world.

Conclusion

In this chapter I have used *Bahok* as an artistic project to exemplify how, within transnational contexts, competing cultural memories embodied within individuals are gradually dismantled due to a lack of shared understanding and common reference point amongst those who occupy this space. This is facilitated through challenging essentialist notions of home, as transnational diasporic agents relocate through choice and mobility, and attach multiple reference points to belonging and identity through their transient selves. These multiple reference points also give rise to complex hybridities that move beyond the dual into the plural spaces that aid identity constructions. What emerges in the place of "cultural memory" is a new shared vocabulary based on the communal experience of occupying the transnational space. This new language, the repertoire, is non-archival, present, and becomes a valuable system of embodied knowledge through which to understand the conditions of the transnational diasporic agent.

Works Cited

About NBC, at: http://www.ballet.org.cn/en/jutuanjieshao.htm (accessed
   20 August 2008).
Anthias, F. (2001) "New Hybridities, Old Concepts: the Limits of
   'Culture,'" *Ethnic and Racial Studies*, 24:4, pp.619-641.
Assmann, J. & J. Czaplicka (1995) "Collective Memory and Cultural
   Identity," *New German Critique*, 65, pp.125-133.
Bakhtin, M. (1981) *The Dialogic Imagination: Four Essays*, trans. Caryl
   Emerson and Michael Holquist, Austin: University of Texas Press.
Bhabha, H. (1994) *The Location of Culture*, London: Routledge.
Brah, Avtar (1996) *Cartographies of Diaspora: Contesting Identities*.
   London & New York: Routledge.
Burkitt, I. (1999) *Bodies of Thought: Embodiment, Identity & Modernity*,
   London: Sage.
Chaudhry, F. (2008) email communication to author, 18 August.
Delmas, G. (Dir.) (2008) *Bahok: Lettres sur le pont (Letters on the
   Bridge)*, DVD produced Lardux Films.
George, R. M. (1996) *The Politics of Home: Postcolonial Relocations and
   Twentieth Century Fiction*, Berkeley and Los Angeles: University of
   California Press.
Gilroy, P. (1993) *The Black Atlantic: Modernity and Double
   Consciousness*, London: Verso.
Grehan, H. (2003) "Rakini Devi: Diasporic Subject and Agent
   Provocateur," *Theatre Research International*, 28:3, pp.229-244.
Hall, S. & P. du Gay (Eds.) (1996) *Questions of Cultural Identity*, London:
   Sage Publications.
Hirsch, M. (2008) "The Generation of Postmemory," *Poetics Today*, 29:1,
   pp.103- 128.
Khan, A. *Personal Profile,* at:
http://www.akramkhancompany.net/html/akram_home.html (accessed 18
   February 2005).
Lo, J. (2000) "Beyond Happy Hybridity: Performing Asian-Australian
   Identities," in Ang, I., S. Chalmers, L. Law & M. Thomas (Eds.)
   *Alter/Asians. Asian-Australian Identities in Art, Media and Popular
   Culture*, Sydney: Pluto Press.
Mercer, K. (1999) "Ethnicity and Internationality: New British Art and
   Diaspora-Based Blackness," *Third Text*, 49.
Mishra, V. (1996) "The Diasporic Imaginary: Theorising the Indian
   Diaspora," *Textual Practice*, 10:3, pp.421-447.

Moreiras, A. (1999) "Hybridity and Double Consciousness," *Cultural Studies*, 13:3, pp.373-407.

Papastergiadis, N. (2005) "Hybridity and Ambivalence: Places and Flows in Contemporary Art and Culture," *Theory Culture Society*, 22:4, pp.39-64.

Taylor, D. (2003) *The Archive and the Repertoire: Performing Cultural Memory in the Americas*, Durham and London: Duke University Press.

Tyndall, K. *The Producers: Farooq Chaudhry*, at: http://www.the-producers.org/FarooqChaudhry (accessed 20 August 2008).

Notes

[1] Ian Burkitt (1999) *Bodies of Thought: Embodiment, Identity & Modernity*, London: Sage.

[2] Jan Assmann & John Czaplicka (1995) "Collective Memory and Cultural Identity," *New German Critique*, No 65, pp.125-133.

[3] Akram Khan Company, based in London, was founded in 2000 by dancer/choreographer Akram Khan and producer Farooq Chaudhry. Khan's own repertoire consists of *Kathak* (a north Indian storytelling dance tradition), European contemporary dance, and the aesthetic and political spaces in between. The company's transnational vision brings together dancers from India, Spain, South Africa, Korea and Slovakia among others. Fuelled by the need to give voice to individual experiences, Akram Khan Company negotiates the spaces between cultures, tradition, modernity, post-modernity and its by-product, subjectivity. The articulation of diaspora is thus at the heart of Khan's artistic vision, and hybridity is an inevitable characteristic in his practice. Through a relatively recent but impressive history of performance projects, Khan's artistic journey has moved from solo explorations in *Loose in Flight* (2000) and *Fix* (2000) to large ensemble choreographies in *Rush* (2000), *Kaash* (2002) and *Ma* (2004), to duet collaborations in *Zero Degrees* (2005), *Sacred Monsters* (2006) and, the most recent, *In-I* (2008). *Bahok* (2008) is a unique departure for the company, as for the first time Khan does not perform but takes on the role of Artistic Director. This allows his artistic enquiry to gain momentum outside his own body, demanding critical distance.

[4] National Ballet of China (NBC) was founded in 1959, and prides itself on being "the only Chinese national ballet." Its artistic mission is twofold. Firstly it wants to promote western classical and contemporary ballet to Chinese audiences; and secondly it wants to explore the "unique fusion possible between classical ballet and Chinese culture." See *About NBC*, at:

http://www.ballet.org.cn/en/jutuanjieshao.htm (accessed 20 August 2008). *Bahok* is described as NBC's first ever dialogue with the language of contemporary dance.

[5] See, for instance, Paul Gilroy (1993), *The Black Atlantic: Modernity and Double Consciousness*, London: Verso; Homi Bhabha (1994) *The Location of Culture*, London: Routledge; Avtar Brah (1996) *Cartographies of Diaspora: Contesting Identities*. London & New York: Routledge.

[6] Helen Grehan (2003) "Rakini Devi: Diasporic Subject and Agent Procateur," *Theatre Research International*, Vol. 28, No 3, p.239.

[7] See Vijay Mishra (1996) "The Diasporic Imaginary: Theorising the Indian Diaspora," *Textual Practice,* Vol. 10, No 3, pp.421-447.

[8] Nikos Papastergiadis (2005) "Hybridity and Ambivalence: Places and Flows in Contemporary Art and Culture," *Theory Culture Society*, Vol. 22, No 4, pp.39-64.

[9] Rosemary Marangoly George (1996) *The Politics of Home: Postcolonial Relocations and Twentieth Century Fiction*, Berkeley and Los Angeles, University of California Press, p.2.

[10] *Ibid.*

[11] *Ibid.*

[12] *Ibid.*, p.199.

[13] *Ibid.*

[14] Giles Delmas (Dir.) (2008) *Bahok: Lettres sur le pont (Letters on the Bridge)*, DVD produced by Lardux Films.

[15] Farooq Chaudhry (2008) email communication with author.

[16] George (1996).

[17] Akram Khan, *Personal Profile* at: http://www.akramkhancompany.net/html/akram_home.html (accessed 18 February 2005).

[18] Papastergiadis (2005), pp.39-64.

[19] See, for example, Bhabha (1994); and, Stuart Hall & Paul du Gay (Eds.) (1996) *Questions of Cultural Identity*, London: Sage; Gilroy (1993).

[20] Alberto Moreiras (1999) "Hybridity and Double Consciousness," *Cultural Studies*, Vol. 13, No 3, p.337.

[21] Floya Anthias (2001) "New Hybridities, Old Concepts: the Limits of 'Culture,'" *Ethnic and Racial Studies*, Vol. 24, No 4, pp.619-641.

[22] Kobena Mercer (1999) "Ethnicity and Internationality: New British Art and Diaspora-Based Blackness," *Third Text*, no 49.

[23] Papastergiadis (2005), p.38.

[24] In an interview on the making of *Bahok*, Khan revealed his affiliations to being a "carrier." His parents moved to the UK when his mother was pregnant with him in the early 1970s, literally carrying him within her. His maternal grandfather was a political activist during the traumatic Partition of Bengal into West Bengal and Bangladesh, and despite enduring extreme physical torture, survived to carry with him stories and experiences of the trauma that gave birth to his nation. Khan goes on to admit that such brave and often traumatic embodiments of the dislocations of his ancestors lends him his desire to articulate the experience of being a *bahok*.

Khan's desire to "carry" through intimate affiliations to his ancestors' memories can be understood through Marianne Hirsch's conceptual condition of postmemory. Hirsch writes that, "Postmemory describes the relationship of the second generation to powerful, often traumatic, experiences that preceded their birth but that were nevertheless transmitted to them so deeply as to seem to constitute memories in their own right." Hirsch (2008), "The Generation of Postmemory," *Poetics Today*, 29:1, p.103.

[25] Mikhail Bakhtin (1981) *The Dialogic Imagination: Four Essays*, trans. Caryl Emerson and Michael Holquist. Austin: University of Texas Press.

[26] Jacqueline Lo (2000) "Beyond Happy Hybridity: Performing Asian-Australian Identities," in I. Ang, S. Chalmers, L. Law & M. Thomas (Eds.) *Alter/Asians. Asian-Australian Identities in Art, Media and Popular Culture*, Sydney: Pluto Press.

TOHU-BOHU:
RACHEL ROSENTHAL'S PERFORMANCES
OF DIASPORIC CULTURAL MEMORY

ROBERTA MOCK

According to Una Chaudhuri, Rachel Rosenthal "began making performances two hundred million years ago, when the break-up of her body formed the continents, the oceans, the earth as we know it."[1] Bonnie Marranca famously referred to Rosenthal's performance art as "autobiology," stating that as she moves beyond the personal, "the face of the earth has become a metaphor for her own physiognomy."[2] I have chosen to use the term "autotopographical" to describe Rosenthal's relationship between autobiography, the body, and place. My focus is on the movements between these concepts, on connected moments of becoming that slip around the tensions between formlessness and materiality. These moments, to me, are complex expressions of cultural memory. In Rosenthal's work, clear patterns can be mapped in, on and between three types of performative spaces: the structures and strategies of the individual performance events Rosenthal has created; her performing body; and, her body of performance work as it constructs a "mythic" narrative. All make meaning by offering their various audiences an embodied sense of process. I propose that these spaces and their mappings are closely connected through a Jewishness which is, significantly, rarely named.

My use of the term "autotopography" is meant to signal the performative location of a particular individual in actual space. For Dee Heddon, autotopographical practice "brings into view the 'self' that plots place and that plots self in place, admitting (and indeed actively embracing) the subjectivity and inevitable partiality or bias of that process."[3] Heddon's work tends to focus on the relationship between site specificity and autobiographical representation, although she suggests that there are other ways in which the concept may prove productive. What we share is an interpretation of "autotopographical" that focuses on the mutual constructions of interior and exterior spaces to create meaning for audiences through geographic tropes. In this chapter I will explore how Rosenthal autotopographically performs a specific form of diasporic cultural memory: that is, one that is Jewish, assimilated, Western Euro-American, post-Holocaust and female.

Duncan and Ley note, in their collection *Place/Culture/Representation*, that hegemonic topographical discourse may be presented as a "science" but it is also a "practice" that produces "knowledge in the service of power that is deeply intertwined in the cultural, social and political webs of a society."[4] For this reason, the topographical "writing of place" may be either subversive or reactionary. Adding "auto" to "topography" is to acknowledge and expose the fact that it is as much a "creative act of interpretation, of perspective, of location" as the "writing of self"; both are contingent, shifting, and always "becoming."[5] These ideas resonate closely with the operation of cultural memory. As Paul Connerton writes in *How Societies Remember*, "Groups provide individuals with frameworks within which their memories are localised and memories are localized by a kind of mapping. We situate what we recollect within the mental spaces provided by the group."[6] Complex and intricate relationships exist between the individual, memorialization and material space; collective "states of mind" often refer to either memories of specific places or the impossibility of being in such places.

These understandings are, I think, also at the heart of Marranca's concept of "autobiology." "Formidable seismologies," she writes of Rosenthal, "erupt from the rhetorical body in this chaotic discourse of signs and shifting surface texts."[7] Lying just beneath and informing both her symbolism and performance strategy are the sedimented layers of Rosenthal's performances of self and the gestural scars these have left over an extended period of time. Indeed, Rosenthal's career as an artist tends to be presented in terms used to describe the earth's strata. Born in 1926, the layers begin accumulating above her childhood during which she studied ballet and was surrounded at home by family friends like Marc Chagall, Leonard Bernstein and Vladimir Horowitz. Having fled the Nazis with her parents, first from Europe and then Brazil, during the first half of the 1940s she attended the High School for Music and Art in New York, along with students such as Allan Kaprow. Then there was her professional initiation by the masters of mid twentieth-century French experimental theatre, Jean-Louis Barrault and Roger Blin, followed by her active participation in the New York avant-garde scene of John Cage,

Jasper Johns, Robert Rauschenberg and Merce Cunningham. During this time she made visual art, danced with Cunningham's Junior Company and also worked as an assistant to Erwin Piscator.

The years between 1956-1966 comprise the phase of Rosenthal's life that she files "under the archeological name of I.T. [Instant Theatre]."[8] Based in Los Angeles (which would henceforth remain her home), she and her then-husband, King Moody, engaged in radical, risky, improvisatory theatre-making and workshopping. In the late 1960s, after the Instant Theatre was closed (due to exhaustion, problems with money and Equity, and the pain Rosenthal suffered due to osteoarthritis), she returned to sculpture.

The early 1970s is notable for her involvement in the southern Californian feminist arts movement during which time she worked with, and was influenced by, Miriam Schapiro and Judy Chicago. In Lisa Bloom's book about Jewish feminist identities in American art, she notes that a disproportionate percentage of feminist art makers on both American coasts were secular Jews. "Many of these Jewish feminist artists," she writes, "left their Jewishness at home and acted, politically, as feminists, and as generic white Americans."[9] Judy Chicago's name change, from Judy Gerowitz in 1970, is emblematic of a high profile artistic career which blossomed when she began to emphasize the visibility of gender to the exclusion of all other "vectors of power" (to use Judith Butler's phrase). Judy Chicago chose to mark her body, her self, through an identification with the place she was born. Rosenthal's choice *not* to change her name, as was common for so many Jewish immigrants in America, seems to arise from the same impulse: that is, the recognition that naming can signify otherness or difference.

For the majority of feminist artists in California, what wasn't named in the 1970s – that is, Jewishness – became subsumed into their difference, as women, and the way this was expressed artistically. The emphasis on life writing, materiality and collage in this environment can be seen to lead to the creation of what can be considered Rosenthal's first pieces of performance art. Between 1976 and 1981, Rosenthal embarked on a series of unfolding autobiographical performances, commenting later that, "if you really saw all these pieces, you would have the whole autobiography, the whole history of my life."[10] I would like to pause here to briefly consider a specific performance of this period. I will return to another, *Charm*, which was made earlier in 1977, later in this chapter.

Figure 1: Rachel Rosenthal. Photo: Amy Fishbein.

My Brazil, which Rosenthal performed in 1979, both foreshadows the autotopographical performances to follow and is exceptional in its unambiguous reference to Rosenthal's Jewishness. *My Brazil* deals with a seven-month period in 1940-41 in which Rosenthal and her family lived in Rio de Janeiro as refugees, before fleeing the anti-Semitism of Brazil's fascist *Estado Novo* dictatorship which once again threatened their lives. The performance charts Rosenthal's growing sensuality and her fantasies. She talks of other Rachels, one who stayed in France and joined the Resistance and another who dies in a concentration camp. She repeatedly dies and is reborn – like her beloved half brother Pierre who was killed in North Africa in 1943 (that is, after Rosenthal actually left Brazil). Before becoming a "cosmic cloud," Pierre picks Rachel up in his arms and flies with her over the earth and to the moon. Visions of Nazi rallies transform into a birds-eye view of oceans, meadows, the Grand Canyon. Rachel returns to earth but predicts that she will one day herself evolve from animal to element:

> I will break into splashes of drops like fireworks, waterworks, sparks. I will shatter and re-form in an infinite variety of ways, landing on my feet, my fins, my claws... I will be a geyser and a waterfall... I will erupt from Krakatoa ... I will become what I have always been and go back to where I never left.[11]

Autobiographical memory, utopian future, landscape and the evolving exiled body are yoked together in this performance text.

In an interview at the time of *My Brazil*, Rosenthal said:

> I take aspects of my life that I feel were useless and worthless, and through performance redeem them. It's a means of understanding and re-creation. Putting them in an art form has a mythmaking quality.

Later in the same interview, she links these acts of representation with the immediacy of presentation: "No matter how much you work on the text, how much you prepare beforehand, the actual transformation is happening right there in front of the audience."[12] This was very much the case when Rosenthal had her hair shaved off at the end of her production, *Leave Her in Naxos*, in 1981. By this pivotal point, Rosenthal seems to be more or less reconciled with her past and has "transformed" her body into the one that has now become iconographic (See *Figure 1*). Her work from this time onwards tends to move between global concerns, which focus on ecological issues and animal welfare, and personal touchstones, anecdotes and references (as opposed to longer autobiographical confessions, purges and exorcisms).

The figure of the ancient Greek earth goddess Gaia is conjured and embodied by Rosenthal in increasingly complex formulations in performances such as *Gaia, Mon Amour* (1983), *L.O.W. in Gaia* (1986) which was based on a three week trip to the Mojave desert, and *Pangaean Dreams* (1990). *Gaia, Mon Amour* emerged as a response to James Lovelock's Gaia hypothesis that proposed a model of the world as a single organism, as well as from a therapeutic impulse, and an involvement with shamanistic belief systems. Her incarnation of Gaia in this piece makes it clear how Rosenthal (the person, the performer) is meant to function as a theatrical signifier: "Embrace me. It is the same as holding yourselves. It is all ONE. I am you. YOU ARE GAIA NOW."[13] In *Pangaean Dreams*, Rosenthal personifies the supercontinent that broke up over 200 million years ago, connecting the disintegration of her own arthritic bones with the action of tectonic plates. This metaphor is used to structure the performance, with the intention that audiences will "identify with the planet" via an identification with Rosenthal as a person: "Because I am identified with the Earth as well as being a human being, if I were to conceive of myself as anything, it would be as a go-between."[14]

Despite Marranca's assertion that "while Rosenthal walks in the realm of myth she is demythologizing herself,"[15] Rosenthal herself seems to have had misgivings about some responses to her strategy. In a 2001 interview, the year after she retired from performing herself, she discusses why she felt the need to return to autobiography in her final touring performance, *Ur-boor*: "So many people want to make of me what I am not – which is a guru or a shaman or … a messiah of some sort… a goddess,"[16] she says uncomfortably. So just as she built archetypal imagery upon autobiography, at the end of her performance career Rosenthal felt the need to dismantle in reverse. In 2009, at the age of 83, she works as a painter who continues to run intensive performance workshops, based on early Instant Theatre experiments, called The DbD Experience (which stands for "Doing by Doing").

It was at her Espace DbD in Los Angeles that, in the mid-1990s, Rosenthal and her company presented a series of performances called *Tohubohu!* – or, perhaps more accurately, a creative process that manifested itself in a series of performances each with the same title. A combination of two nearly synonymous words, *tohu-bohu* is an imitative construction itself treated as a contracted synonym for the Hebrew phrase *tohu-va'vohu.* This appears in the second line of the book of *Genesis* and it commonly refers to the primeval chaotic state from which the world was created: *Ve-ha'aretz hayta tohu-va'vohu* ("and the earth was without form, and void"). Rosenthal explained her evocation of the concept literally; the aim of her project was to create improvised performances that emerged from a "spontaneous and collective ordering of chaos." Like the biblical language from which it is borrowed, the meaning of *tohu-bohu* when applied to Rosenthal's work is poetic and open to interpretation, and I will return to it later in the chapter.

According to reviewer Meiling Cheng, who saw *Tohubohu!* on more than one occasion, it "explored the evolution of artistic consciousness as a standing metaphor for the cosmos." However, it also has a distinct prior identity and history rooted in Rosenthal's stature as a pioneering feminist performance artist in Los Angeles ... shaped by her dreams for a vital theatre and by her ecofeminist beliefs; her autobiographical details provide the basic tropes.[17]

In other words, *Tohubohu!* emerges as much as a performative assemblage of Rosenthal's life work in a specific location as from the ordering of disparate elements available to its improvising creators in the moment. Furthermore, this life work must itself be read as a process that both builds upon and constantly refers back to itself. Thus the bald-headed shamanic crone of *L.O.W. in Gaia* could only manifest herself as a result of a series of earlier autobiographical performances which, significantly, are both haunted and driven by a Jewishness that is rarely named explicitly. An autotopography that could appear essentialist is built upon and contains the autobiographical. This is why, in this chapter, I am mainly focusing on early pieces such as *My Brazil* and *Charm*, the performance that tackled her childhood memories for the first time.

According to Rosenthal, despite practicing Zen Buddhism in the 1950s and '60s, her "inclination was always away from religion of any sort." This eventually developed into a recognition that Earth is her "deity," although she has said that "It's not really a religion: it's a veneration, a spiritual approach."[18] Rosenthal claims that when she was younger, as she had no religion, it was "talent" that was venerated. Her father was an atheist and she was brought up with "no sense of being Jewish at all." She said in an interview that

> We were completely 'assimilated' Jews... I didn't even know I was Jewish until I noticed that the little girls who took their First Communion had these lovely little dresses and little white hats and everything. I asked my mother, 'When am I gonna do that? This looks neat,' you know, and she said, 'You can't. You're Jewish.' And I said, 'What's that?'[19]

This anecdote is also told in a version of *Charm*, which is significant for being one of her first autobiographical performances, one that moves her work further away from "theatre" (if only in the sense that Rosenthal is performing a persona closely aligned to her "self" and is discussing her own history rather than playing a fictional character). Interestingly, it is heard only in the radio version of the play: the dematerialized version. There are important differences between the live version of *Charm*, which was performed only once, and the radio version made a decade later.[20]

In the *Zohar*, the work upon which all subsequent kabbalistic writing is based, *tohu-bohu* (actually, in particular, *tohu*) is considered "formless matter," a world of pure spirit from which progressively more material emanates. The oxymoronic tensions between "formlessness" and "matter" are echoed for me in *Charm*, with each of its three sections framed by a male voice reading a newspaper article about subnuclear physics. Some of the particles he describes, named quarks, are "strange" and "charmed" in that they do not decay like others. It is clear from Rosenthal's performance text that she was raised to personify "charm" and that she considered herself "charmed"; both relate to her "strangeness" which forms the basis of her identity and which she attempts to reject. This strangeness derives from her family's great wealth as well as her Jewishness (which are not presented as related). The latter, however, is never explicitly named in the staged performance. Jewishness is, rather, remarkable for its absence, upon which Rosenthal herself comments when she recounts finding her mother in bed crying:

> And somebody mentioned that it had to do with mother's sister, my aunt Hanka, in Poland. They said she was dead. Something to do with the Nazis... I didn't understand what that was.

> And strangely enough, for the next few days I expected somebody would say something. But nobody mentioned anything.[21]

This anecdote mirrors the overall theme of *Charm* and the motifs that emerge from it: that lurking beneath a glamorous public life were untold horrors and fears that needed to be hidden from view. It is an example of what Leo Spitzer calls "critical memory" – that is, "nostalgia's complicating other side" that incorporates negative and bitter memories.[22]

Throughout the tales of her "fun" family and abuse at the hands of her governess, Rosenthal stuffs herself compulsively with sweets brought to her by an increasingly disgusted servant. Opening her dictionary at the start of the performance, she notes that the word "charm" appears between "charlotte russe" and "charnel house": "Nothing, but I mean NOTHING could be more appropriate!" she says. I must agree. Here again is an oblique reference to Jewishness which is indeed presented as a non-thing, conspicuous in its absence, alluding to death camps and the compulsive *boulimie* of the hysteric which we are about to see enacted.[23]

The food has been cut from the radio version of the play; although references to various delicacies remain, Rosenthal's speeches are not performed while eating. What is *added* to the radio version, like the story of the Communion dress, is perhaps more interesting: another male voice, paralleling the speeches about "strange" particles, reads texts about Nazi doctors. While it is inappropriate to make connections that are too literal in Rosenthal's work, in this version Jewishness is much more clearly aligned to otherness, danger, growing up. In the credits at the end of the broadcast, Rosenthal states that the performance is dedicated to her parents and also to all the members of her family killed in "the Holocaust and World War II." This is also written on the cover of my cassette of the performance, which features a montage of a little girl in a satin party frock over an image of a swastika.

There is much to say about the relationship between Holocaust photography, trauma and cultural memory. Particularly relevant here is Marianne Hirsch's application of Kaja Silverman's understanding of "heteropathic memory" to the analysis of images of children made during the Shoah:

> [W]here the subject is not split just between past and present, adult and child, but also between self and other, the layers of recollection and the subjective topography are even more complicated. The adult subject of postmemory encounters the image of the child victim *as* the child witness, and thus the split subjectivity characterizing the structure of memory is triangulated. And that triangulation identifies postmemory as necessarily cultural.[24]

While technically speaking Rosenthal can be considered a Holocaust survivor, her sense of distancing and her narratives of childhood incomprehension more closely resemble the operation of postmemory which Hirsch uses to describe the relationship of children of survivors of cultural or collective trauma to the experiences of their parents. Because I do not have space to pursue this further now, I would like to simply draw attention to Hirsch's use of the word "topography" to express the relationship between time, image, altarity and subjectivity in representations of Holocaust memory that involve children.

The live performance of *Charm* ends with the taped voice-over questioning whether there is an ultimate particle or whether nature is "an endless series of seeds within seeds within seeds…" While the recording plays itself out, according to the published stage directions, Rosenthal holds a mangled chocolate cake "before her at arm's length, squatting, her eyes open, not seeing, her mouth open and empty. She's turned into a monster."[25] I can't help but remember one of the etymologies of *tohu-bohu* that I have encountered:

> It is possible that *tohu* is connected to Hebrew *tehom,* the watery abyss on which the world rests (itself related to the name of the ancient Babylonian sea-dragon goddess Tiamat), *bohu* being an alliterative reduplication; alternately, both words may be connected to the two verbs *taha* (to wonder, to make no sense of) and *baha* (to stare blankly).[26]

The associations become more insistent as I reflect upon the text that Rosenthal speaks and dances in *Pangaean Dreams* many years later:

> Under the sea a Dragon lives/ Coiled around the Globe/... Her name, the Mid-Ocean Ridge./ Sometimes her spine pokes out/ like Nessie of the Loch./ These sightings have been given names... The millennium approaches. I grow older. The plates move. As one moves, all move. That's the law of Chaos and I accept... With the Pangaean dinosaur ensconced in my brain. In the Earth. Of the Earth.[27]

Rosenthal seems to be embodying the concerns and observations of cultural geographer Doreen Massey. In her book *For Space*, Massey reminds us that topographies of space are always a process, an unfinished business. Places are not fixed areas on a map but integrations of space and time: that is, "spatio-temporal events."[28] According to Massey, "immigrant rocks" are – like people but much more slowly – passing through places, changing all the time. One of the reasons it is impossible to go "back" home is because it will have moved on from where we left it.[29]

Alisa Solomon has noted that familiarity with Rosenthal's accumulated body of work influences one's reading of individual performances. Thus, even when "she doesn't mention it, we know what would have happened if she hadn't escaped Europe." Reflecting on *Pangaean Dreams*, Solomon makes explicit connections between the performer's personal catastrophe as a refugee and the earth breaking itself apart; Rosenthal speaks "at once for the creature severed from geological wholeness and for the adolescent girl schlepped, in a personal continental drift, to Portugal then Brazil then New York." She hears "strains of klezmer" under Rosenthal's words even while acknowledging that the artist herself intended to send a message about the "experience of refugees from *any* cataclysm" (but, in particular, that of First Nations people during and after the European colonization of the Americas).[30]

Solomon's analysis of Rosenthal's work mirrors, and has influenced, my own long term project which is to expose, trace and establish distinct connections between female Jewish performers in the modern Diaspora.[31] She is interested in how "the Jew goes missing" in discussions of the ways in which women artists like Rosenthal present their bodies and deconstruct gender. I have already referred to the fact that this was to a great extent a strategy for a generation of women artists, especially those based in Southern California in the early 1970s. For Solomon, "the disruptive figure of the Jew glimmers through their work" *despite* its lack of specifically "Jewish content." While I can't quite go along with her assertion that "Rosenthal is a postmodern [Sarah] Bernhardt" (due to their radically different agendae and positioning within hegemonic cultures), my own argument is strongly implied in Solomon's collapsed association: that as Jewishness was suppressed from the late 19th century onwards, it began to manifest itself performatively in a number of different ways which then began to be quoted by subsequent generations of Jewish women. Jewishness becomes what Marjorie Garber has called a "spectral visibility": that is, "the visibility of the ghost."[32]

These haunted performances are an example of the "repertoire" in action, another expression of cultural memory and one central to Diana Taylor's thesis in her influential book *The Archive and the Repertoire.* In contrast to archival memory which exists materially in the form of documents such as literary texts, letters, films, and (perhaps significantly) maps, the repertoire "enacts embodied memory: performances, gestures, orality, movement, dance, singing – in short, all those acts usually thought of as ephemeral, nonreproducible knowledge." Repertoire allows for individual agency and "requires presence: people participate in the production and reproduction of knowledge by 'being there', being part of the transmission."[33] For Taylor, it is impossible to think about cultural memory and identity as disembodied. The body in cultural memory is specific, pivotal, and subject to change. It is a product of certain taxonomic, disciplinary, and mnemonic systems. Furthermore, Taylor is adamant about the impossibility of separating cultural memory from race and gender.[34]

Rosenthal can be seen to be working in a historical tradition which intertextually responds to and exploits the stereotype of the hysteric Jewish woman that was consolidated in the late 19th century and often conflated with representations of "universal womanhood." Most of these anxieties coalesce in the *fin de siècle* vamp/ire which paradoxically presents the *femme fatale* Jewess as simultaneously hyperfeminine and powerfully masculine. By *Gaia, Mon Amour*, Rosenthal is drawing our attention to Lilith, the original Jewish vamp/ire, as an earth mother figure capable of both destruction and redemption. Earlier, in *The Death Show* (1978), she identifies the "Fat Vampire" as a stifling self-image based on the unhealthy acceptance of conformity and external projections. She is killed via a touchingly funny ritual that evokes compulsively eaten fattening foods.

Historically, Jewish women (like Bernhardt, Rachel Felix and Anna Held, all of whom like Rosenthal had complicated relationships with French nationality due to their Jewishness) have tended to achieve the most success when performing in styles and genres that are realistic but not naturalistic – that is, when they offer the illusion of "being" rather than "replicating." Since the dawn of 20th century, their bodies (often distorted through extreme relationships with food) and these styles tended to present sexual difference through "grotesque" displays of otherness. Una Chaudhuri's discussion of Rosenthal's Gaia could come straight from Bakhtin's writings on the carnivalesque body in grotesque realism: "One 'monstrosity' that is particularly dear to Rosenthal is that most hated of cultural icons: the hag, the ugly, vulgar, hectoring, badgering, and above all shameless old woman who tells the truth and doesn't give a damn."[35] This leads to a final observation about the careers of Jewish female performers: they are often unusually long since they do not rely on the conventions of dominant representations of femininity and beauty.[36]

Indeed, issues of aging, beauty and femininity collide in Rosenthal's baldness. Those present in the audience of *Leave Her in Naxos* on 13 February 1981 recognized the shaving of her head as a symbolic act. According to Ruth Weisberg:

> [W]e saw Rosenthal looking like a lama, ascetic and spiritual. She appeared very masculine with her bald head, but was still absurdly dressed in her garish, spangled costume. The shaving of Rosenthal's hair seemed an experience of death for the audience. It was fully accepted and even desired by Rosenthal; nevertheless, this gesture of loving violence appeared to be a violation and a denial. The result was an image powerful in its duality and its ability to disturb.[37]

The vocabulary in this account makes it clear why Alisa Solomon connects Rosenthal's lack of hair with Jewishness (for her, both Holocaust imagery and *fin de siècle* caricatures).[38] This connection is intuitive: dominant representations of Jewish women, as well as regulations within orthodox Judaism, focus on the eroticism of hair and the complex relationship between its apparent absence and presence operates in unpredictable ways according to cultural location. Still, Solomon's comment that Rosenthal's use of hair helps her to "challenge cozy assumptions about gender categories and about the hierarchical structures such classifications breed" is appropriate in that it works on the associative level of Rosenthal's own performances of self.

It is in this intuitive and associative spirit that I offer the following observation about Rosenthal's baldness. It revolves around *Time*, a painting made by Miriam Schapiro between 1988-91 as part of her "Collaboration Series: Frida Kahlo and Me." Schapiro is a few years older than Rosenthal and they have known each other since the late 1940s. *Time* is an autobiographical painting that is concerned with the aging process of an intellectual creative woman. It features a bald self-representation of Schapiro in male attire and a dancing woman whom she is presumably painting (possibly an earlier incarnation of herself). The painting seems to ambivalently signal the transformation of a defiant woman who has lost her sexual power and thus becomes ambiguously gender-identified.

According to Thalia Gouma-Peterson, Schapiro's "collaboration" with women artists like Frida Kahlo is her "most overt engagement with representation as a means by which the self can be constructed and made visible." Fundamental to the understanding of this image is the knowledge that it is based on Frida Kahlo's *Self-Portrait with Cropped Hair* (1940), which records both Kahlo's cutting of her long hair following her divorce from Diego Rivera and her assertion as an independent art-maker. Schapiro merges her own face with Kahlo's in order to establish a sense of personal identity as a woman artist through the recognition of a legitimate ancestry. As important to Schapiro was the often overlooked fact that Kahlo was part Jewish. For Gouma-Peterson, "these double self-portraits are a means for Schapiro to merge with a female prototype – a type of mother figure. Ironically, the merging occurs in *Time* at a moment when the mother is masquerading as a man." [39]

Ironic perhaps, but not unique; these are the very tropes at work in Rosenthal's self-presentation at the same time.[40] Kahlo, Schapiro and Rosenthal seem to be performing what Diana Taylor has identified as another strategy of cultural memory, a meaning-making paradigm closely related to the concept of repertoire: the scenario. "Instead of privileging *texts* and *narratives*," the scenario structures "social environments, behaviours, and potential outcomes... Its portable framework bears the weight of accumulative repast" and "makes visible, yet again, what is already there: the ghosts, the images, the stereotypes."[41] Jewish scenarios, whether religious, cultural or political, tend to be diasporic; they perform situations of exile, usually grounded by the threat of genocide. As we have already seen, this type of scenario has shaped Rosenthal's performance work. However, by comparing Rosenthal's autobiographical embodiment to Schapiro's we see another scenario at work, one in which a specific type of womanhood is being signalled in two ways: through its association, first, with masculinity and, secondly, with what *isn't* there, an absence of something that matters and is matter.

It is precisely at the point Rosenthal begins presenting herself with no hair and in army fatigues (adopted "formally" onstage at the end of her transformation from a "Tarzana housewife" into a hustling artist in *Soldier of Fortune*, also 1981) that she feels most "herself":

> I felt for the first time that I looked like how I felt inside, and it was immensely liberating… Because somehow the physical image worked from the outside in. There was a good feedback loop … creating an entity, which was Rachel Rosenthal that I had never felt before was a true me or that was authentic or believable or comfortable. And suddenly there I was, at my age (which was getting more and more advanced!), and yet it was as though everything was new and opening up for me and indeed it was.[42]

It is perhaps this "authentic" reconciliation of spirit and matter that allowed for the most explicit and "comfortable" Jewish reference in Rosenthal's oeuvre.

In *KabbaLAmobile* (1984) she "deconstructed" texts from *Sefer Yetzira* (*Book of Creation*), the writings of the 13th century kabbalist Abraham Abulafia, and journalistic copy from automotive magazines. Face painted like a warrior, in billowing robes, Rosenthal chanted from these texts and danced shamanically on top of a high platform. Beneath her, a team of seven stunt drivers performed a synchronized spectacle that was choreographed to echo Rosenthal's text:

> The engine is like two 3-cylinder units joined. The intake and exhaust valves are sodium-coded and are actuated by twin overhead camshafts located in an aluminum box extending over both cylinder banks. The cylinders themselves are Nikasil-coated and are welded by electron beam to the individual 4-valve cylinder heads.

Here is your soul
Blood is her name
Here are your mother and father
vessels to the name and memory of it.[43]

Commentators frequently remark upon the sublime synthesis of form and content, visual imagery and spoken words, space and movement in *KabbaLAmobile*.

It could be added that *KabbaLAmobile* includes no personal references whatsoever and is in many ways Rosenthal's most unified and coherently presented "concept" as a performance. Her own recitations seem designed to replace the taped voice-overs and projected slides of written scientific and philosophical discourses that feature prominently in other performances. According to Rosenthal,

> I discovered that the literatures that deal with both subjects [Kabbalah and cars] are very similar insofar as they are both ecstatic and completely esoteric. No one can understand either one until one is an initiate. In the long run, spirituality isn't found exclusively in this or that, so why not in cars? Cars, too, reflect the universe.[44]

And so it seems that, perhaps as a precursor to *Tohubohu!* over a decade later, Rosenthal found a way to encompass Jewishness in her worldview – or perhaps, a way that Jewishness could encompass her worldview.[45] In both cases she adopts the language of the Bible but avoids naming Judaism, focusing instead on its mystical ancientness. Jewishness here becomes an immaterial vessel that holds Rosenthal (as a person/performer/art maker), her identification with Gaia, and their performance manifestations.

At the heart of these manifestations is always contradiction, self-reflection, a challenge. This is the case even in as coherent a package as *KabbaLAmobile* in which the cars that represent an aspect of the universe's spirituality are also simultaneously destroying the earth; in which the shamanic figure refuses an identification as a shaman. Perhaps to fully understand this performance, one must read it in conjunction with *The Others*, also made in 1984, a piece about ethics and animal rights in which Rosenthal performs with forty animals and their owners. The relationship between machines made to be seen to be using up the earth's resources for pleasure and the creatures with which human beings share this earth is a complex one.

It is here that I would like to return to the concept of *tohu-bohu*. In later kabbalistic literature and many Chassidic communities, it is considered an "intermediate stage between the ultimate good of pure spirit and the ultimate evil of pure matter," expressing life's challenge of achieving an even balance between "sins and merits."[46] In a 1994 interview, Rosenthal articulates the drive behind her performance making:

> I was born into an affluent family and realized early on that not everybody lived as we did. And I felt very guilty. The other guilt came from the fact that we were able to leave France while so many people were killed in the Holocaust. My very big guilt was that we were saved... A lot of the family were sent to Auschwitz and the rest went through a great deal of horror... The final issue was that I always wanted to be an artist and that I was very male-identified... For a long time I hid those shameful secrets. In 1975, when I started to do performance, for some reason I did a flip-flop and began to use myself as material for performance and began to air those shameful secrets. I realized they were also everybody else's shameful secrets. That was a big liberation for me and a way of reaching people.[47]

As Mieke Bal has noted, "Memories do not allow the distinction between private and public...Cultural memory is collective, yet, by definition, subjective."[48] Rosenthal's work seems to emanate from the desire to balance her "uglies," her secrets, her guilt, her shame – what she seems to perceive as her, and our, "sins" – with the "merits" of recognition, transformation, and the acceptance of responsibility. In it, there are no neat binaries that assume "spirit" is "good" and "matter" is "bad"; in fact, her message is that the balance can only be achieved when "spirit" and "matter" are unified rather than opposed. For me, Rosenthal's Jewishness appears to be the unnamed formlessness that provoked her shared performative *journey* of the self, that which needed to be examined and expressed materially through and as performance, as a manifestation of cultural memory.

Or perhaps it would be more accurate to use anthropologist Tim Ingold's term, "way-finding," to describe Rosenthal's autotopographical practices and certainly my approach to charting them. This *moving between places* "more closely resembles story-telling than map-using, as one situates one's position within the context of journeys previously made."[49] Rosenthal's experiences correspond with the overlapping concepts of diaspora currently in scholarly operation: the first signifies the collective trauma of exile; the second, the "disembedding" of social and national networks which are then reformulated in a globalized economy.[50] According to writers such as Paul Gilroy and Stuart Hall, diasporic people "belong to more than one world, speak more than one language (literally and metaphorically); inhabit more than one identity, have more than one home"; they "have succeeded in remaking themselves."[51]

Rosenthal expresses this sense of plurality through a holistic engagement with a single concept of space: the planet. It is, however, still a space of "becoming," even as it absorbs and transcends specific places. Its fundamental characteristic is transitional. As Pile and Thrift note in *Mapping the Subject*, liminal spaces exceed allegorical functions when related to migrants, diasporas, and political refugees.[52] Importantly, for these people there is no "real" place to return: the diasporic subject is always-already here and there. Through an autotopographical embodiment of both "home" and "exile," Rosenthal has performed the role, as she says, of "go-between." Hers is the *recherche* identified by Andreas Huyssen in his book *Twilight Memories*, a mode of memory quite different from what he describes as recuperation. It is the "tenuous fissure between past and present," he writes, that constitutes cultural memory and makes it "powerfully alive."[53] In Rosenthal's performance work, she is always-already here and there, temporally and spatially, and moving between both.[54]

Works Cited

"Artist's Project: Rachel Rosenthal" (date unknown) *Modiya*, at: http://hdl.handle.net/1964/446 (accessed 24 April 2006).

Bal, M. (1999) "Memories in the Museum: Preposterous Histories for Today," in Bal, Crewe and Spitzer (Eds.) *Acts of Memory: Cultural Recall in the Present*, Hanover: University Press of New England.

Bal, M., J. Crewe and L. Spitzer (Eds.) (1999) *Acts of Memory: Cultural Recall in the Present*, Hanover: University Press of New England.

Bloom, L. E. (2006) *Jewish Identities in American Feminist Art: Ghosts of Ethnicity*, New York & London: Routledge.

Cheng, M. (1997) "Performance Review," *Theatre Journal*, 49.2.

Connerton, P. (1989) *How Societies Remember*, Cambridge: Cambridge University Press.

Duncan, J. and D. Ley (1993) "Introduction: Representing the Place of Culture," in Duncan & Ley (Eds.) *Place/Culture/Representation*, New York & London: Routledge.

Garber, M. (1999) *Symptoms of Culture*, Harmondsworth: Penguin.

Gouma-Peterson, T. (1999) *Miriam Schapiro: Shaping the Fragments of Arts and Life*, New York: Harry N. Abrams Inc.

Hall, S. (1996) "New Cultures for Old," in Massey, D. and P. Jess (Eds.) *A Place in the World: Places, Culture and Globalization*, Oxford: Oxford University Press.

Heddon, D. (2008) *Autobiography and Performance*, London: Palgrave Macmillan.

—. (2009) "One Square Foot: Thousands of Routes," in Mock, R. (Ed.) *Walking, Writing & Performance: Autobiographical Texts by Deirdre Heddon, Carl Lavery & Phil Smith*, Bristol: Intellect.

Hidle, K. "Place, Geography and the Concept of Diaspora – A Methodological Approach," at: http://www.nhh.no/geo/Nyesider/GIBframe/GIB.full.pdf/244.pdf (accessed 15 February 2007).

Hirsch, M. (1999) "Projected Memory: Holocaust Photographs in Personal and Public Fantasy," in Bal, Crewe and Spitzer (Eds.) *Acts of Memory: Cultural Recall in the Present*, Hanover: University Press of New England.

Huyssen, A. (1995) *Twilight Memories: Marking Time in a Culture of Amnesia*, New York: Routledge.

Massey, D. (2005) *For Space*, London: Sage Publications.

Mock, R. (2007) *Jewish Women on Stage, Film and Television*, New York: Palgrave Macmillan.

Pearson, M. (2006) *"In Comes I": Performance, Memory and Landscape*, Exeter: University of Exeter Press.

Philologos (2006) "Is 'Limbo' On Its Way Out?" *The Forward*, 6 January, at: http://www.forward.com/articles/7126 (accessed 21 April 2006).

Pile, S. and N. Thrift (1995) "Mapping the Subject," in Pile and Thrift (Eds.) *Mapping the Subject: Geographies of Cultural Transformation*, London & New York: Routledge.

Rosenthal, R. (1987) *Charm* (audio cassette), in Heathfield, A. with F. Templeton and A. Quick (Eds.) (1997) *Shattered Anatomies: Traces of the Body in Performance*, Bristol: Arnolfini Live.

—. (1989) Interview conducted by Moira Roth in Los Angeles, California (September 2, 1989), *Smithsonian Archives of American Art*, at: http://www.aaa.si.edu/collections/oralhistories/transcripts/rosent89.htm (accessed 1 May 2006).

—. (2001) *Location One Interview: Rachel Rosenthal interviewed by Bonnie Marranca* (video), 5 January 2001, at: http://www.location1.org/locution/rosenthal.html (accessed 1 May 2006).

—. (2001) *Rachel's Brain and Other Storms*, London & New York: Continuum.

—. (date unknown) Performance description of *KabbaLAmobile*, at: http://www.w3art.com/rr01/rr01t07.html (accessed 25 July 2006).

Roth, M. (Ed.) (1997) *Rachel Rosenthal*, Baltimore: The Johns Hopkins University Press.

Solomon, A. (1997) *Re-Dressing the Canon: Essays on Theatre and Gender*, London & New York: Routledge.

Spitzer, L. (1999) "Back Through the Future: Nostalgic Memory and Critical Memory in a Refuge from Nazism," in Bal, Crewe and Spitzer (Eds.), *Acts of Memory: Cultural Recall in the Present*, Hanover: University Press of New England.

Taylor, D. (2003) *The Archive and the Repertoire: Performing Cultural Memory in the Americas*, Durham: Duke University Press.

Notes

[1] Una Chaudhuri (2001) "Introduction: Instant Rachel," in Rachel Rosenthal (2001) *Rachel's Brain and Other Storms*, London & New York: Continuum, p.1.

[2] Bonnie Marranca (1996) "A Cosmography of Herself: The Autobiology of Rachel Rosenthal," in Moira Roth (Ed.) (1996) *Rachel Rosenthal*, Baltimore: The Johns Hopkins University Press, p.80.

[3] Deirdre Heddon (2008) *Autobiography and Performance*, London: Palgrave Macmillan, p.92.

[4] James Duncan and David Ley (1993) "Introduction: Representing the Place of Culture," in Duncan & Ley (Eds.) (1993) *Place/Culture/Representation*, New York & London: Routledge, p.1.

[5] Deirdre Heddon (2009) "One Square Foot: Thousands of Routes" in Roberta Mock (Ed.) (2009) *Walking, Writing & Performance: Autobiographical Texts*, Bristol: Intellect.

[6] Paul Connerton (1989) *How Societies Remember*, Cambridge: Cambridge University Press, p.37.

[7] Bonnie Marranca (1996), p.88.

[8] Rachel Rosenthal (1974) "Excerpts from "Rachel Rosenthal," in Roth (Ed.) (1996), p.155.

[9] Lisa E. Bloom (2006) *Jewish Identities in American Feminist Art: Ghosts of Ethnicity*, New York & London: Routledge, p.32.

[10] Interview with Rachel Rosenthal conducted by Moira Roth in Los Angeles, California (September 2, 1989), *Smithsonian Archives of American Art*, at: http://www.aaa.si.edu/collections/oralhistories/transcripts/rosent89.htm (accessed 1 May 2006).

[11] Rachel Rosenthal (1979) "*My Brazil,*" in Rosenthal (2001), p.53.

[12] Rachel Rosenthal quoted in Ruth Askey (1983) "Excerpts from 'Exoticism and Fear in Rio'," in Roth (Ed.) (1996), p.106.

[13] Rachel Rosenthal (1983) "*Gaia, Mon Amour*," in Rosenthal (2001), p.159.

[14] Alexandra Grilikhes (1994-95) "Taboo Subjects: An Interview with Rachel Rosenthal," in Roth (Ed.) (1996), pp.60-61.

[15] Bonnie Marranca (1996), p.85.

[16] *Location One Interview: Rachel Rosenthal interviewed by Bonnie Marranca*, 5 January 2001, video at: http://www.location1.org/locution/rosenthal.html (accessed 1 May 2006).

[17] Meiling Cheng (1997) "Performance Review," *Theatre Journal* 49.2, p.218.

[18] Grilikhes (1994-95), p.60.

[19] Interview with Rachel Rosenthal, conducted by Moira Roth (September 2, 1989), *Smithsonian Archives of American Art*.

[20] A cassette of the radio version of *Charm* was included in Adrian Heathfield with Fiona Templeton and Andrew Quick (Eds.) (1997) *Shattered Anatomies: Traces of the Body in Performance*, Bristol: Arnolfini Live. This recording of *Charm* was co-produced by High Performance and Jacki Apple (1987) High Performance Audio.

[21] Rachel Rosenthal (1977) "*Charm*," in Rosenthal (2001), p.24.

[22] Leo Spitzer (1996) "Back Through the Future: Nostalgic Memory and Critical Memory in a Refuge from Nazism," in Mieke Bal, Jonathan Crewe and Leo Spitzer (Eds.) (1996) *Acts of Memory: Cultural Recall in the Present*, Hanover: University Press of New England, p.96.

[23] The majority of patients upon whom Sigmund Freud and Josef Breuer based their theories of hysteria (such as Ida Bauer and Bertha Pappenheim) were Jewish women.

[24] Marianne Hirsch (1996) "Projected Memory: Holocaust Photographs in Personal and Public Fantasy," in Bal, Crewe and Spitzer (Eds.) (1996), p.15.

[25] Rosenthal (1977) "*Charm,*" in Rosenthal (2001), pp.30-31.

[26] Philologos (2006) "Is 'Limbo' On Its Way Out?" *The Forward,* 6 January, at: http://www.forward.com/articles/7126 (accessed 21 April 2006).

[27] Rachel Rosenthal (1990) "*Pangaean Dreams,*" in Rosenthal (2001), pp.194-195.

[28] Doreen Massey (2005) *For Space*, London: Sage Publications, p.130.

[29] *Ibid.,* p.137.

[30] Alisa Solomon (1997) *Re-Dressing the Canon: Essays on Theatre and Gender*, London & New York: Routledge, pp.126-128. My emphasis.

[31] See Roberta Mock (2007) *Jewish Women on Stage, Film and Television*, New York: Palgrave Macmillan. This book focuses specifically on high profile performers working in mainstream contexts.

[32] Marjorie Garber (1999) *Symptoms of Culture*, Harmondsworth: Penguin.

[33] Diana Taylor (2003) *The Archive and the Repertoire: Performing Cultural Memory in the Americas*, Durham: Duke University Press, p.20.

[34] *Ibid.*, p.86.

[35] Una Chaudhuri (2001) "Commentary: Freaks of Nature," in Rosenthal (2001), pp.197-198.

[36] Sarah Bernhardt, Sophie Tucker, Joan Rivers, Judith Malina and Barbra Streisand are some obvious examples.

[37] Ruth Weisberg (1981) "Reaching for Revelations," in Roth (Ed.) (1996), p.111.

[38] Alisa Solomon (1997) *Re-Dressing the Canon: Essays on Theatre and Gender*, London & New York: Routledge, p.123 & p.126.

[39] Thalia Gouma-Peterson (1999) *Miriam Schapiro: Shaping the Fragments of Arts and Life*, New York: Harry N. Abrams Inc., pp.124-128.

[40] I do not know whether Schapiro's image was made, consciously or not, with Rosenthal in mind.

[41] Diana Taylor (2003), p.28.

[42] Interview with Rachel Rosenthal, Conducted by Moira Roth in Los Angeles, California (September 2, 1989), *Smithsonian Archives of American Art*.

[43] Rachel Rosenthal, Performance Description of *KabbaLAmobile*, at: http://www.w3art.com/rr01/rr01t07.html (accessed 25 July 2006).

[44] Quoted in "Artist's Project: Rachel Rosenthal," *Modiya*, at: http://hdl.handle.net/1964/446 (accessed 24 April 2006). An edited excerpt of *KabbaLAmobile* on video is available to watch from this page.

[45] There are, of course, many non-Jewish followers of "Kabbalah," especially in California (I have used quotation marks to indicate that this version of Kabbalah is obviously light years away from its meaning and usage in the lives of Chassidic Jews.) Rosenthal's interest seems to emerge at the start of this trend.

[46] Philologos (2006).

[47] Quoted in Grilikhes (1994-95), pp.62-63.

[48] Mieke Bal (1999) "Memories in the Museum: Preposterous Histories for Today," in Bal, Crewe and Spitzer (Eds.) (1999), p.180.

[49] Mike Pearson (2006) *"In Comes I": Performance, Memory and Landscape*, Exeter: University of Exeter Press, p.6.

[50] See Knut Hidle, "Place, Geography and the Concept of Diaspora – A Methodological Approach," p.2, at: http://www.nhh.no/geo/Nyesider/GIBframe/GIB.full.pdf/244.pdf (accessed 15 February 2007).

[51] Stuart Hall (1996) "New Cultures for Old," in Doreen Massey and Pat Jess (Eds.) *A Place in the World: Places, Culture and Globalization*, Oxford: Oxford University Press, p.47.

[52] Steve Pile and Nigel Thrift (1995) "Mapping the Subject," in Pile and Thrift (Eds.), *Mapping the Subject: Geographies of Cultural Transformation*, London & New York: Routledge, pp.18-19.

[53] Andreas Huyssen (1995) *Twilight Memories: Marking Time in a Culture of Amnesia*, New York: Routledge, p.3.

[54] Many different versions of this chapter have been presented at conferences and seminars, including to the Jewish Intercultural Working Party (IFTR, Helsinki, 2006), Performance & the Body Working Group (TaPRA, London, 2006), University of Wolverhampton (2007), Theatre & Performance Research Group at the University of Plymouth (2007) and the Centre for Critical Cultural Research Symposium at the University of Plymouth (2008). I am grateful to the many colleagues who offered suggestions and helpful comments and would particularly like to thank Joshua Sofaer, Colin Counsell, Phil Smith, Royona Mitra and Mariana Ifolde.

BELATED SPACES: EMBODYING EMBODIMENT IN HOLOCAUST TOURISM

BRYONI TREZISE

If to remember is to provide the disembodied 'wound' with a psychic residence, then to remember other people's memories is to be wounded by their wounds.... Finally, to remember other people's memories is to inhabit time... The function of recollection... is to transform not reproduce. (Kaja Silverman)[1]

Embodying Embodiment

Theatre and performance theorists have long debated the complex role of the body in enabling the transmission of cultural memory. As a memory form in itself, theatre has been described as being "ghosted" in a way that sets it outside of other visual media. Marvin Carlson has famously written of theatre's hauntedness, which owes to its capacity for not only recall, but for a particular kind of repetition staged in the retelling, re-enactment and re-experience privileged by embodied practice.[2] Scholars such as Alice Rayner understand the complexity of this repetition less through conceptions of mimesis, and more through notions of ontology, which position the theatrical double not as an imitation of an original, but as "an appearance of a dynamic contradiction... that cannot come to rest in either what is visible or invisible."[3] This tension between visible and invisible, appeared and disappeared, aligns theatre with a mythology of ghostliness but also bespeaks the deeper connections it holds to questions of existentiality – that is, concerns fundamental to the enactment of cultural memory. In this, theatre stages what Peggy Phelan terms the "the drama of corporeality,"[4] such that it might be argued that performing cultural memory demonstrates, to some degree, the tautological embodying of embodiment itself.

For Phelan, the ontology of disappearance enabled by the live performing body is evidence of its capacity to operate beyond representation. "Performance cannot... participate in the circulation of representations," she writes, "once it does so, it becomes something other than performance."[5] Phelan's argument suggests that what theatre "loses" by way of ephemerality is central to how we understand the contingencies of the knowledges that it constructs. Knowledge, for Phelan, is necessarily built by the ways that performing bodies stage themselves *through* acts of (dis)appearance. In this, the quotidian performer entertains an ontological loss that is correlative to broader memory concerns. Theorists such as Richard Schechner and Joseph Roach read embodiment differently, taking the operations of liveness in the opposite direction. Rather than emphasise the transience of all performance, Schechner focalises notions of "twice behaved behaviour"[6] to argue that while one particular body may disappear, the corporeal knowledges that it holds still remain. Roach applies notions of surrogacy and substitution to flesh out how it is that communal behaviours are remembered across time. In his argument, actions are repeated to enable continuity, while at the same time, the very act of substitution suppresses its own secondariness. A substitute can only ever stand in for that which was formerly there by ironically pretending that they were always there.[7]

For Diana Taylor, the practices of substitution present in restored behaviour represent cultural repertoire – the way in which performance "enacts embodied memory: ... gestures, orality, movement, dance, singing... all those acts usually thought of as ephemeral, nonreproducible knowledge."[8] Taylor positions repertoire in tension with the archive, which "exists as documents, maps, literary texts, letters ... all those items supposedly resistant to change... [W]e might conclude that the archival, from the beginning, sustains power."[9] While Taylor's writing registers a lament for the (lost) role of the body in sustaining knowledges of import, she also concedes that "[w]hat changes over time is the value, relevance, or meaning of the archive, how the items it contains get interpreted, even embodied."[10] In this regard, while an emphasis on embodiment as the *modus operandi* of performance reveals its particular manipulations of disappearance (Phelan), or restoration (Roach), the body can be seen to more productively function as the site by which the archive is enacted as affective knowledge, or doubly, as the site through which the archive formulates corporeal metascripts: the continuous enactment of social norms that enables dominant cultural meanings to prevail.

In the case studies that follow, I argue that the problematically emphasised idea of embodiment can be used to understand contemporary spatial sites dedicated to the public remembrance of cultural trauma. In doing so, I suggest that a paradigm of *embodying embodiment* can be detected in the spatial and performative strategies manipulated by the sites under discussion. My analysis focuses on the narratives offered for re-embodiment by three tourist memorials situated in Germany and Poland: Peter Eisenman's *Memorial to the Murdered Jews of Europe* (Berlin), Christian Boltanski's *Missing House* (Berlin) and the Auschwitz-Birkenau Memorial and Museum (Oswiecem). Through these sites I argue that the stakes of embodiment as a mnemonic tool rest in how it figures identification with the subject positions of victim and perpetrator: in essence, how it invites tourists to align themselves with Polish-German, or German-Polish cultural perspectives. In each, it is the conflation of two "dramas of corporeality" (the past and the present) that stages the tourist *as a body* who must remember. In this, the sites not only differ in the implementation of embodiment for cultural ends, but reveal embodiment's role in the narration of power that attends the histories of the sites themselves.

Inheriting Memory

In recent Polish-German Holocaust discourse, scholars widely debate the role of history in assembling perceptions of victim-perpetrator responsibilities. For Steven Sampson, there exists a degree of contention around "the culpability of perpetrators," but the controversy of the topic also enables "[a]lternative versions of truth" through "generating new 'conversations' in German and Polish societies about who is guilty of what."[11] While this discourse encompasses the complex refractions of economic, geographic, pre-World War II and religious histories that frame the two countries, and indeed has attempted to move beyond a simplistic rendering of victim-perpetrator roles, the spatial histories offered for tourist embodiment often fail to encompass the breadth of such discussion. In this regard, writers such as Omar Bartov argue that such a stringent "discourse on enemies and victims" is no longer a tenable standpoint. As one of "the most crucial issues of this century," Bartov provocatively argues for its role in the perpetuation of violence, guiding "conduct in and perceptions of war and genocide" by "redefin[ing] our views of victimhood and identity."[12] In this light, an ethico-political critique of embodiment explains not only how tourists engage with the aesthetics of remembrance, but how they are enabled to take on the social subject position – and hence cultural identity – embedded within the tenets of a site's aesthetic program.

The prevalence of embodiment as a strategy for recollection has arisen out of an interest in the cultural role of the aesthetic as one paradigm of expressing intergenerational relationships to the past. Marianne Hirsch terms this fraught space between forbears and new family members "postmemory," typified as a legacy of inheriting traumatic pasts from a position of the present that is inflected with doubt, ambivalence, guilt or rage. Hirsch explains that postmemory is "distinguished from memory by generational distance... its connection to its object or source is mediated not through recollection but through an imaginative investment and creation."[13] The role of embodiment in disseminating this kind of legacy has been figured as paramount to effecting *affect* in the body of the spectator and so to activating a transaction that operates beyond mere cognitive identification.

Scholars have well noted the shifts in strategies made by museum curators, art makers and architects for the preservation of shrinking knowledge about horrific pasts. The highly discussed Holocaust museum in Washington and the well documented Jewish Museum in Berlin are both cases in point for moving the domain of Holocaust representation from one of narrative cognition to one of embodied knowledge. Alison Landsberg argues that this trend in American mass culture "reflects a change in what constitutes knowledge."[14] The body of the visitor is figured as primary to the implementation of historical understanding by "complement[ing] the cognitive with affect, sensuousness and tactility."[15]

Kaja Silverman writes evocatively of the intimate viscerality that needs to occur for such intergenerational, empathic acts of recollection to take place. Silverman argues that such acts privilege "a profoundly dialectical relationship to the other" that speaks hauntingly of the disembodied wound which seeks landing in unknown bodily terrain. The terminology of a "psychic residence" here suggests homecoming and welcome, but also points to the political grain of Silverman's argument. "We" – the witness, the spectator, the listener, the visitor – are to be physically impressed by this wound so that it changes us and so that we change it. The force of this exchange is to be such that both past and present revisit each other to enable the transformative potential in mutated memories, prosthetic recollections and infiltrated histories to be activated.[16] Jill Bennett considers this potential in artworks that mark a discursive shift from semiotic effects to empathic affect. Bennett argues that these works source a "communicable language of sensation… with which to register something of the experience of traumatic memory."[17] Within this language, what Bennett importantly describes as Deleuze's version of the "*encountered sign*" works not as an enabler of sympathy, but rather as an enabler of empathy grounded in "a *feeling for* another that entails an encounter with something irreducible and different, often inaccessible."[18]

From Bennett's perspective, while the aim of affect is to summons the spectator to witness trauma with bodily knowledge, this might nonetheless involve a lessening of the narrative at stake and instead operate in aid of a more Brechtian form of understanding.[19] Such a premise of distance – of embodying *embodiment* if you will – bears particularly high stakes when, in the words of Dominic LaCapra, the work of memory should enable the recognition of the "'Himmler' in oneself" as much as the Himmler in the Other.[20] Such arguments implicitly suggest that "true" recognition of victimhood only arises with the recognition first of the "'Himmler' in oneself." Employing the corporeal whilst also rupturing its psychic force is a complex manoeuvre for memorial aesthetics to maintain, and yet Bennett's reading acknowledges the complicity of embodiment within co-constructions of hierarchies of knowledge and difference. To this degree, an empathic politics of embodiment begins with a double premise: cultural memory sites perform embodiment as equally as embodiment is *performative*: that is, as a cultural strategy it is deeply embedded within relations of power.

Missing the Missing: Christian Boltanski's Absence

I walk along Berlin's Grosshamburger Strasse and I miss it. I walk back again and still miss it. There are no signposts to this memorial, but I know that it exists. I walk again and realise that my pursuit of what I continue to miss – Christian Boltanski's *The Missing House* – is filled with decent irony. We are supposed to miss it; it is supposed to be missed. When I finally see it, or, when I finally see the *absence* of it, Boltanski's *Missing House* strikes for its suburban character. The artwork is placed in the centre of living quarters tucked away on a narrow strip with cafés and high-end fashion. The memorial house is homage to an original house destroyed in bombing raids in 1945. Now I behold the house's absence and feel as if I am trespassing not on sacred ground as much as on private property. The missing house is gated and its space has become a landscaped garden that bridges the apartment blocks on either side. Close-up, the house is suggested by 12 mounted plaques on the neighbour's façade which list its former inhabitants, their profession and their period of tenancy. Their names signify absent bodies, representing a future that did not eventuate.

Figure 1: Christian Boltanski *Missing House*, Grosshamburger Strasse, Berlin, 2005. Photo: Bryoni Trezise.

Alison Lewis characterises the Holocaust as the foundational point of German identity. In this it is a "negative myth of origin and a primal phantasmatic scene of guilt and shame around which German national identifications are organised."[21] For the tourist Berlin performs multiple temporal and experiential relations to this foundational point. As Deputy Director of the Jüdisches Museum Berlin, Tom Freudenheim states, "[i]f you are in Berlin you can't escape the Holocaust. All of Berlin is a memorial site."[22] In this regard, the specific history of Boltanski's *Missing House* is important to understanding the memorial *poesis* the house creates for its contemporary viewers. The house characterises a number of vantage points that position German identity as both victim and perpetrator in relation to the act of destruction that the house signifies. Abigail Solomon-

Godeau explains that 15/16 Grosshamburger Strasse was destroyed in the allied bombings of 3 February 1945, a raid which itself de-housed over 120,000 civilians:

> Two of the building's central staircases and the apartments on their landings were destroyed; those people in those apartments on those stairwells were perhaps maimed or killed; those living on either side were spared.[23]

For Solomon-Godeau, what becomes important of the house's history is the different categories of victimhood that it inscribes:

> … prior to 1942 many of the building's residents were Jews. By the time of the bombings, however, those tenants had been evicted, displaced, deported, and presumably liquidated. Thus, when the allied bombings occurred, many of the tenants were German Aryans who had replaced the now-vanished Jewish residents.[24]

In being a memorial to the lives of Aryan-Germans re-inhabiting the site of already decimated Jewish-Germans, *Missing House* unintentionally charts an uncanny sense of double death in the categories of victimhood it generates. Indeed it constructs a layer of mourning around *both* Aryan and Jewish categories within German cultural identity more generally, while at the same time positioning both Allied Forces and Nazis as central perpetrators of the violence now being re-witnessed.

At the same time, the sense of duplicitous haunting is not overtly present in the artwork itself. In fact, none of the abovementioned facts detail the specificity of the lives that were lost, or how they were lost. As Boltanski explains:

> What interested me about this project was that you can take any house in Paris, New York, or Berlin, and with that one house, you can reconstruct an entire historical situation.[25]

Boltanski's flippancy is essential to reading the politics embedded within this work. To behold the house is to behold its *denouement* and my participation within its denouement. As a viewer, in order to recreate the house, I need to first reassemble its absence. "My work is not about, it is after," Boltanski has said.[26] Boltanski's work remakes the event of disappearance by foregrounding the role of embodiment as central to the process of enacting remains. As tourists, we arrive in the *eftermaele* to reassemble the pieces. This is a simultaneous act of resurrection and destruction. As a participant I am made complicit in the act of absence making. I have no choice in my subject position: I am guilty of making the work *work*, which is also to say, I am guilty of making the house re-disappear.

The art of making disappearance re-disappear as opposed to reconstructing the disappeared is geared towards foregrounding affect rather than mimesis as a privileged mode of remembrance. As a participant in Boltanski's memorial I do not merely peruse the life of the victim, I am contributor to their immanent destruction. In this sense, embodiment does not place me directly inside the house, but rather places me as an executor of the violence enacted upon it. The power relation that I come to inhabit in relation to these absent bodies forces me to inscribe a victim-perpetrator opposition through how my *affective* encounter with the work is central to my ability to read it. In wanting to tell a history, this site reproduces the power-relations of that history in performative terms. Furthermore, when understanding the historical weight of the house, I begin to understand that the very absence that I am forced to remake masks the more sinister absence of the originary Jewish inhabitants (who are made doubly absent by being un-recollected by the memorial itself). When contemplating the ethico-political role of embodiment in constructions of German memory, I become complicit not only in the destruction of the Aryan inhabitants, but *complicit* in the surreptitious "secret" surrounding the lost Jewish bodies that the house unwittingly maintains.

Acts of Return: Photographs from the Wound-point

In ethnographic discourse, embodiment is aligned with the function of transmitting cultural memory. Discussing the spirit possession rituals of the Hauka tribe of West Africa, Paul Stoller explains that embodiment constitutes a relation between "the centrality of the sentient body" and political power. In doing this, it becomes "an arena in which cultural memory is... refashioned" by formulating the body as a site through which power is contested.[27] Via Stoller, in this second example of spatially produced Polish-German relations, I point to the tautology by which embodiment becomes *embodied*. If memory is always an embodied practice, then a discursive repetition of embodiment as a cultural trauma strategy ultimately draws continuity between the *experience* of the bodies that were lost, and the *experience* of the bodies given to recollect loss. In this, embodiment holds a heightened semiotic value when positioned as an outright stratagem of traumatic memory. The presence of tourist bodies on a traumascape comes to signify loss itself, staging one "drama of corporeality" in relation to the historicity of a former one. In Stoller's work, cultural memory forms employ the embodied as a way of continuing social narratives and contesting power. In sites of traumatic memory, the very materiality of the bodily performs itself in contrast to the absent bodies that comprise the scene of trauma itself. Liveness ultimately stages its ontology as an act of return in place of the disappeared.

The slippage between such corporeal repetitions is nowhere clearer than at the Auschwitz-Birkenau memorial in Oswiecem, Poland, a site positioned as the oppositional wound-point to Berlin's hypersaturated memoryscape. Auschwitz is situated on the city edge so that the journey towards it strikes a temporal and spatial dislocation. While *Missing House* invited tourists to become co-conspirators of atrocity, at Auschwitz tourists are invited take on the emotional visage of Holocaust victims themselves. As a first step in this kind of embodiment the process of arrival (indeed, even the lengthy queues of tourists who swarm these sites) stages the act of return as an ambivalent reminder of the bodies who never left. Auschwitz-Birkenau comprises two components: the first, a tour of Auschwitz I, comprising educational information, museum displays and guides; the second a visit to the Birkenau site – an emotively barren landscape save crumbling buildings, the end of a train line and a memorial.

While both sites seek to educate tourists into the atrocities of the Holocaust, they also work in tandem to establish the context for embodied performance that the tourist then plays out. Unlike the *Missing House*, this form of embodiment is figured around an investment in victimhood, where the tourist is educated into the narrative of the Holocaust, and is then transported to the traumascape as if to inhabit the predisposition of the victims they themselves. While in the first sequence, tourists are taught about the levels of destruction, the minority groups targeted and the numbers of those who died, in the second sequence, tourists apply this cognitive knowledge to the way that they then inhabit the authenticities of historical space.

Auschwitz-Birkenau is a deeply emotional experience for many visitors. At the same time it limits its capacity for remembrance by stunting the ethico-political possibilities of embodiment and denying tourists a range of subject positions from which to experience its history. The projection of victimhood as one key component of Polish identity, and doubly, the projection of victim-perpetrator paradigms as ground points from which to envisage Polish-German relations are here made manifestly clear. Understanding the "Himmler in oneself" is offensive, as is the even more problematic disposition of attempting to recognise the humanity in a Himmler. The overwhelmingly numb feeling of despair often felt at this site is given no space from which to destabilise the past, and so to, again in the words of Silverman, transformatively *produce* it. When Silverman argues that embodying the wound of another should enable transformative recollection, what she means is that *through* the very process of embodiment, the categories by which it is established should be made playful, arbitrary, unstable. At Auschwitz-Birkenau, tourist bodies are neither free to chart a new bodily action nor are they compelled to inhabit the scriptural, behavioural terms for the bodies who once suffered there. If performance is an act of surrogacy akin to Roach's argument, visiting concentration camps might be here understood as a collective re-inhabitation of the bodily scripts of the dead.

So, what does the tourist body do to resituate the broader dynamics of Polish-German memory? Tourists take photographs. These are photographs of the family *emplaced* within the site – a performance of family literally remaking the archive through repertoire. Marianne Hirsch describes the experience of family photography for Holocaust survivors as often experienced as pockmarked catalogues of trauma. The current Auschwitz photographs are now precisely staged. One, in front of the crematorium drum: a mother, a father and their two children. *They smile*. As Roland Barthes has made clear, the eye of the camera says "[t]his will be and this has been."[28] It attests to presence against the absence-making of time.

So what to make of these snapshots, photographs re-wedged into the scene of destruction? The relationships between embodied performance and the historico-materiality of the site here become telling. Firstly, the new photographs perform as a revenant correcting the "this was [not] here" to a "this is here now" signified by the photograph as a sign of familial survival. In this transition, repertoire enables an updating of the archive by re-emplacing archival remains at the expense of what has been corporeally lost. Secondly, as *performance*, the social enactment of photography itself wrestles with the overriding behavioural script of the place. In this, the lines of body and sight that walk the space become re-written as contemporary tourist bodies *trace over* the originating mnemonic register of the landscape.

The Empty Signification of Peter Eisenman's Boxes

Figures 2 & 3: Peter Eisenman *Memorial to the Murdered Jews of Europe*, Berlin, 2005. Photos: Bryoni Trezise.

Are they supposed to resemble coffins? This is a question put to our guide on approaching Berlin's newest holocaust monument, *Memorial to the Murdered Jews in Europe*, opened in 2005. They are definitely coffin-like, the stern black rectangular boxes rising into the sky at different heights from a grid platform. Architect Peter Eisenman designed the 2711 concrete stelae and their measurements are precisely geometric: 95 centimetres by 2.98 metres, forming endless corridors in a paradoxically predictable and yet maze-like formation. The boxes ascend, and coupled against each other create waves of undulation as they move into height and down again. Their pattern is mesmeric and their presence awesome, expanding over almost five acres of Berlin's Potsdamer Platz, a former dead zone in front of the Berlin Wall. From a distance the boxes consume a whole neighbourhood, writing a blanket of grey disturbance across the rhythms of daily life. Up close and inside, they are strangely inanimate. Bodies become alone and anonymous walking through their drab pathways. It is cold and empty inside the shadows. There is nothing to behold. No mystery, no trick, and certainly no labyrinthine secret exit.

While the memorial was designed for the purpose of remembrance, the catalogue explains that it instead "raise[s] the question of remembrance and its location" through "wholly avoiding creating an impression of finality."[29] The memorial is disturbing for its resistance of finality on a number of levels. There is no plaque dedicating the monument to its history. As one online blogger has commented: "I'm here. In Berlin. Spent 5 hours at the Memorial yesterday. It's wonderful – because it's the only place in Berlin where I did NOT think of the Holocaust..."[30] Eisenman explains that the memorial "attempts to decontextualise the Holocaust... Not to try and locate it, not to try and make it a thing of nostalgia, not to try and make it be rationalized."[31] While it holds an underground museum dedicated to the history of murdered Jews, the memorial itself acknowledges nothing of this history bar the image of the boxes themselves.

In this sense, the gravestones can simply perform as a creatively inhabitable civic space: "I like to think that people will use it for short cuts, as an everyday experience, not as a holy place."[32] Children play and jump in this strange landscape, however formidable the sharp cement edges may be. Differently, the design has also caused outrage. While the memorial might be largely unreadable, the history of the anti-graffiti paint used to preserve the boxes has not been so ambiguous. Provided by a company formerly associated with the provision of Zyclon B to the Nazi concentration camps, there stands a point of commonality not without irony.

The memorial arrived in Berlin's heightened memory boom as a point of controversy and as a distinct intervention into what the catalogue terms "Berlin's new satisfaction with itself":

> The *Memorial*... intends to disturb and discompose. Before the city and country lean back and act as if things were back to normal – could ever be back to normal – the question is raised here, cast in stone: what does the city have in mind as it re-moves the ruins of history and makes itself a cosy sitting room again?[33]

The catalogue argues that the memorial draws a "line in stone under the past"[34] in a way that suggests that its purpose is to draw a line under how memory itself should function. But "what message could an abstract monument not associated with a particular place or event be expected to have?"[35] What is it to inhabit, to make meaning from, to peruse or eat lunch on a space which insists upon refusal, ambivalence or improvisational play? Who does it make me become as I walk, eat, jump or forget along its greyness? What does it signify in its failure to signify?

For memory to work here, it intentionally resists nostalgic longings and instead refuses what it is most used to naming. The pretence of the memorial suggests that it is precisely inside the moment in which memory is refused that another kind of memory emerges: one built out of improvisational gestures given in how the body informs, moves through and ultimately writes the space. This is the conjectural space of inhabiting the suspension of signification itself. As an architectural play, the memorial's blank architecture plays with the architecture of memory: it is an invitation to replay new memories against the structures of old ones.

In light of the notion that Berlin is not only embedded *in* memory, but performs a relationship *to* memory, this memorial clearly unpacks the relationship between these two parameters. Where we formerly understood the positioning of the Holocaust as a "primal phantasmatic scene of guilt and shame," Eisenman's memorial instantiates a practice of both enacting and resisting memory that places at Berlin's centre, not the Holocaust, but a centre of multiplicity and paradox. The monument not only raises questions of how to remember, when to remember and who to remember, but its design itself asks the question of what memory *is*, what it *is* to remember. While the structure was designed specifically to memorialise murdered Jews, it instead enacts memorialisation as a statement against prolonging longing itself. What is it to resist the reinstantiation of loss as a version of contemporary memorial practice? What is it to "lose" the "loss" that memory would otherwise need to keep intact?

Different to Boltanksi's house, the memorial cannot be physically missed. Boltanksi's house needs to be searched out, a glimmer discernible to the clever eye only. Eisenman's memorial is a grandiose statement pitched in the heart of the city. While the house made an absence present, Eisenman uses overt presence to signify into a potential, but not named, absence. This tendency is an *ambivalent absence*, a hallmark of a postmemorial aesthetic. While Boltanski's design locates a response to the ruin in terms of referential loss, Eisenman's design is not the reconstruction of a lost object but an inhabitable landscape that signifies multiply and invites multiple behaviours into its corridors. The memorial can be read as a gloomy rendition of coffin boxes *or* as a statement that ignores its lost object altogether. More than anything, it signifies its own ambivalence about signification. I am both victim and perpetrator, caught within my desire to re-experience the loss of another. Walking in this landscape of tiered and blankly ominous boxes, I recollect all of the different memorial sites I have visited. Auschwitz appears in my mind, but here it is given the possibility to replay itself in how I re-script this intensely ambivalent space. In this, the victim-perpetrator, Polish-German narrative that I have been embodying becomes a re-mapping of the claims memory holds towards embodiment. As a newly remembering body, I am enabled to write and explore the multiplicity of histories held spatially herein.

Works Cited

Barthes, R. (1981) *Camera Lucida* [1980], trans. Richard Howard, New York: Hill and Wang.

Bartov, O. (1998) "Defining Enemies, Making Victims: Germans, Jews, and the Holocaust," *The American Historical Review*, 103.3: pp.771-816.

BBC News (2005) "Berlin Opens Holocaust Memorial," *BBC World News*, 10 May, at:
http://www.news.bbc.co.uk/2/hi/europe/4531669.stm (accessed 22 April 2006).

Bennett, J. (2005) *Empathic Vision: Affect, Trauma and Contemporary Art*, Stanford: Stanford University Press.

Carlson, M. (2001) *The Haunted Stage: Theatre as Memory Machine*, Ann Arbor: University of Michigan Press.

A Daily Dose of Architecture Blog, at:
http://www.archidose.blogspot.com/2005/05/stelae.html (accessed 22 April 2006).

Hirsch, M. (1997) *Family Frames: Photography, Narrative and Postmemory*, Cambridge, Massachusetts and London: Harvard University Press.

Hollander, J. (2003) "Peter Eisenman, Architecture'60, Designs New Holocaust Memorial in Berlin," *Columbia University News*, at:
http://www.columbia.edu/cu/news/03/07/peterEisenman.html (accessed 22 April 2006).

Kaiser, S. (2005) *Postmemories of Terror: A New Generation Copes with the Legacies of the "Dirty War,"* New York: Palgrave Macmillan.

Kapralski, S. (2001) "Battlefields of Memory: Landscape and Identity in Polish-Jewish Relations," *History & Memory*, 13.2, pp.35-38

LaCapra, D. (1998) *History and Memory After Auschwitz*, Ithaca and London: Cornell University Press

Landsberg, A. (1997) "America, the Holocaust, and the Mass Culture of Memory: Toward a Radical Politics of Empathy," *New German Critique*, 71, pp.63-86.

Lewis, A. (2003) "Germany's Metamorphosis," *Cultural Studies Review*, 9:2, pp.102-122.

Lury, C. (1998) *Prosthetic Culture: Photography, Memory and Identity*, New York and London: Routledge.

Marranca, B. and G. Dasgupta (2000) "Berlin's New Jewish Museum: An Interview with Tom Freudenheim," *PAJ: A Journal of Performance and Art*, 22:2, pp.39-47.

Phelan, P. (1993) *Unmarked*, New York and London: Routledge.

—. (1997) *Mourning Sex: Performing Public Memories*, New York and London: Routledge.

Rayner, A. (2006) *Ghosts*, Minneapolis: University of Minnesota Press.

Roach, J. (1996) *Cities of the Dead: Circum-Atlantic Performance*, New York: Columbia University Press.

Sampson, S. (2003) "From Reconciliation to Coexistence," *Public Culture*, 15:1, pp. 181-186.

Schechner, R. (2006) *Performance Studies: An Introduction* [2002], New York and London: Routledge.

Schlör, J. (2005) *Memorial to the Murdered Jews of Europe*, trans. Paul Aston, Munich, London, Berlin and New York: Prestel.

Silverman, K. (1996) *The Threshold of the Visible World*, New York and London: Routledge.

Solomon-Godeau, A. (1998) "Mourning or Melancholia: Christian Boltanski's 'Missing House'," *Oxford Art Journal*, 21.2, pp.3-20.

Stoller, P. (1995) *Embodying Colonial Memories*, New York and London: Routledge.

Taylor, D. (2003) *The Archive and the Repertoire: Performing Cultural Memory in the Americas*, Durham and London: Duke University Press.

Tumarkin, M. (2005) *Traumascapes*, Victoria: Melbourne University Press.

Young, J.E. (1999) "Memory, Counter-Memory and the End of the Monument," *Harvard Design Magazine*, 9, pp.1-10, at: http://www.gsd.harvard.edu/research/publications/hdm/back/9young.pdf (accessed 3 April 2009).

Notes

[1] Kaja Silverman (1996) *The Threshold of the Visible World*, New York and London: Routledge, p.189.
[2] Marvin Carlson (2001) *The Haunted Stage: Theatre as Memory Machine*, Ann Arbor: University of Michigan Press, p.3.
[3] Alice Rayner (2006) *Ghosts*, Minneapolis: University of Minnesota Press, p.xii.
[4] Peggy Phelan (1997) *Mourning Sex*, New York and London: Routledge, p.4.
[5] Peggy Phelan (1993) *Unmarked*, New York and London: Routledge, p.146.
[6] Richard Schechner (2006) *Performance Studies: An Introduction* [2002], New York and London: Routledge, p.34.
[7] Joseph Roach (1996) *Cities of the Dead*, New York: Columbia University Press, p.5.
[8] Diana Taylor (2003) *The Archive and the Repertoire*, Durham and London: Duke University Press, p.20.
[9] *Ibid.*, p.19.
[10] *Ibid.*
[11] Steven Sampson (1998) "From Reconciliation to Coexistence," *Public Culture*, 15.1, p.183.
[12] Omar Bartov (1998) "Defining Enemies, Making Victims: Germans, Jews, and the Holocaust," *The American Historical Review*, 103, p.772.
[13] Marianne Hirsch (1997) *Family Frames: Photography, Narrative and Postmemory*, Cambridge, Massachusetts and London: Harvard University Press, p.22.
[14] Alison Landsberg (1997) "America, the Holocaust, and the Mass Culture of Memory: Toward a Radical Politics of Empathy," *New German Critique*, 71, p.77.
[15] *Ibid.*, p.76.
[16] See Celia Lury (1998) *Prosthetic Culture: Photography, Memory and Identity*, New York and London: Routledge, for a discussion on prosthetic memory.
[17] Jill Bennett (2005) *Empathic Vision: Affect, Trauma and Contemporary Art*, Stanford: Stanford University Press, p.2.
[18] *Ibid.*, p.7 & p.10 (italics original).
[19] *Ibid.*, p.10.
[20] Dominic LaCapra (1998) *History and Memory After Auschwitz,* Ithaca and London: Cornell University Press, p.34.
[21] Alison Lewis (2003) "Germany's Metamorphosis," *Cultural Studies Review*, 9.2, p.105.
[22] Bonnie Marranca and Gautam Dasgupta (2000) "Berlin's New Jewish Museum: An Interview with Tom Freudenheim," *PAJ: A Journal of Performance and Art*, 22.2, p.46.
[23] Abigail Solomon-Godeau (1998) "Mourning or Melancholia: Christian Boltanski's 'Missing House'," *Oxford Art Journal*, 21.2, p.3.
[24] *Ibid.*

[25] As quoted in Solomon-Godeau (1998), p.7.

[26] As quoted in Hirsch (1997), p.259.

[27] Paul Stoller (1995) *Embodying Colonial Memories*, New York and London: Routledge, p.21.

[28] Roland Barthes (1981) *Camera Lucida*, New York: Hill and Wang, p.96.

[29] Joachim Schlör (2005) *Memorial to the Murdered Jews of Europe*, Munich, London, Berlin and New York: Prestel, p.38.

[30] Edward, comment on *A Daily Dose of Architecture Blog*, comment posted 10 May 2005, http://www.archidose.blogspot.com/2005/05/stelae.html (accessed April 22, 2006).

[31] Jason Hollander "Peter Eisenman Designs New Holocaust Memorial in Berlin", *Columbia University News*, at:
http://www.columbia.edu/cu/news/03/07/peterEisenman.html (accessed 22 April 2006).

[32] Peter Eisenman quoted in "Berlin Opens Holocaust Memorial," *BBC World News*, at: http://www.news.bbc.co.uk/2/hi/europe/4531669.stm (accessed 22 April 2006).

[33] Schlör (2005), p.5.

[34] *Ibid.*, p.38.

[35] *Ibid.*, p.33.

BARCELONA:
EARTH, PUPPETS AND EMBODIMENT

CARIAD ASTLES

Barcelona is a haunted city. As the capital of Catalonia, it has been respectively colonised, annexed, invaded, re-colonised, assimilated; it has reached autonomy, been re-annexed, and now enjoys an uneasy status as a "nation without a state," linked tangibly to the Spanish state yet with a high degree of separation. Spectres of the Civil War and the brutal repression of Catalan people and their cultural identity still haunt its streets and institutions, despite attempts by the *Generalitat* (government) to symbolically erase traces of those traumatic times.

Apart from a decade of effervescent protest during the 1970s, Catalans have hesitated to examine too much the experiences of the repression under the dictatorship, with artists preferring on the whole to instead reaffirm their identity as Catalan, drawing inspiration from their cultural environment. The puppeteer-painter Joan Baixas has been a pioneering force within Catalan theatre since the late 1960s, and his work is emblematic of the Catalans' ongoing attempt to understand both their past and their current identity. This chapter will examine the work of Joan Baixas and related Catalan artists in response to the themes suggested by the title of this book: performance and cultural memory, and embodiment. Puppet theatre has played a significant role within the development of Catalan theatre since the last days of the Franco regime, and Baixas has been one of the main players in establishing Barcelona as a site of theatre memory and conscious re-negotiation.

Marvin Carlson notes the complex and close relationship between space, geography and cultural memory:

> theatre spaces, like dramatic texts and acting bodies, are deeply involved with the preservation and configuration of cultural memory, and so they also are almost invariably haunted in one way or another, and this haunting

of the space of performance makes its own important contribution to the overall reception of the dramatic event.[1]

Carlson here is primarily referring to theatre buildings, but his comment could equally refer to the spaces used by Catalan theatre artists in Barcelona for performance. I earlier referred to Barcelona as a haunted city. Notwithstanding that it could be argued that any place is haunted by the traces of acts and enunciations gone before, Barcelona is *specifically* haunted by memories of the cultural repression undergone by Catalans during the dictatorship of General Franco, which lasted from 1939 until his death in 1975.

It is important here to convey a certain amount of historical information to set in context the performances I will discuss. Both Catalan as a language and Catalan cultural practices were banned during the first decade of Franco's dictatorship, and later suppressed through a cultural policy of subjugation and dominance in which Spanish culture and language were promoted as the culture of education, authority and governance. Immediately prior to the Spanish Civil War, Barcelona was under the control of a Republican government which promoted education and culture in Catalan as part of its mission. Following the defeat of the Republican and Communist forces by the Nationalists, however, Catalan was repressed through a system of censorship of books and theatre, and through propaganda spread by Nationalist troops. The city of Barcelona was re-inscribed as a Spanish city; streets were symbolically re-named after Spanish military victories or Spanish Nationalists.[2]

This process was akin to colonisation as described by Smith and Katz:

> [Colonisation] is predicated on the deliberate, physical, cultural and symbolic appropriation of space … metaphors of colonisation rescript this territorial incursion as an invasion and insidious habitation of the social and psychic space of oppressed groups, while decolonisation becomes a metaphor for the process of recognising and dislodging dominant ideas, assumptions and ideologies as externally imposed – literally of making a cultural and psychic space of one's own.[3]

The Catalan flag and the national anthem were banned, as was any public use of Catalan outside a strictly domestic environment, including all state institutions such as schools and universities. New signs promoting the use of Spanish and denigration of Catalan were installed in public places. These policies towards the abolition of Catalan identity have been described as "cultural genocide" and are discussed in detail by scholars of

Catalan political studies since democracy in Spain.[4] Since 1978, the *Generalitat* in Barcelona has attempted to re-inscribe the city with Catalan identity through re-naming the streets, squares and public places with their former names or with names of Catalan writers, artists and intellectuals, symbolically linking Barcelona with the development of art and thought through its own citizens. The *Generalitat* has also promoted festivals and exhibitions of Catalan culture, ranging from popular festivals such as the September festival of *La Mercé* (the patron saint of Barcelona), which is by and large a celebration of Catalan performance culture, with competitions of "human towers," fire-running, displays by dragons and other mythical beasts from Catalan popular culture, and processions of giant puppets and "bigheads." The *Generalitat* also makes frequent use for public ceremonies of buildings which were originally built in the *moderniste* style. This was part of the Catalan *Renaixença* (Renaissance) in the nineteenth century, a period which saw a resurgence in Catalan national identity coinciding with a growth in experimentation in the visual arts and architecture.

Barcelona has thus become a site for contested identity where the ghosts of the Civil War and past repression mingle on the streets with the ghosts of contemporary Catalan culture. In her discussion of a popular festival, the *Patum* of Berga, Noyes notes that the influence of Francoism still haunts performance: "Anyone over thirty carries traces in their memory of the Francoist performances imposed on them in school and church and the military."[5] Despite positive approaches towards promoting Barcelona as a city of Catalan culture, in-depth research into deaths and disappearances during the Civil War and the years following have been avoided, as they have been throughout Spain in general. It is only in recent years that people have begun to demand the excavation of mass graves and identification of bodies, with full investigations into the events leading to disappearances and massacres. The current polemic surrounding the excavation of the mass grave in which it is believed that the body of the poet and playwright García Lorca was thrown is an example of this.

Joan Baixas

Joan Baixas spent his childhood under the dictatorship and as a young student was quickly absorbed into the antifascist movements beginning to grow at the end of the 1960s. Baixas' work as a puppeteer is symbolic of the processes over the last forty years in Barcelona, for he has consistently addressed questions of cultural memory (not only Catalan) and identity.

Baixas uses objects, puppets and matter (such as sand, paint and water) to articulate contemporary concerns which are directly influenced by past and current events within and beyond Catalonia.

The question of embodiment in relation to puppetry needs a little discussion here. The embodied performer is usually understood as a live, performing body whose experience is transmitted through the phenomenological expression of "liveness." Puppets clearly are not "live" but are constructed beings, built by their maker and expressed through the hands of their performer. I suggest, however, that puppets should be seen as objects of cultural memory which bear the traces of their making, and thus of cultural remnants, in the matter from which they are constructed, the locus of their making/finding, and the presence of their performing. Puppets thus can be both of the "archive" and the "repertoire" as described by Diana Taylor: of the archive as they are physical, material objects referencing particular performances; and of the repertoire as their performance is in no way less ephemeral than those of live bodies.[6] Meaning in puppet performance is therefore articulated through a relationship between the material structures of the objects and the choreography/enactments of the performance itself.

Puppets and animated matter can be seen as "embodiments" in three ways in the work of Joan Baixas. First, as performers made for a specific purpose, with clear intentions, they embody the characters or concepts they represent. Second, through the interference/involvement of their makers – in the case of Baixas, a consciously Catalan artist collaborating with other Catalan artists in the pursuit of artistic endeavour – the puppets/things embody those artists' presence and experience, and traces of their identity, through the process of making. Third, they comprise embodiments in their inscription on the very materials used. Baixas does not work predominantly with figurative puppetry but within visual theatre in a wider sense.

He uses matter such as sand and mud which has been trodden on, marked, sifted or shifted, and so on. In his commentary on walking, De Certeau notes how it is "enunciated" by the choreography and shape-shifting that has been part and parcel of its creation: "the act of walking is to the urban system what the speech act is to language or the statements uttered... it is a process of *appropriation* of the topographical system on the part of the pedestrian."[7] Similarly, in using matter like sand and mud, Baixas demonstrates that his own stories are inscribed into the material as part of the shared stories created through the memory of all who have walked through or across it, or used it in any way.

I will now discuss three phases of Baixas' work, characterised by the performances *Mori el Merma* (*Death to the Tyrant*) which opened in 1978, *Laberint* (*Labyrinth*, 1986) and *Terra Prenyada* (*Pregnant Earth*, 1996), and Baixas' current projects, *Smash!* and *Casadelobos* (2009). These three phases show Baixas' engagement with his own cultural memory, his links as an artist and as a human being to the cultural memories of others, and his use of puppets and matter to evoke and embody cultural memory. I discuss these pieces chronologically, but the analyses weave between the phases of his work.

Baixas and his late partner, Teresa Calafell, formed the puppet theatre *La Claca* in 1967. From the outset his work shunned conventional narrative and sought instead to draw on popular Catalan traditions such as the popular puppet show *Pulxinel.lis*. At this time Catalan society began to re-organise, and interest in educational and creative activities grew dramatically. Catalan associations began to look at their cultural heritage and a generation of new artists, among them Baixas, explored possibilities for creative expression. *La Claca* experimented with masks and puppets, incorporating ideas from visual art practices. Baixas actively sought renewal and renovation, and his work is widely seen in Barcelona as a catalyst of a cultural moment in Catalan life.[8] More than any other artist of his time, he embraced the idea that visual art and performance could work together, and that identity could be re-negotiated through performance.

Catalan Culture and the Carnivalesque

La Claca deliberately chose to perform Catalan stories and folklore, and Baixas and Calafell researched popular traditions such as the bigheads and giant puppets in order to recreate processional, outdoor shows aimed at exorcising the trauma of the past and reclaiming public space. This period of his artistic activity can be described as "carnivalesque" in that it was a comic and festive subversion of the status quo within which Catalan culture was still hidden from public eye by the long practice of censorship and cultural dominance. Baixas' early shows featured grotesque and comic stereotypes, sexual and scatological imagery, and themes which in some way undermined the patriarchal state. These included *l'Espardenyeta* (1969), a show full of childish curses and Catalan colloquialisms, and *Puppet Striptease* (1971). The use of Catalan imagery, such as giant puppets and bigheads, and of Catalan expressions in the performances, demonstrates the embodiment and reclaiming of Catalan culture after years of censorship.[9]

Perhaps most important of all choices made by *La Claca* was their decision to present only in Catalan or without words, not in Castilian, the language of the dictatorship. During the 1970s Baixas acted as a focus for puppetry initiatives, including the founding of the biennial festival of puppetry and visual theatre in Barcelona and the establishment of a puppetry department at the *Institut del Teatre*. One of the exhibitions organised at the 1975 puppet festival served as a starting point for his collaboration with the Catalan artist Joan Miró and his most emblematic show, *Mori el Merma*. This carnivalesque and grotesque show, premiered in Mallorca in 1978, marked a moment of transition in Catalan culture. Baixas' vision of Catalan puppet theatre was always one which made use of heterogeneous forms, and linked the popular to high art:

> I must be clear that when I talk about figures, I make no distinction between puppets and masks, between objects and abstract forms. The art of figures consists in an emotion created by the scenic play of objects charged with meanings and taken on by an actor.[10]

Mori el Merma is a vehemently political play through its carnivalesque portrayal of the figure of Franco himself. In creating this show, Baixas recognises that the ghosts of the past, in the form of grotesque figures of the dictatorship, needed to be exorcised in a way that allowed positive laughter. Without sidestepping the atrocities of the Franco regime, which had just ended with the dictator dying in his bed, not through some act of political rejection by the Spanish or Catalan people, Baixas sought to ridicule and critique the excesses and nonsensical diktats of fascist governments universally, while making it absolutely clear throughout that this referred to the government of Franco. The ghosts of cultural memory thus became comic, laughable figures who had lost their power to cause fear and dominate. They were portrayed as large, overgrown puppets, splashed with Miró's bright colours and childish forms. Thus Franco was portrayed as a gross monster through the use of cultural forms he despised: Catalan art and popular festival.

As stated earlier, the show was a collaboration between Miró and *La Claca*. Baixas has consciously aimed to work with Catalan artists such as painters and musicians in the creation of new pieces. Miró was a deeply politically engaged artist; during the years of the dictatorship he lived in exile in Paris. He wanted Franco to be remembered as a ridiculous and repulsive figure. The performance – which attracted differing responses from the press and audience, ranging from the "shit, shit, shit" of one Barcelona paper to the *Times*' comment that: "London has never seen anything so intense"[11] – marked Miró as a painter of intense Catalan sentiment and sensibility, and one who saw his art as part of a deep social engagement.

Mori el Merma represents the carnivalesque spirit in Catalan theatre post-Franco, creating a grotesque world where authority, patriarchy and official institutions of church and state were ridiculed. Baixas says of the process towards performance:

> This Ubu that we shared with Joan Miró was really none other than Franco, who had died a year before the beginning of our collaboration. We envisioned the piece as our Requiem Mass for Francoism.[12]

Baixas has made it clear that the show was never designed as a political analysis; instead, their aim was more immediate: "To become aware of the monster which had grown inside ourselves ...."[13] This comment notes a significant aspect of Baixas' approach to cultural memory: that the community itself holds some of the responsibility for the ghosts which haunt them. Thus, as Taylor suggests, performances can enter into dialogue with the history of trauma and both re-negotiate meaning and responsibility through the function of witnessing. In the case of *Mori el Merma*, the puppet Merma, the monster, embodied collective fears and revulsion at the spectres of the Civil War and the years of repression. The puppet itself, a giant figure, distorted and overgrown, was made by Baixas and painted by Miró, thus marking the embodiment of the dictatorship with Catalan rewriting. This re-inscription directly onto the body of the puppet was a means by which Baixas and Miró hoped to mark history and mark a clear path for the future, affirming Catalan festive culture over Spanish, Catholic domination. Puppets can thus be re-inscribed with cultural memory and stories re-written directly on their bodies through physical re-configuration.

The story of *Merma* is created through visual theatre; within the story the cruelty and excess of the monster ultimately leads to his fall. Other characters, also grotesque giant puppet figures, include Mrs Merma and Merma's Ministers, who rebel against him. Michael Billington wrote in *The Guardian* that "anti-fascist sentiments can be instilled with carnival energy ... the experience combines fury, fun, energy and wit with that

sense of highly coloured dislocation you get from … Miró's paintings."[14]
Mori el Merma was significant in the late 1970s because it bridged a
moment of profound change in Catalan political and cultural life. Its
resonance at the time of its creation was in its break with the ghosts of the
past and in looking forward to a Catalan future.

It is important to note that Baixas was not alone in his approach to
performance during the 1970s. A number of other significant visual theatre
companies, notably *Els Comediants,* were also working with popular,
festive imagery drawn from Catalan culture, and reclaiming public space
to assert their identity and power. Most puppet theatre at this time focused
on open-air spectacle, researching and re-presenting Catalan folk and
traditional tales through the lens of a renewal of Catalan culture, drawn
from cultural memory. The popular puppet show thus became an
embodiment of Catalan culture itself. No show, however, caused such a
reaction or had such an effect in marking the break with the past as *Mori el
Merma.*

Baixas sees puppet theatre as a process of mark-making. Through the use
of tangible, material elements in performance, a statement of identity is
marked on stage in physical media. His performances, as commented
earlier, make meaning through the dialogue between the human (live) and
choreographed elements, and the material, physical marks made. Cultural
identity, memory and embodiment are enacted through this dialogue.

In his later work, Baixas develops this process by distancing himself more
from figurative puppetry and extending his research into live painting and
installation work. His experience of collaborating with Miró encouraged
him to continue working with painters and visual artists, such as Da Matta
and Tàpies. After the establishment of democracy in Catalonia, Baixas was
increasingly drawn to the metaphors of journey, and the language of
anthropology and myth. Faced with a new cultural reality in which Catalan
artists, freed from the repression of dictatorship, were trying to understand
their own place within the post-Franco world, Baixas tried to identify
those elements that could work across cultures. Catalan institutions and
government during the 1980s and 1990s were deeply concerned with
establishing Barcelona as a multi-cultural and modern city, which could
play on the world stage with other European capitals such as Paris and
London. Catalans were encouraged to travel for study and work, and
international presence in Catalonia was also encouraged. Catalans looked

outwards, and this period is largely identified with the re-establishment of Catalan identity as progressive, educated and cosmopolitan.

Materiality & Journeys

These preoccupations were identified in Catalan puppetry through a series of shows which explored the nature of identity and the role of the artist in the world. In 1986 Baixas created the show *Laberint* with Roberto Da Matta. This performance took place as an installation, a labyrinth in which the audience got lost within a synaesthetic experience. Inside the labyrinth, individuals were asked to consider their ideology, their relationship with others and their role within society.[15] During the 1990s, Baixas created a series of painting-journey semi-autobiographical shows which are still in performance. These involved him in painting live on vast screens, including fragments of his local and international travels.

When Baixas travels, he collects mud from the places he visits and paints on stage with this mud, using brooms, sponges and other tools strapped onto long poles to paint with. His memories are thus embodied materially in the paintings created. These painting-performances go under different titles for different audiences: *Dopamina Suite*, *Painted Music* and *Pregnant Earth*. *Pregnant Earth* was performed in 2002 using earth from Sarajevo (in which, he was told, were human ashes from the Balkan wars), Russia, Australia (where he worked with an aboriginal group) and Catalonia. In *Pregnant Earth*, Baixas narrates his journeys, occasionally presenting himself at the front of the stage as a crude and poorly manipulated string marionette, a parody of puppetry activity. Behind him, on the vast screen of his memory, he paints with real matter images from his subconscious, alongside the cultural and anthropological memory of others. In so doing, he marks the actual physical traces of his journeying, noting where his steps have crossed other lives in the much-trodden mud. He thus marks not only his own place in the world as a travelling artist, but that of Catalonia as a place of transit, and of mixed cultural heritage.

As gateway to the Iberian peninsula, Catalonia has traditionally been a place for people to pass through, leaving traces of their cultures and existence. Baixas marks the cultural palimpsest of Catalonia by linking it mythically to other cultures. He also notes the fragility of the individual before the vastness of collective myth. By painting with earth from different continents and telling stories from those continents, he enters into dialogue with questions of globalisation and collective trauma.[16] Through these performances, Baixas seeks to find and create through matter people's shared myths, traumas and realities. The clay with which he paints is testimony to the idea that the journeys of individual and collective life stories are traces which can be wiped and rewritten, but which never completely fade. As he paints on the enormous stage canvas, he inscribes new images over old ones, suggesting that human beings are the complex interaction of all the stories and influences of their lives. As a metaphor for Barcelona, this is particularly powerful, due not only to the cultural rewriting and re-imaging engaged in by the Spanish military authorities earlier in the twentieth century and later by the Catalan government, but also to the city's history of multiple cultural confluence, reception and transculturation.

This intertextuality is the result of a process of creation deeply concerned with memory.[17] Baixas' approach shares much with the Catalan visual artist Antoni Tàpies, who also explored the creative possibilities of matter, creating "matter paintings" using sand, crushed marble, coloured clay, canvas, and so on. Through collages and three-dimensional sculptures, Tàpies used the real, everyday elements of the world surrounding him, in the belief that in the everyday, the deep structures of culture could be made material. Throughout his career, Tàpies became more concerned with the local as a way of understanding the global, an approach which is shared by Baixas; the latter's wanderings show him approaching the global through his own miniature experiences as a fragile puppet wandering through the great mythic landscapes of human culture. Other companies such as Catalan performance group *La Cubana* and puppet companies *Teatrenu* and *La Cònica/lacònica* have also focused on the banal and quotidian to express Catalan culture through their use of everyday objects found on the streets of Barcelona. The work of these artists shows both the fragility of the human condition, as beings made of matter, and the importance for the artist of being deeply engaged in their society through a synthesis of political philosophy and personal encounter.

Tàpies used the iconography of Catalan culture in many of his paintings, such as *Els Solcs* (*The Furrows*), which represents either the stripes on the Catalan flag or the ploughed fields of rural Catalonia. He experimented with putting matter onto his canvases then painting over it, and waiting for the surfaces to crack to show their structures, believing that the deep structures of society are seen through its matter. Both Baixas and Tàpies questioned constantly the role and positioning of the Catalan artist in a post-Franco world, using layering and matter as a means to understanding their condition. Within puppetry, the puppet body or matter itself was understood as the body of the cultural Catalan, narrating and discussing themes within Catalan consciousness.

The Fragmented or Absent Body

Baixas' ongoing work reflects current concerns regarding mediated imagery, and the body as fragmented, projected or absent. In a world where reality and imagery is mediated obsessively and continuously by technology, Baixas questions the presence of the body in performance by creating interactive shows in which images are projected onto robot bodies, or suggested through their absence.

In 2004, Barcelona staged an international exhibition and celebration of world culture, *Fòrum de les cultures*. This highly-publicised event was designed to celebrate world cultures and point forwards to systems of greater communication and respect between cultures. A series of intense political and philosophical debates throughout the event considered questions of interculturalism, the economic relationship between the North and the South, and the challenges facing Barcelona as a city of world cultures. *Fòrum*, however, was fiercely criticised by many of the multicultural communities within Barcelona for a number of reasons. Tickets were prohibitively expensive, and many groups and cultural organisations within Barcelona itself were excluded. For instance, communities of Arabs and Africans, and racially mixed communities, were largely excluded on economic grounds from participating in discussions about their own identity.

Baixas noted that *Fòrum* was marked by the absence of world cultures, despite its claims. The organisation of the festival itself excluded world culture through mass commercial marketing and catering which offered only fast food, and groups and individuals that were considered too challenging or confrontational were also excluded. The event thus became a showcase or façade rather than a deep interrogation of the real issues that preoccupy Barcelona in terms of cultural identity. The same year, scores of West Africans were held in detention centres pending discussion of their legal status as economic migrants and racist attacks have increased in the last five years as the population of Catalonia grows through mass immigration from North and West Africa, Asia and China. Baixas suggests that cultural identity on the world stage is marked by absence, fragmentation and exclusion, while mediatised images are dominated by a façade of interculturalism.[18]

Within puppet theatre, the body of the puppet has also become fragmented and disembodied, represented through projections, shadows or sometimes broken or discarded objects. Commenting on the city, De Certeau notes that "the surface of [its] order is everywhere punched and torn open by ellipses, drifts and leaks of meaning: it is a sieve-order; the relics compose the story, being tied to lost stories and opaque acts."[19] The body in recent Catalan puppet theatre has similarly been "torn open." Instead of traditional puppets it uses projections or objects, items of memory found around Barcelona in bins, scrap heaps and flea markets, or else distant robotised creations that are reminiscent of the human but not "live."

The use of objects in performance is not new. The father of contemporary Catalan visual theatre, Joan Brossa, experimented with object-poems and plays before the contemporary visions of puppetry in the twenty-first century. Brossa worked across forms throughout his artistic career, and his influence is apparent in the work of Baixas and other contemporary puppetry artists such as *La Cònica/lacònica* and *Playground Teatre*. Brossa enjoyed the disorder created by unexpected connections and the distortion of words and letters. One of his early pieces for puppet theatre, *La Barba de cordills o les olles a l'escut* (*The String Beard, or the Cooking-Pot Shields*, 1947) involved characters listing names of objects one after another, creating a dislocation of things and their meanings. Brossa's main influence on contemporary puppetry, however, was his obsession with using real objects from daily life in Barcelona. He walked through the city every day, collecting objects. Brossa saw in real objects the imprint of the Catalan, the culture of Barcelona in action. Created and used by people in Barcelona, for Brossa objects comprised embodied memory, even if they were discarded, for their rejected status made them more useful as artistic, performing objects.

This pattern is mirrored in the work of *La Cònica/lacònica*, who wandered the streets of Barcelona at night, seeking objects representative of the city, to create distorted and unusual shadows in their most widely-toured and acclaimed piece, *Shadows of Found Objects* (1995). *La Cònica/lacònica* also creates site-specific actions in "lost" locations around Barcelona through their use of light, shadows and objects. According to Alba Zapater, one of the founders of the group, their concern is to present the utility of the useless; to project onto different kinds of surfaces and materials; to express an unusual world, subtle and ephemeral, and constantly in change.[20]

Contemporary Practices

Baixas is currently working on two projects. The first, *Smash! Antoni, Child of Sand*, is based on the animation of sand from the beach in Barcelona in collaboration with architectural ideas developed by the Catalan architect Antoni Gaudí. In this piece Baixas again uses matter to develop the idea that the human condition is marked by the matter of which we are made, the location and the manner of the making, and the links through matter to Catalan identity. His second project, *Casadelobos*, is an interactive tent-installation to be set up in public space, where the audience can enter their thoughts and ideas, and engage in dialogue directly with a robot and with projected images. Questions of liveness, fragmentation and distortion through projection are key to this project. Baixas comments on the difficulties faced by contemporary puppet theatre through its loss of the body and return to the use of matter and things:

> We might be tempted to think … that the monster has been banished from our society's culture … Not a bit of it. The monster possesses a vitality which is enviable these days. We live in a world where the mysteries of days gone by are transformed into definite realities. …How can Hamlet avenge his father if he's the son of a sperm bank and a surrogate mother or, even worse, a clone of his uncle? We have to change our conduct to adapt to this situation. The contemporary world calls for other forms of representation.[21]

Casadelobos is formed by an igloo of translucent plastic through which an audiovisual collage consisting of photos, videos and music is projected. The artist, Baixas himself, appears from time to time as part of the collage, projected through the screens but never fully present.

The absence of the body is also central to the work of the company *Playground* in which Xavier Bobes performs as an actor within an animistic environment. In this world, his objects represent the lost worlds of the Catalan city and he is respectively confused, traumatised, excited and restored by the objects which tell multiple narratives. Bobes frequently uses dolls and dismembered body parts of dolls which are manipulated not as puppet characters but as things. He comments that the knowledge of *broken* things is an essential part of his performance, as they are small, useless and silent.[22] The lost child in his performance is a broken toy; useless and silent objects become cultural commentators.

The obsession with found objects, matter, fragmentation and projection among Catalan puppet companies alludes to a sense of dislocation and an awareness that cultural identity and individual and collective memory are made up of fragments, things and matter trodden and used by others in concrete circumstances. The groups' use of visual imagery and dramaturgical elements is predicated upon a European world dominated by migration, loss of identity related to place, the object and technology. The eliding of identity with place offers little to those excluded from traditional interpretations of place. Michael Keith and Steve Pile suggest that:

> Politically, there is a reactionary vocabulary of both the identity politics of place and a spatialized politics of identity grounded in particular notions of space. It is the rhetoric of origins, of exclusion, of boundary-making, of invasion and succession, of purity and contamination.[23]

The tendencies discussed in this chapter show the development of puppet theatre in Catalonia, and particularly Barcelona, as exemplified in the work of Baixas. Initially puppet theatre presented its bodies as grotesque and laughable, reclaiming and celebrating Catalan popular culture. It then moved on to a preoccupation with embodiment and the inscription of cultural memory on matter. Finally, it became concerned with the disruption, dismembering and projection of the body, with memory and collage becoming principal factors in developing narrative, and with technological and live bodies juxtaposed against matter or objects taken from the Barcelona's streets, beaches and parks. These practices allow for the imprints of the excluded, with marginalised objects and trodden matter functioning as narrators and embodiments of cultural memory.

Works Cited

Baixas, J. (1989) "¡El trabajo teatral es asunto vuestro! Miró, Saura, Matta y el 'Teatro de la Claca'," *Puck* No. 2, Charleville-Mezières: Institut International de la Marionnette, pp.14-20.

—. (1998) *Escenes de l'Imaginari*, Barcelona: Institut del Teatre.

Benach, J. A. (1986) "Perderse con 'Don Qui' en el laberinto de La Claca," in G. Ferrer and M. Rom (Eds.), *Laberint La Claca*, Barcelona: Enginyers de Catalunya.

Billington, M. (1978) "Riverside: *Mori el Merma*," *The Guardian*, 24 November.

Bravo, I. (1996) "Un home del teatre anomenat Joan Miró," in *Miró en Escena*, Barcelona: Fundació Joan Miró, pp.17-46.

Bueno, P. (1989) "Miró: los trabajos ineditos del pintor para el teatro," *Diseño Interior*, No. 43.

Carlson, M. (2001) *The Haunted Stage: The Theatre as Memory Machine*, Ann Arbor: University of Michigan Press.

Crameri, K. (2008) *Catalonia: National Identity and Cultural Policy 1980 – 2003*, Cardiff: University of Wales Press.

De Certeau, M. (1984) *The Practice of Everyday Life,* Berkeley and Los Angeles: University of California Press.

—. (1988) *The Writing of History*, New York: Columbia University Press.

Diamond, E. (1996) *Performance and Cultural Politics*, London: Routledge.

George, D. and J. London (Eds.) (1996) *Contemporary Catalan Theatre: An Introduction*, Sheffield: The Anglo-Catalan Society.

Graham, H. and J. Labanyi (Eds.) (1995) *Spanish Cultural Studies: An Introduction; The Struggle for Modernity*, Oxford: Oxford University Press.

Keith, M. and S. Pile (Eds.) (1993) *Place and the Politics of Identity*, London: Routledge.

McRoberts, K. (2001) *Catalonia: Nation Building Without a State*, Oxford: Oxford University Press.

Noyes, P. (1997) "Reciprocal tourism and the fear of the floating local: Networkers and *Integristes* in a Catalan Provincial Town," *Performance Research*, Vol. 2, No. 2, Summer, pp.54-63.

Saumell, M. (1996) "Performance Groups in Catalonia," in George and London (Eds.) (1996) *Contemporary Catalan Theatre: An Introduction*, Sheffield: The Anglo-Catalan Society, pp.103-128.

Smith, N. and C. Katz (1993) "Grounding Metaphor: Towards a Spatialized Politics," in M. Keith and S. Pile (Eds.) *Place and the Politics of Identity*, London: Routledge.

Taylor, D. (2003) *The Archive and the Repertoire: Performing Cultural Memory in the Americas*, Durham and London: Duke University Press.

Interviews with the author

Interview with Joan Baixas, at *Fòrum de les Cultures*, Barcelona, 19 May 2004.

Interview with Joan Baixas, Barcelona, 10 October 2008.

Interview with Xavi Bobes, Barcelona, 20 September 2008

Interview with Alba Zapater, Barcelona, 21 September 2008.

Notes

All translations from the original texts in Catalan or Spanish are by the author.

[1] Marvin Carlson (2001) *The Haunted Stage: The Theatre as Memory Machine*, Michigan: University of Michigan Press, p.134.

[2] As David George and John London note, "This was not just a question of translation from Catalan into Spanish. It is indicative of the radical nationalization enforced on Barcelona that the 'Plaça de Catalunya' should be changed to the 'Plaza del Ejército Español' (Square of the Spanish Army)." See "Introduction," in D. George and J. London (Eds.) (1996) *Contemporary Catalan Theatre: An Introduction*, Sheffield: The Anglo-Catalan Society, p.14. This "radical nationalization" reflects the process of symbolic re-inscription described by Michel De Certeau. He notes that "on this threshold ... the conqueror will write the body of the other and trace there his own history." See De Certeau (1988) *The Writing of History*, New York: Columbia University Press, p.xxv.

[3] Neil Smith and Cindi Katz (1993) "Grounding Metaphor: Towards a Spatialized Politics," in M. Keith and S. Pile (Eds.) (1993) *Place and the Politics of Identity*, London: Routledge, pp.70-1.

[4] See, for example, Kenneth McRoberts (2001) *Catalonia: Nation Building without a State*, Oxford: Oxford University Press; Heather Graham and Jo Labanyi (Eds.) (1995) *Spanish Cultural Studies: An Introduction; The Struggle for Modernity*, Oxford: Oxford University Press; and Kathryn Crameri (2008) *Catalonia: National Identity and Cultural Policy 1980 – 2003*, Cardiff: University of Wales Press.

[5] Patricia Noyes (1997) "Reciprocal Tourism and the Fear of the Floating Local: Networkers and *Integristes* in a Catalan Provincial Town," in *Performance Research*, Vol. 2, No. 2, Summer, p.63.

[6] Diana Taylor (2003) *The Archive and the Repertoire: Performing Cultural Memory in the Americas*, Durham and London: Duke University Press.

[7] Michel De Certeau (1984) *The Practice of Everyday Life,* Berkeley and Los Angeles: University of California Press, p.97.

[8] As Elin Diamond notes, performances are "cultural practices that conservatively re-inscribe or passionately reinvent the ideas, symbols and gestures that shape social life." Diamond (1996) *Performance and Cultural Politics*, London: Routledge, p.1.

[9] Writing of this kind of practice, Mercè Saumell notes, "Gramsci's theories on bourgeois supremacy and its suppression of popular art and language (by considering them inferior) were decisive; one of the most important aims of this ... theatre was to subvert cultural repression by reviving popular forms linked more to oral than written literature." See Saumell (1996) "Performance Groups in Catalonia," in George and London (Eds.) (1996) *Contemporary Catalan Theatre*, p.105.

[10] Joan Baixas (1989), "¡El trabajo teatral es asunto vuestro! Miró, Saura, Matta y el 'Teatro de la Claca'," in *Puck*, No. 2, Charleville-Mezières: Institut International de la Marionnette, p.14.

[11] Pepa Bueno (1989) "Miró: los trabajos ineditos del pintor para el teatro," in *Diseño Interior*, No. 43, p.27.

[12] Baixas (1989), p.16.

[13] *Ibid.*

[14] Michael Billington (1978) "Riverside: *Mori el Merma*," *The Guardian*, 24 November, p.31.

[15] Joan Antoni Benach (1986) "Perderse con 'Don Qui' en el laberinto de La Claca," in G. Ferrer and M. Rom (Eds.) *Laberint La Claca*, Barcelona: Enginyers de Catalunya, p.76.

[16] Diana Taylor notes that "Performance as a lens enables commentators to explore not only isolated events and limit cases, but also the scenarios that make up individual and collective imaginaries." Taylor (2003), p.278.

[17] Marvin Carlson notes that postmodern theatre is "almost obsessed by citation, with gestural, physical and textual material consciously recycled, often almost like pieces of a collage, into new combinations with little attempts to hide the fragmentary and 'quoted' nature of these pieces." Carlson (2001), p.14.

[18] Baixas interview with author, 19 May 2004.

[19] De Certeau (1984), p.107.

[20] Zapater interview with author, 21 September 2008.

[21] Baixas (1998), p.195.

[22] Bobes interview with author, Barcelona, 20 September 2008.

[23] Michael Keith and Steve Pile (1993), "Introduction Part 1: The politics of place...," in Keith and Pile (Eds.) (1993) *Place and the Politics of Identity*, pp.19-20.

DEAD BODIES/LIVE BODIES: MYTHS, MEMORY AND RESURRECTION IN CONTEMPORARY MEXICAN PERFORMANCE

RUTH HELLIER-TINOCO

Who am I?
Where do I come from?
I am Antonin Artaud
and I say this
as I know how to say this
immediately
you will see my present body burst into fragments
and remake itself
in ten thousand notorious
aspects
a new body
where you will
never
forget me
(from *To Have Done with the Judgement of God* by Antonin Artaud, 1947)

In Twenty-first Century Mexico, traces of mythical and prehispanic pasts mingle and merge with a globalized, postmodern and capitalist present, in a ceaseless drive towards an enhanced future. Within the context of a complex, sophisticated and contradictory nation, many Mexicans continue an ongoing search for collective and individual identities, in which cultural memory, as a lived national memory, relies on bodies, ghosts, shadows, presences, statues and souls of indigenous and prehispanic pasts. The purpose of such figures is to create the present, driven by the questions "Who am I?" and "Where do I come from?" "Indigenous" Mexican bodies – living and long-since dead – have been utilised for decades as performers, exhibits and source material in performances that re-member, revive, resurrect, represent, resuscitate, reincarnate and reconstruct an embodiment of a real and imagined prehispanic past, shaping and forming a communal experience and site/sight of present and future "Mexico." Depictions and bodies of indigenous Mexico act as potent loci of reminiscence, and networks of performing bodies act as "symbols of the 'past,' mythically infused with timelessness,"[1] functioning to engender and enable traces of a past to be revived and recreated. Represented on stages, flesh and blood bodies of the present are transmuted into artefacts, cohering with bodies monumentalised in stone statues, frozen-in-time in postcard photos, re-produced as *un recuerdo* – a souvenir – a memory, and captured in processes of decontextualization and re-signification.[2]

Throughout the twentieth century and continuing into the twenty-first, staged and theatrical performances have engaged icons, myths, stories, figures and locations of prehispanic and mythical Mexico as rich material for exploring themes and generating notions of cultural memory. In these performances, actors, dancers and performers personify roles as indigenous and prehispanic figures. Simultaneously, "authentic" indigenous people have been the focus of attention as exhibits and artefacts of a prehispanic past engaged in contemporary yet timeless ritual. Here I place four performances under the spotlight: two overt theatre pieces – *Nezahualcóyotl* and *Orfeo Indígena (Indigenous Orpheus)* – and two ostensibly authentic displays of indigenous life – *Noche de Muertos* (Night of the Dead) on the island of Janitzio, and *Soul of Mexico*, a film exhibition of Night of the Dead on the island of Janitzio. All four explicitly engage with the performance of memory through embodied practices.

Nezahualcóyotl, a devised physical theatre piece, was described by the directors Juliana Faesler and Clarissa Malheiros as "a scenographic equation of memory and times."[3] Staged in the renowned theatre of the National Autonomous University of Mexico (UNAM) in 2007 with a company of five highly trained performers, and engaging a physical style drawing on LeCoq techniques, the piece created a heightened emotional atmosphere, fused with comedic moments, to explore themes of prehispanic rulers and deities and twenty-first century lives in Mexico. *Orfeo Indígena*, a "Multimedia Ritual for the Third Millennium" directed by Elisa Lipkau, employed interdisciplinary dramaturgical practices in the site-specific setting of the colonial Cloister of Sor Juana in the heart of Mexico City to create a poignant and powerful staged experience. Juxtaposing and merging live performance with filmed projections, and live performing bodies with filmed images of living, carved-in-stone, and painted-in-codices bodies, [4] the piece played with the story of the creation narrative/myth of the first Mesoamerican human.

As a contrast to these "theatrical" performances, the once-yearly event of Night of the Dead on the tiny island of Janitzio, Lake Pátzcuaro, Michoacán some two hundred miles west of Mexico City, is presented as authentic custom. [5] On 2 November each year P'urhépecha islanders undertake the night-long memorial ritual of Night of the Dead, a communal celebration of their dead ancestors, involving a candlelit vigil in the tiny cemetery. As part of the postrevolutionary nationalistic strategies of the 1920s the private observance ritual of remembrance was transformed into an ethnographic and touristic public spectacle and attraction. In the twenty-first century, the activities of the P'urhépecha islanders in the cemetery are observed by hundreds of thousands of tourists, visitors and voyeurs who travel across the waters of the lake to experience the commemoration, crowding into the diminutive graveyard to witness what is framed as an uninterrupted practice carried out in an untouched way from time immemorial.

In 2000, the film *Soul of Mexico* captured the activities of the P'urhépecha women undertaking Night of the Dead in the cemetery on their tiny island of Janitzio and transported them across the ocean to Germany. As a display of pseudo-ethnography, or perhaps poetic, technological artistry, the video exhibition was screened in the Mexican pavilion at EXPO 2000, the World's Fair in Hanover. Spectators could ostensibly experience the ritual "as if they were there," [6] and by wearing special glasses the 2D bodies were transformed into 3D "real" bodies. Both Night of the Dead and *Soul of Mexico* deal specifically with a ritualized meditation and experience of death, ancestors and communing with the dead/souls, provoking viewers into reflection of their own mortality and origins.

At the heart of all four performance events are experiences and explorations of memory which engaged the most potent of questions – "who am I?" – movingly posed by poet, playwright, performer and director Antonin Artaud. In creating *Orfeo Indígena*, Elisa Lipkau was inspired by Artaud's work, and with his entreaty to view theatre and ritual as magical forms of transforming the world. Artaud regarded theatre as a physical expression in space, calling for strange and disturbing lighting, sound, physical and vocal elements, believing that theatre should affect the audience as much as possible. [7] For Artaud, imagination was reality, and dreams, thoughts and delusions no less real than the "outside" world.

Whilst Lipkau's piece engages many of Artaud's beliefs by design –
using multiple realities with lighting, video projection, live performances,
heightened vocalizations and extreme physicality – the three other
performances under consideration here also encompass core elements of
Artaud's dramaturgical and philosophical thinking. Throughout
Nezahualcóyotl there is a heightened tension through the vocality,
bodywork and lighting, that engages with notions of profound and
extreme experience. Night of the Dead places the spectators in a position
of visceral engagement, where the darkness of the night, flickering
candles, smells of incense, cold, misty air, gentle movement through the
cemetery and the presence of the (imagined) souls of the ancestors
coalesce to produce a site-specific experience where the audience are in
the heart of the action. With *Soul of Mexico* the state-of-the-art
technology purportedly allowed audiences to experience the ritual as if
they were there, plunged into the heart of the action, communing with the
souls of the dead.

As vital acts of transfer, transmitting social knowledge, memory, and a
sense of identity, these embodied practices offered ways of knowing –
knowing about who we are.[8] Each of these performances deliberately and
explicitly aimed to create contexts for the contemplation of a concept of
memory through the specific use of bodies: bodies read as openly
performing bodies, engaging in pretence and representation of
"prehispanic and indigenous bodies," and bodies framed as authentically
indigenous and therefore interpreted as being "of the past," engaged in
acts of communing with dead and immortal ancestors. Embedded in all
four performances lay an efficacy, poignancy and poetry of prehispanic
Mexico, historical and mythical, in which themes and bodies of
past/present, death/life, and souls/shadows enabled traces of memory-
shaping.

Cultural inheritance and legacy

Mexico is a nation of superimpositions, juxtapositions and contradictions,
of masks, facades and revelations, in which identities, histories and
memories are wrought and moulded through rhetoric, images, literature,
media, dance and music to perform complex ideological and political
agendas. Mexican identities and memories are rooted in multiple histories
of wars, conflicts, invasion, changing territorial boundaries, shifting
allegiances, independence, revolution, corruption and migration. There is
a sense of constant and inevitable loss, and of searching for identity

through memory.[9] All four performances form strands within particular historical, political and ideological webs in which a distinctive quest and longing for a sense of identity is fundamentally part of the tapestry.

Cultural inheritance and legacy always traces back to a moment of imposition, incursion and invasion, when the Spanish *conquistadores* and missionaries set foot in the "New World." Temporally there is a "before" and an "after" – the prehispanic and posthispanic. Reaching back in time to understand the "before" is ever present and wholly part of "now," particularly when the "before" engages the question "who am I?" In the notion of the prehispanic there is another "before," relating to divinities, gods and goddesses, all of whom interface with the "historical figures" of prehispanic civilizations. Mexico is a context in which everything that has come "after" implicitly or explicitly, covertly or overtly references the "before"; as a nostalgic era of sophistication, as mythical and divine contexts, as communities of blood-thirsty pagans, as backwards peoples, or as highly developed civilizations of astronomers and mathematicians. Memory draws on a time of great crisis, of a world forever lost, with fragments remaining as tangible vestiges in stones of pyramids and ceremonial buildings, artefacts, drawings in codices and narratives of Spanish soldiers and priests, and intangible traces in stories, music, and dances transmitted through ephemeral and fallible processes of sensory acts. Lying between and often reconciling the tangible and intangible are the corporeal traces, the living flesh-and-blood bodies of twenty-first century Mexicans whose ancestry, blood-line or cultural setting designates them as "indigenous."[10]

In the trajectory from "the prehispanic past" to the present day the trail twists through colonisation, independence from Spain, bloody revolution, twentieth-century nationalism and capitalist modernization to a twenty-first century nation of multinational corporations, transnational mass media and multiple inequalities. Racial and ethnic divides, and the classification of bodies, has always been an intrinsic element of identity. In the colonial period, notions of miscegenation led to the formation of a caste system with three roots – indigenous, African and Spanish. During independence, *indigenismo*, an ideological movement which placed value on the indigenous past, created a focus for the formation of a developing national identity. Living indigenous peoples were discriminated against whilst memories of a prehispanic past, captured in stones and artefacts, were treasured.

Following the revolutionary wars of 1910 to 1920, the construction of a unified Mexican nation was the supreme objective, with the creation of *lo mexicano* – "Mexicanness" – as the ultimate goal. Through the shaping of imagined communities, in what was a contradictory and complex era, policies for modernization, industrialization and economic capitalism jostled with ideologies of *indigenismo* and *mestizaje* (miscegenation or mixing). A nationalistic infrastructure was fashioned, with a definition of nationhood in which the indigenous and the modern were inextricably linked. Whilst *mestizaje* concerned the concept and practice of creating a mixed authentic Mexican nation, *indigenismo* entailed both valorising and incorporating contemporary indigenous peoples and cultures into the newly developing nation state. Whereas previous *indigenismo* had focused upon indigenous practices and people of the past, postrevolutionary twentieth-century *indigenismo* encompassed living indigenous peoples.

In this network of signification, material and ethereal traces of indigenous lives and bodies would form an essential and fundamental core of cultural heritage and memory. Tangible artefacts still related to stones and objects, and to archaeological sites managed by the National Institute of Anthropology and History. Alongside these the narratives, stories and histories of prehispanic civilizations, captured in codices, statues, sculptures and art work continued to be deployed. In addition, the bodies of living people were valued as sites and sights of memory, appropriated and utilized as objects and artefacts of the nation's heritage, displayed in anthropological and folkloric contexts. Concurrently, self-representation and the struggle for land, political rights, and a place and space within the developing modern Mexican nation's economy and society, was often over-shadowed by the nationalist ideology.

Twentieth-century processes of nationalism and tourism required the shaping and promotion of representative icons, of symbols of Mexicanness, and of an essentialising embodiment of Mexico. Blurring the boundaries between contemporary living indigenous bodies and prehispanic bodies, ethnographic photographic images of indigenous peoples were published in journals and books; monuments recreated indigenous bodies; folkloric festivals placed indigenous bodies on proscenium arch stages; and theatricalised site-specific performances took place in archaeological sites using prehispanic themes.[11] In contexts of burgeoning national and international tourism, the creation and shaping of authentic attractions and the staging of authenticity necessitated the exploitation of indigenous difference and exoticism for the tourist gaze.

Postcards, guide-books and souvenirs recreated indigenous places, objects and bodies as tangible artefacts to entice and to re-member experiences.[12]

Narratives of a Nation's Past

In many contexts of twentieth- and twenty-first century Mexico, cultural memory has equated with a form of national memory, engaging with notions of the narratives of the nation's past.[13] Characterizing the era of 1920 to 1940, Claudio Lomnitz has commented on the contention over memory "or, to be more precise, the contention over the connection between stories about the past, the interpretation of the present, and expectations for the future."[14] Such concerns relate to a sophisticated, complex and contradictory relationship between the present and a past. Angst over a national memory and notions of a collective identity and of individual identities relates to the concept of a nation of trauma and rupture, of the pain of lost identity, and the search for identity. In this context, community and individuals are unified in a shared history, each person making sense of their own place in the nation, yet doing so within the construction and framework of a state-shaped national memory. With the need to find roots and the need to trace the untraceable and know the unknowable, there was and is a hope that it could and can be found in the narratives of the prehispanic rulers, in the myths of the gods of past eras and in the rituals and bodies of the twenty-first century indigenous peoples. In performance, all have become iconic, embodied referents of national belonging and cultural memory.

Death-Soul-Memory

Three interrelated concepts and themes permeate the performances of *Nezahualcóyotl*, *Orfeo Indigena*, Night of the Dead and *Soul of Mexico*, all of which are fundamentally potent for exploring notions of memory: past-present, death-life, souls-shadows. In each performance the past and present interface and merge and the past is intrinsically and inextricably part of the present in a tangible, visible, embodied form: through the presence of souls in the cemetery; through skull masks placed over a living face; through a live body generating shadows; and through filmed photography projected live, yet capturing a trace of a past activity.[15] In these performances notions of a prehispanic and mythical past, as documented and inscribed in drawings in codices, sculptures and stones, capture an intrinsic element of memory. The cold stones of ceremonial buildings, artefacts of cloth, bones and precious metals, and the flesh-and-blood bodies of living people interface with phantasmagorical bodies and souls of the past. In the death-life continuum, death points to the transient nature of life, inherently indexing memory and shadows of the past. In popular practices of remembrance, the dead continue to exist alongside the living, and the dead are simultaneously "on stage" with the living. The dead, who represent and are memory, preserve the past alongside the living, serving to provide a collective memory threatened by extinction through the dislocations of modernization in postrevolutionary Mexico.

Indigenous bodies become objects of the past, embodying the "souls of the ancestors," hinting at notions of immortality, and enabling a trace and residue of preincursion Mexico. Bodies of living individuals are transformed into the "soul" of Mexico in a representation and re-membering of the collectivity of the Mexican nation. In a century of loss of soul through modern alienation, engaging with indigenous bodies and with performances that connect to prehispanic bodies generates compelling sites of cultural memory. Following a Darwinian trajectory, there has been a particular potency of living "authentic" bodies or specimens, as evidenced in the performances of Night of the Dead and *Soul of Mexico*. The body itself, as a physical entity, acts as "the ultimate signifier of identity and the final authenticator," engaging with "the intractability of the notion of the 'body' as that which is really 'real', a repository of truth."[16] Particulars of each body, of physiognomy and of skin colour, lead to an interpretation of embodiment of authenticity. With the specific framing, where ethnographic display encourages a reading of an "authentic" body, the performing body references another time and place, acting as a vestige of memory and personifying past bodies.[17] With *Nezahualcóyotl* and *Orfeo Indígena*, whilst the overt performance frame signalled the role of the bodies as "non-authentic" indigenous bodies, specific dramaturgical elements encompassed notions of an authenticity of experience.

As performing bodies resonate as icons and embodiments of memory, so too locations and spaces act as kinaesthetic and sensorial material experiential sites of memory for audience members. Both *Nezahualcóyotl* and *Orfeo Indígena* overtly recreated and explored familiar, quotidian sites of modern Mexico, such as the metro system, and merged these with tangible and intangible sites of prehispanic Mexico. For audiences in Mexico City, their everyday lives were referenced, imaged, performed, setting up poignant resonances. Mexico City, home to some twenty million people, is wholly enmeshed in an environment of amalgamating modernity and prehispanicity. As the site of the heart of the Aztec empire and location of the bitter struggle between Spanish conquistadores and indigenous peoples, a memory of loss is ever present. In the core of Mexico City is a location of profound significance – *El Centro Histórico* – The Historic Centre. The prehispanic stone remains of the Principal Aztec Temple or pyramid – *El Templo Mayor* – (virtually destroyed by the Spanish conquistadores and only unmasked in 1978), nestle against the sixteenth-century Roman Catholic cathedral on one side of the huge central plaza or *zócalo*.

With the sunlight glinting on the centuries-old stone, the carved Wall of Skulls of the *Templo Mayor* lays bare a residue of bodies and preserves an icon of death. Each morning, just a few hundred yards away soldiers of the Mexican Army hoist a massive flag of the Republic of Mexico high in the centre of the *zócalo*, displaying the Aztec foundational imagery of an eagle with a serpent in its beak, perched on a cactus, in the centre of a lake. Evidence of a lake below the *zócalo* is visible in the stones of the slowly sinking colonial cathedral. Each day in the Historic Centre, performers of the reconstructed Aztec Dance of the *Concheros*, wearing long feathered headdresses and tunics, dance a form of ritual and political choreography to the beat of deeply-resonating drums which rebound off the stones of the cathedral and the *Templo Mayor*.

Night of the Dead on the island of Janitzio presents another form of kinaesthetic memory, producing a corporeal experience for audience members. In contrast to the urban metropolis of Mexico City, Lake Pátzcuaro is a deeply rural area, where little islands lie within the waters of the lake, and tiny village communities nestle along the shoreline surrounded by rolling hills. As an "authentic indigenous site" where P'urhépecha islanders have lived for centuries, bounded by water, and separated and ostensibly isolated from outsiders, the island of Janitzio encompasses notions of a pristine land imbued with the past, unadulterated and unaltered with the passing of time. Simply setting foot on the island stimulates an experience of an encounter with the past. Being present in this place throughout the hours of darkness for Night of the Dead heightens the notion of communing with ghosts of the ancestors.

Nezahualcóyotl

Nezahualcóyotl forms part of "The Mexican Trilogy," and acts as a "reflection upon our present history and our day by day relationship with our prehispanic past."[18] It was devised by the company *La Máquina de Teatro* (The Theatre Machine), an interdisciplinary ensemble which the directors perceive as "*un cuerpo* – a body – a collection of parts, and an organic system."[19] With a company of five performers, the performance utilizes physical theatre, spoken text, extended vocal work, integral scenographic elements and puppetry. The piece was created for performance in the theatre of the National Autonomous University of Mexico (UNAM), with a standard, open stage and an auditorium of forward-facing rows of seats.

The narrative hovers around the figure of Nezahualcóyotl, the fifteenth-century King of Texcoco (an area of central Mexico) and an eminent ruler, poet, and philosopher.[20] Yet Nezahualcóyotl is rendered ahistorical as he encounters prehispanic gods such as Quetzalcóatl (the plumed serpent), and a *peso*-less woman begging on a street in twenty-first century Mexico City. As the performers constantly transform themselves, they take on the roles of contemporary humans living quotidian lives in Mexico City, gods of myths, timeless dead/skull-masked beings, prehispanic Kings and even their "real selves" through use of their "real" names. There is a sense of temporal merging and blending, where historical time periods are indistinguishable and irrelevant.

Setting up the exploration and interface between present and past, the performance programme provides a clear and poetic framing for interpretation of the piece, making specific references to memories and practices of prehispanic locations, dances, music, and images in Twenty-first Century Mexico:

To think *Nezahualcóyotl* is to converse with history… to talk with what has been lost, with the ceaseless conquest. To think *Nezahualcóyotl* is to recapture one's self; it is also the strategy of exchange between the stage and the street, between history, myths and the divine; between the living and life. Close your eyes, think of the word, speak it: *Nezahualcóyotl*. Are we him and his contemporaries and are they us? Yes and no; Yes, because the passions, the human emotions, the richness and the poverty are the same, the territory is the same. No, because we do not perceive of the universe and our environment in the same way; no, because we have utterly transformed this region. And yet we are they and they are us; we are simply people travelling through history.
    Walk through the Historic Centre of Mexico City. Feel the stones, the cries, always with the souls of the dead. Lean against the walls and hear the voices of the depths. Take a sideways glance at… the smiles of the people. I am incorporated.[21] What is left in the depths: the *templo mayor*. Hear the

persistent rhythm of the drum and the breathiness of the flute. Someone
approaches – they reach out their hand grasping a tin containing some
coins. The feathers and flag undulate.[22]

Audience members are provoked and encouraged to view themselves
within the performance, in direct relation with the various embodiments,
through their connections with recognizable emotions and locations, and
to use that frame to experience and interpret the performance. Familiar
twenty-first century objects (such as a school bag and a shopping bag),
references to the metro system and the style of everyday colloquial street
conversation locate the time in the present, yet the presence of gods and
prehispanic figures in the same scenario confuses the temporal nature.
Each of the performers is contiguously and simultaneously mythical,
prehispanic and contemporary. The costume design allows each to retain
a basic and distinctive identity throughout, which is instantly
transformable by the removal or addition of a single item. One wears a
skirt and cardigan; another a tunic; yet another a shirt and trousers. With
the superimposition of a mask or a headdress the performer instantly shifts
from god to contemporary woman to prehispanic King. Huitzilopochtli, a
god of Aztec mythology, is instantly represented through the addition of a
fantastical headdress copied from images in Aztec codices, created with
long, multicoloured, balloons, indexing frivolity and fragility. Each body
is also inscribed with "otherness" from the outset with whole-body
painting: one has blue arms and feet, with a stripe down the centre of her
face, painted yellow on either side, referencing and emulating deities
represented in painted codices.

Numerous dramaturgical elements place the primary focus on the bodies
of the performers. The minimalist stage design presents an empty space
with a simple half-circle of large blank panels. Striking and dramatic
lighting creates geometric paths of light and accentuates the shapes and
actions of the bodies. Bodies dart out from behind the panels, skim across
the space, or peer round the corner. Body shapes and choreographic
designs draw on the in-profile, 2D bodies etched in stone carvings and
painted in the codices, bringing the long-dead and mythical bodies to life.
In the opening sequence, one performer walks through the space between
the two centre panels, making a trajectory from the back of the stage
down a path of light. As she walks, two other crisp dark figures appear in
profile on the panels, moving as she moves. They are perfectly formed
shadow-figures, replicating the 2D images of the gods of the codices. The
imagery of shadows display complete body-shapes yet they are virtual
bodies, formed only by the light. There is a sense of the body-object itself

being present, yet it produces a ghostly trace. It is moving in real time, yet the shadow-body is just a shape-shifter. Death also figures throughout the piece as the performers place a simple skull-mask over their faces (See *Figure 1*). Each mask, a flat-face skull drawn in a cartoon-style, is pushed into place over the nose, enabling an easy transformation from unmasked to masked; the clothing and body remain the same.[23]   Death haunts contemporary inhabitants of Mexico City as it did in prehispanic eras. Yet these dead/live bodies joke with each other, seeking their own shadows and witnessing their own aliveness.

Figure 1: Nezahualcóyotl, Mexico City, 2007. Photo: Crista Cowrie.

At the end of the piece, as a significant contrast to the flesh-and-blood bodies of the actors, and their virtual shadow-bodies, the body of Nezahualcóyotl takes the form of a one-foot high figurine or puppet, manipulated by all of the performers. He is dressed and placed down-stage centre. The tiny plastic body becomes the focus of attention, and with this little object, the immeasurable and illusive narrative of the life of the prehispanic king and the notion of collective memory is captured and signified – the diminutive, life-less, body-object is empowered with signification merging past and present, as a representation of an unbroken and relentless search for connection.

Orfeo Indígena

In contrast to *Nezahualcóyotl*, *Orfeo Indígena* was a site-specific piece, performed at night in the University of the Cloister of Sor Juana, in the Historic Centre of Mexico City.[24] Forming part of the First Dance Festival in Urban Spaces (entitled "*Urbe y Cuerpo*," "Metropolis and Body") and the "Festival of Mexico of the Historic Centre" the piece explicitly explored extremes of corporeal presences, utilising an unsettling style that moved between live performers and video projection.

As with *Nezahualcóyotl*, the printed programme framed the piece for audience members:

> Through movement, music and video we invite you to relive a fundamental myth of the Aztec culture and therefore of our contemporary identity: the descent of Quetzalcóatl to Mictlán or the underworld, to recover the sacred bones of the primitive beings and to create with them our mythical ancestors: the first Mesoamerican human being.[25]

Also paralleling *Nezahualcóyotl*, an overt connection between past and present Mexico was posited, and a direct provocation to audience members was given to position themselves within the piece and to make connections with their own senses of identity and memory. Using the creation myth of Quetzalcóatl as the central narrative, an eternal and central idea of cultural and communal memory – "who am I and where did I come from?" – formed the core of the piece. The piece presented a constant interface of past and present, whereby the past memories of stories and myths are wholly part of everyday life in Mexico.

Four characters form the central core of the piece: the god Quetzalcóatl; his brother/shadow Xolotl; the goddess Quilaztli, who creates the new human being; and the Lord of the Dead-Unliving. Only Quetzalcóatl and Quilaztli appear as live performers, interfacing with video images which are projected onto various surfaces, including the white-painted wall of the cloister, a fluttering line of washing, and the gently wavering *rebozo* (shawl) of the goddess Quilaztli. In the darkness of the twenty-first century Mexican night, the pulsating body of Quetzalcóatl interfaces with his virtual self and with his shadow Xolotl in video projections, as he stands atop a mountain, runs through prehispanic stone ruins and takes a journey into the underworld by descending the escalators of a metro station and taking an underground train to another world.[26] One sequence encompasses a potent fusing of past and present through the setting in the vast mountain-top archaeological/prehispanic site of Xochicalco. Twenty-first century filmed images show the contemporary remains of ancient stones, outlines of walls, a ball court and pyramids. In one shot, the 2D body of Quetzalcóatl carved in stone on the side of a pyramid is juxtaposed with the filmed-live body of Quetzalcóatl as performer, who emulates the corporeal position of the carved body.

Figure 2: Orfeo Indígena, Mexico City, 2007. Photo: Miguel A. Medina.

Many scenographic elements create familiarity with the present, which are juxtaposed with iconic images of prehispanicity. Quetzalcóatl is costumed in black T-shirt and jeans, and his face is covered with a black ski mask, an iconic indigenous image since 1994. Worn by *subcomandante* Marcos, the leader of the indigenous rights movement of the Zapatista Army of National Liberation (EZLN), the mask has come to represent the struggle for indigenous rights, identity and plurality (See *Figure 2*). The goddess Quilaztli is costumed in a pan-prehispanic style, with braided hair, white tunic, bare feet and *rebozo*. Materializing only in murky shots as video projections, the body of the Lord of the Dead-

Unliving appears in the realm of the fantastical, with full body- and face-paint of red and black.

As an instance of the rich iconicity which the piece encompasses, the bones for the creation of the Mesoamerican human being are given form as heads of maize. As the staple food of contemporary Mexicans, and as a foodstuff central to the lives of prehispanic peoples, maize is a profound signifier of survival, land rights, sustenance, and continuity. Maize represents a trace of, and continuation from, prehispanic life.[27] Bones represent the trace of a body, left behind after death, yet in this instance they are crucial for the creation of new life. In another moment of weighty imagery, a red plastic grocery bag, ubiquitous amongst poor and middle-class Mexicans for carrying fruit, vegetables, tortillas, and groceries, is used to transport the sacred bones – a bag full of maize heads. Quetzalcóatl runs through the underground station with the bag, and falls heavily, dropping the bag and spilling the bones/maize over the polished floor. What of the future of the human race? Fragility, ephemerality and virtuality imbue the performance.

Through the video and live images there is a constant juxtaposition and merging of narrative, creating an effect of past and present as one, of memory being just around the corner, and of ritual and performance. In the live performance, torches and dim lighting create a world of half-light and shadows, and of endeavouring to make out the real images through the darkness. A silhouetted body of a *concheros* dancer with iconic feathered headdress stands on a balcony, half-seen, half-unseen.

Video images mingle overt theatrical performance using actors with "ethnographic" images of contemporary pilgrims dancing in Mexico City on their way to the Basilica of the Virgin of Guadalupe, blurring and merging notions of ritual, performance, icons and bodies.[28] In one extraordinary moment, the unforgettable scene of the body melting into the mirror from Jean Cocteau's film, *Orpheus*, displays the literal transmutation of live body into mythical depths of memory. In the final section of the piece, as a projection of the credits runs up the side of the white-walled cloister, the live body of the performer playing Quetzalcóatl dangles precariously from high above the space, turning somersaults and walking over the names of each individual involved in the performance. As an embodiment of the creation of new life, Quetzalcóatl hangs by a thread, seemingly connecting past and present, yet highlighting the transient performance that is already over, leaving behind nothing but a trace and a shared memory.

Night of the Dead

Whilst *Orfeo Indígena* and *Nezahualcóyotl* are overt theatre pieces, Night of the Dead on the island of Janitzio, Lake Pátzcuaro, is presented as an authentic indigenous (P'urhépecha) ritualized celebration of dead ancestors, promoted by the Michoacán and Mexican Tourist Boards.[29] Many P'urhépecha people believe that the souls of the dead will revisit the earth, and so undertake a communal event of remembrance and celebration, offering food and flowers. Whilst the whole island is the site of the performance, attention is focused on the tiny cemetery which clings to the side of the sharply sloping face of the land. Visitors and onlookers make the thirty-minute journey to island by boat, ferried through the night in a constant stream of launches piloted by the men of Janitzio. Once on the island there is no entrance barrier or fee and visitors are free to wander at will. On the basketball court, a staged Festival of Music and Dance runs through the night to entertain the crowds of tourists.

While the P'urhépecha music and dance event is rehearsed, choreographed and directed for visitors, the activities in the cemetery are interpreted as authentic ritual, carried out unaltered year-upon-year from time immemorial. Within the walls of the cemetery, the bodies of P'urhépecha women and children are gazed upon as authentic bodies, and their corporeal actions read as unrehearsed and undirected custom. The actions are simple yet poignant – as night falls, smalls huddles of P'urhépecha women and children make their way to the cemetery, carrying candles, bundles of bright orange *cempasuchitl* (marigold) flowers, baskets of bread and ornate *ofrendas* (offerings for the dead). Each group settles itself by the graves of deceased family members, adorning the burial place with dozens of candles, flowers and offerings, kneeling and sitting, sometimes praying, sometimes chatting, sometimes sleeping. Each woman is clothed in the everyday wear of P'urhépecha islanders – a full-pleated skirt and apron, embroidered blouse and the ubiquitous blue P'urhépecha *rebozo* which shrouds, frames and half-masks each face. Dimly lit with the flickering glow of thousands of candles the whole scene creates an atmosphere filled with living shadowy figures communing with dead ancestors.

As potent romanticized imagery this once-a-year event appears in tourist brochures, guide books, postcards and posters: images depict shawled P'urhépecha women, with heads bowed, kneeling beside gravesides in the darkness, surrounded by marigolds, candles and offerings. Just out of the frame and absent from the myth-making imagery are the other bodies that are also in the cemetery – the thousands upon thousands of visitors, voyeurs and onlookers who have travelled to the island, attracted by the expectation of observing and experiencing a unique, indigenous/ prehispanic ritual, performed by authentic living P'urhépecha inhabitants, communing with dead ancestors.

Wholly immersed in embodying and performing cultural memory (a prehispanic yet contemporary memory) through a sensorial experience and through the viewing of indigenous bodies engaged in ritual memorial activities, the event provides the ultimate location for contemplation of the "who am I? and where do I come from?" subject. Mexican and international visitors travel to this site of memory to come into contact with traces of "the past" through an inscribed space and landscape – interpreted through the isolation and separation of the waters of the lake, facilitating the preservation of the peoples and customs in a pristine and prehispanic state. For the audience, the experience provides opportunities for a sense of spiritual pilgrimage, of journeying to a place from which one can return home after a profound encounter with oneself. In this setting of corporeal experiences visitors encounter other bodies and the physical world in a multi-sensuous manner, tapping into half-imagined memories, generated through networks of images and stories.

A journey through the night by boat across the waters of the lake allows for an experience of remoteness and dislocation as the island emerges out of the darkness lit by thousands of candles. Visitors travel through the mists of time and disembark into another world – a world of the past, of authentic indigenous bodies and of the souls of the ancestors. All the senses are engaged through the feel of the cold of the night, the smell the incense and flowers, the taste of hot fruit punch or *ponche*, the sound of music drifting through the air, and the sight of shadowy figures in the graveyard. In this world all things are ephemeral, and the figures and place are shadowy, masked by the darkness. Living bodies of the P'urhépecha islanders merge with souls and ghosts of the ancestors, where the memory of death is at the heart of the celebration.

In an ethnographic article from the 1920s, US folklorist Frances Toor characterized the whole event as "a distant world of fantasy" in which "the scene of the night was like a strangely beautiful dream in an unreal world."[30] In 2007, in a national newspaper article, journalist Ignacio Roque described the women and children undertaking the Night of the Dead on Janitzio as like "phantasmagorical figures."[31] In writing such as this, the people of Janitzio and the event of Night of the Dead are firmly and decisively positioned outside contemporary Mexico, existing in the same temporal space, yet confined to a state of a dream and to the embodiment of collective memory. Yet, the year-upon-year repetition of the performance of Night of the Dead for the hundreds of thousands of visitors ensures the survival of the islanders on Janitzio in their home-village without the need for migration. As the whole event is the biggest money-making activity of the year, the economic return for performing a premodern and prehispanic memory is considerable. As dawn materializes, the women and children of Janitzio tread gently back to their homes, and the visitors leave the scene, travelling back to the twenty-first century in launches piloted by the men of Janitzio. Night of the Dead and the bodies of the islanders remain as traces in their memories as imagined and ritualized embodiments of the past.

Soul of Mexico

In an extension of Night of the Dead as embodied performance of cultural memory, the film *Soul of Mexico* exhibited the P'urhépecha islanders in a 3D "real time" performance at the World's Fair in Germany. Live bodies of the Janitzio islanders were captured and displayed in a virtual setting, performing an essence and memory of "Mexico" on the world stage. Within the Mexican pavilion, which itself encompassed the design of a prehispanic pyramid, an "immersive gallery" projected real time images of Night of the Dead on Janitzio onto screens, using technology that was able to "plunge visitors into the heart of this celebration of the dead so that they feel 'as if they were there.'"[32] Visitors could walk through the tunnel "as if" walking through the cemetery, observing the P'urhépecha women kneeling and praying, lighting candles and laying flowers, at the "ancestral celebration" and experiencing a "living diorama."[33] No trace of the bodies of the thousands of onlookers in the cemetery on Janitzio entered the frame.

By wearing special glasses, visitors could view the figures of women and children as 3D bodies rather than 2D profiles, seeing their bodies as "lifelike" moving-in-real-time humans. *Soul of Mexico* presented the event as authentic and genuine ritual, passed on through the mists of time. As a diorama is a museum and theatre display device or model utilized with the intention of giving the impression of the real, then a living diorama not only gives the impression but "is real." The audience was engaged in virtual travel, being transported back in time, making a pilgrimage to another place and world. Using the most advanced technology to access this ancestral celebration highlighted the temporal and spatial distance between the real world and the world of memory and of the past.[34]

As the island world was presented as a virtual yet factual world, with souls of the ancestors creating connections with the present, so the very images of bodies that were claimed as being so "lifelike" were simultaneously connected to death through the focus of the ceremony (Night of the Dead) and the presumed unbroken link to the dead bodies of the past who had carried out those very activities in the same site since time immemorial. A collective and global communion through death and ritual engendered reception as a shared, embodied memorial celebration of life, and the global village could be united in cultural memory through the distant imagining of ancient bodies and treasures of the past, as the "living" diorama encapsulated images of death. Life and death, presence and absence, past and present were held within the same frame through the bodies of the P'urhépecha islanders on Janitzio projected as filmic images.

Reviving Buried Treasures

Long before time ever started... Quetzalcóatl, the Feathered Serpent, and Xolotl, Shadow, his twin brother, met each other in the clouds. The two gods had to agree on how to create the new human being who would live on the earth.[35]

As narrated text, these gently spoken words open the performance of *Orfeo Indígena*, drifting into the night sky in the historic heart of Mexico City, unattached to any visible body, yet shaping a memory of the creation of human bodies, connecting time immemorial to twenty-first century pulsating, breathing bodies. In the performances of *Nezahualcóyotl*, *Orfeo Indígena*, *Night of the Dead* and *Soul of Mexico*, bodies provide the connection between stories from and of the past, interpretations of the present, and expectations for the future. Bodies act as memory, as a trace, as an icon, as an index, as a symbol, and as "reality."

Re-membering a prehispanic past and living the memory in contemporary Mexico involves complex temporal and spatial performance processes, in which live bodies merge with and metamorphose into dead bodies, mythical bodies and stone bodies. As creative experimental devised theatre pieces, *Nezahualcóyotl* and *Orfeo Indígena* deal directly with delving into the rich depths of the storehouse of ancient myths and histories to revive and resurrect prehispanic bodies. Night of the Dead and *Soul of Mexico*, revolve around their framing and interpretation as authentic indigenous practices. As these performances engage indigenous bodies and representations of indigenous and prehispanic bodies, so the material construction of sites of collective memory and of explorations of the eternal question "who am I?" enables twenty-first century Mexicans to grapple with the complexities and contradictions of living in contemporary Mexico.[36]

Works Cited

Barthes, R. (1984) *Camera Lucida*, trans. Richard Howard, London: Harper Collins.

Bullé Goyri, A. O. (2003) "El teatro indigenista mexicana de los años veinte: ¿Orígenes del teatro popular actual?," *Latin American Theatre Review* 37/1, pp.75-93.

Campos, R. M. (1930) *El Folklore Musical de las Ciudades: Investigación acerca de la música mexicana para bailar y cantar*, México: Publicaciones de la Secretaría de Educación Pública.

Cohen, A. (1985) *The Symbolic Construction of Community*, New York: Tavistock Publications.

de pinxi (2000), Press release: "Hanover 2000," at: http://www.depinxi.be/presspdf/hanover_en.pdf (accessed 8 April 2009).

Desmond, J. (1999) *Staging Tourism*, Chicago and London: University of Chicago Press.

Foster, G. M. (1948) *Empire's Children: The People of Tzintzuntzan*, Washington DC: Smithsonian Institution, Institute of Social Anthropology.

Fusco, C. (1995) *English is Broken Here*, New York City: The New Press.

Hellier, R. (2001) "Removing the Mask: La Danza de los Viejitos in Post-Revolution Mexico, 1920 – 1940," unpublished PhD thesis, University of Central England.

Hellier-Tinoco, R. (forthcoming 2009) *Embodying Mexico: Tourism, Nationalism and Performance*, New York: Oxford University Press.

—. (2008) "¡Saludos de México (el auténtico)!: postales, anuncios espectaculares, turismo y cuerpos actuantes," *Fractal*, No. 47/48.

—. (2005) "Embodied artefacts of the Viejitos Dance of Lake Pátzcuaro, Michoacán, Mexico," *Proceedings of the 23rd Symposium of the ICTM (International Council for Traditional Music) Study Group on Ethnochoreology 2004*.

—. (2004) "Power Needs Names: Hegemony, Folklorisation and the *Viejitos* Dance of Michoacán, Mexico," in Randall, A.J. (Ed.) *Music, Power and Politics*, New York and London: Routledge, pp.47-64.

La Máquina de Teatro website, at: www.lamaquinadeteatro.com (accessed 28 November 2007).

Lomnitz, C. (2006) "Final Reflections: What was Mexico's Cultural Revolution?" in Vaughan and Lewis (Eds.) *The Eagle and the Virgin: Nation and Cultural Revolution in Mexico, 1920-1940*, Durham and London: Duke University Press, pp.335-349.

Nezahualcóyotl Programme (2007) Teatro UNAM, Universidad Autónoma de México *Orfeo Indígena* programme 2007, Primer Festival de Danza en Espacios Urbanos "URBE Y CUERPO."

Phelan, P. (1995) "Thirteen Ways of Looking at Choreographing Writing," in Foster, S. (Ed.) *Choreographing History*, Bloomington: Indiana University Press, pp.200-210.

Rodriguez, J. and T. Fortier (2007) *Cultural Memory: Resistance, Faith & Identity*, Austin: University of Texas Press.

Roque, I. (2007) "Pátzcuaro y Janitzio reviven su tradicional 'Noche de Muertos,'" *La Crónica de Hoy*, 3 November.

Rowe, W. and V. Schelling (1991*) Memory and Modernity: Popular Culture in Latin America*, Verso: New York.

Taylor, D. (2003) *The Archive and the Repertoire: Performing Cultural Memory in the Americas*, Durham and London: Duke University Press.

Toor, F. (1928) "Noticias de los Pueblos," *Mexican Folkways*, 4:1, pp.65-70.

Vaughan, M. K. and S. Lewis (Eds.) (2006) *The Eagle and the Virgin: Nation and Cultural Revolution in Mexico, 1920-1940*, Durham and London: Duke University Press.

Performances

Nezahualcóyotl. Directed by Juliana Faesler, in collaboration with Clarissa Malheiros, La Máquina de Teatro. Performed at Teatro UNAM, Universidad Nacional Autónoma de México, 2007.

Orfeo Indígena. Directed by Elisa Lipkau. Performed at el Primer Festival
 de Danza en Espacios Urbanos "URBE Y CUERPO," and XXII
 Festival de México en el Centro Histórico, Mexico City, 2007.
Noche de Muertos. Island of Janitzio, Lake Pátzcuaro, Michoacán,
 Mexico. Performed yearly.
Soul of Mexico. Designed and produced by de pinxi, Belgium, for the
 Mexican Pavilion, EXPO 2000, World's Fair, Hanover, Germany.

Notes

All translations from the original texts in Spanish are by the author unless
otherwise noted.

[1] Anthony Cohen (1985) *The Symbolic Construction of Community*. New York:
Tavistock Publications, p.102.
[2] See Ruth Hellier-Tinoco (2008) "¡Saludos de México (el auténtico)!: postales,
anuncios espectaculares, turismo y cuerpos actuantes," *Fractal*, No. 47/48; and (in
press) *Embodying Mexico: Tourism, Nationalism and Performance*, New York:
Oxford University Press.
[3] See La Máquina de Teatro website, at: www.lamaquinadeteatro.com (accessed
28 November 2007).
[4] Painted codices, produced prior to and after the Spanish incursion, use a pictorial
style to narrate events and key figures.
[5] The state of Michoacán is a large and diverse region, steeped in pre-hispanic,
colonial and post-colonial history. Prior to the arrival of Spaniards, the
P'urhépecha Empire dominated the territory of what is present day Michoacán and
the surrounding states. Although decimated by the Spanish incursion of 1522, the
P'urhépecha peoples survived and today form an important element of
contemporary Michoacán and Mexico, and have migrated to the USA in large
numbers.
[6] EXPO 2000 programme.
[7] There is a direct connection between Artaud and Mexico, for in 1936 he
travelled to Mexico, where he lived with and studied Tarahumaran peoples in the
state of Chihuahua, northern Mexico.
[8] See Diana Taylor (2003) *The Archive and the Repertoire: Performing Cultural
Memory in the Americas*, Durham and London: Duke University Press.
[9] Many of Mexico's most eminent writers, historians and philosophers have dealt
with these themes in their work, notably Roger Bartra, Enrique Florescano, Carlos
Fuentes, Claudio Lomnitz, Carlos Monsiváis, and Octavio Paz.
[10] The classification "indigenous" may be a self-designation (particularly by those
involved with struggling for indigenous rights) or an external and state
designation.

[11] A representation of Aztec culture took place in 1925 in the open-air Theatre of the Pyramids of Teotihuacán (close to Mexico City), and a presentation of Maya culture was given in 1929 in Oaxaca. See Rubén M. Campos (1930) *El Folklore Musical de las Ciudades: Investigación acerca de la música mexicana para bailar y cantar*, México: Publicaciones de la Secretaría de Educación Pública, and Alejandro Ortiz Bullé Goyri (2003) "El teatro indigenista mexicana de los años veinte: ¿Orígenes del teatro popular actual? *Latin American Theatre Review* 37/1.

[12] See Hellier-Tinoco (2005) "Embodied artefacts of the Viejitos Dance of Lake Pátzcuaro, Michoacán, Mexico," *Proceedings of the 23rd Symposium of the ICTM (International Council for Traditional Music) Study Group on Ethnochoreology*; Hellier-Tinoco (2004) "Power Needs Names: Hegemony, Folklorisation and the *Viejitos* Dance of Michoacán, Mexico," in A.J. Randall (Ed.) *Music, Power and Politics*, Routledge: New York and London, pp.47-64; Hellier (2001) "Removing the Mask: La Danza de los Viejitos in Post-Revolution Mexico, 1920 – 1940," unpublished PhD thesis, University of Central England.

[13] See Mary Kay Vaughan and Stephen Lewis (2006) *The Eagle and the Virgin: Nation and Cultural Revolution in Mexico, 1920-1940*. Durham and London: Duke University Press, p.6.

[14] Claudio Lomnitz (2006) "Final Reflections: What was Mexico's Cultural Revolution?" in Vaughan and Lewis, p.345.

[15] As Peggy Phelan has observed, "the photograph....shows us the moment that has faded, the death and disappearance of that particular configuration of subjectivity frozen by the camera. ...No longer fluid and moving, the image 'dies' in order to be seen again." Phelan (1995) "Thirteen Ways of Looking at Choreographing Writing," in Susan Foster (Ed.) *Choreographing History*, Bloomington: Indiana University Press, p.202. Roland Barthes wrote that "however 'lifelike' we strive to make it (and this frenzy to be lifelike can only be our mythic denial of an apprehension of death), photography is a kind of primitive theater, a kind of Tableau Vivant, a figuration of the motionless and made-up face beneath which we see the dead." Barthes (1984) *Camera Lucida*, London: Harper Collins, p.32.

[16] Jane Desmond (1999) *Staging Tourism*, Chicago and London: University of Chicago, pp.xiv-v.

[17] A particularly striking example of a performance context leading to a reading of bodies as "real, indigenous, authentic Mexican bodies" occurred in 1992, with the performance *Two Amerindians Visit*...by Coco Fusco and Guillermo Gómez Peña. Despite their efforts to create a piece of overt performance, the bodies of Fusco and Gómez Peña were read and interpreted as authentic indigenous bodies. As Fusco later noted, "we did not anticipate that we... could be believable." Coco Fusco (1995) *English is Broken Here*, New York City: The New Press, p.134.

[18] Faesler and Malheiros on La Máquina de Teatro website.

[19] *Ibid.*

[20] As with many names of prehispanic of rulers, in the twentieth century Nezahualcóyotl was used to name a municipality in the state of Mexico. Nezahualcóyotl City, or Neza City, currently has a population of over a million.

[21] The original Spanish phrase is "Me incorporo" from the verb incorporarse, which translates as "to include one's self." The inclusion of the term "corp" – body – in the centre of the word, points to a notion of embodiment, and thus the concept "me incorporo" wholly embraces the idea of the body within a place and history.

[22] *Nezahualcóyotl* programme 2007.

[23] Skeleton and skull imagery is a common in Mexico, and was made popular through the litho prints of José Guadalupe Posada, a graphic artist, famous for images of skeletons as contemporary figures undertaking quotidian activities. Throughout Mexico, during celebrations of Day and Night of the Dead, sugar skulls are sold in street markets and imagery of skeletons wearing contemporary clothing and carrying everyday tasks is ubiquitous.

[24] Providing another interesting layer, Sor Juana Inés de la Cruz was a sixteenth century nun, poet, scholar and playwright, who lived and died in the very site of the performance.

[25] *Orfeo Indígena* programme 2007.

[26] The underground system in Mexico City has particular resonances as a familiar and necessary element of every life for the survival of millions of residents (used particularly by some of the poorest residents to move around the city). It is also resonant of the Aztec city, through the association with the layer below the contemporary city, through the naming of many stations with prehispanic names as locators and through the display of prehispanic artefacts in various stations. Notably, the station "*La Raza*" ("the Mexican race") figures in certain shots. As a highly potent political term in both Mexican and USA politics, *La Raza* is signifier of great importance.

[27] One of the most influential works of renowned Mexican performance artist Jesusa Rodríguez is "El Maíz" or "Maize."

[28] The Virgin of Guadalupe (also known as *La Virgen Morena* – the Brown-skinned Virgin) is Mexico's foremost figure and icon of devotion and Mexicanness. Forming a link between prehispanicity and colonialism, her body is a sight and site of utmost piety, affection and attachment, forming an essential element of Mexican cultural memory. On 12 December each year, millions of Mexicans make a pilgrimage to the Basilica of Guadalupe in Mexico City where the original image of the Virgin is held. For an analysis of the power of the Virgin of Guadalupe as cultural memory see Rodriguez and Fortier (2007) *Cultural Memory: Resistance, Faith & Identity*, Austin: University of Texas Press.

[29] Lake Pátzcuaro became the focus of attention in 1920s postrevolutionary era of nationalism and burgeoning tourism. The area was visited by folklorists, ethnographers, artists, scholars, politicians, and pedagogues. The P'urhépecha peoples were regarded as in need of incorporation into the national body, and also as useful bodies within the movement of in indigenismo, with a direct bloodline to the prehispanic past. In the 1920s Night of the Dead on Janitzio was viewed by outsiders, and documented as an ethnographic and folkloric event. A representation of Night of the Dead on Janitzio was performed on stage in Mexico City (for example, in the *Cine Olimpia* and *Teatro Sintético del Murciélago*

[1924] and *Hamarándecua* [1930]). As part of the *costumbrista* genre, contemporary rural and indigenous dance, music and ritual practices were appropriated and commodified to create spectacles for public consumption. In the performances and texts of the programmes, there was a blurring and obfuscation of the boundaries between contemporary and prehispanic peoples designated as indigenous, intermingling present and past. In this era, other contemporary performances, particularly pantomimes and ballets, explicitly dealt with scenes of prehispanic Mexico, often drawing directly upon indigenous imagery, and recreating and imagining notions of a preconquest past. By way of an example, in the same year that *Hamarándecua* was produced, a ballet entitled *Quetzalcoatl* was performed, in which prehispanic Aztec dances were represented. In the 1930s the focus for Night of the Dead on Janitzio turned back onto the authentic event on the island itself. Janitzio was transformed into site of attraction for tourists and visitors, and was captured and framed in films (*Janitzio* [1935], *The Three Caballeros* [1944], and *Maclovia* [1948]). By the 1940s Night of the Dead of Lake Pátzcuaro had become a prominent visitor attraction, with US anthropologist George Foster, noting that it had become "one of the most famous spectacles of Mexican indigenous life....Great crowds of tourists have come, and the Tarascan [P'urhépecha] women show no hesitancy in talking with them." See G.M. Foster (1948) *Empire's Children: The People of Tzintzuntzan*, Washington DC: Smithsonian Institution, Institute of Social Anthropology, pp. 220-221. By the 1980s one hundred thousand visitors attended for Night of the Dead, a figure that has persisted into the twentyfirst century.

[30] Frances Toor (1928) "Noticias de los Pueblos," *Mexican Folkways*, 4, no.1, pp.68-9.

[31] Ignacio Roque (2007) "Pátzcuaro y Janitzio reviven su tradicional 'Noche de Muertos'," *La Crónica de Hoy*, 3 November.

[32] See de pinxi (2000), Press release: "Hanover 2000," at: http://www.depinxi.be/presspdf/hanover_en.pdf (accessed 8 April 2009). Quotations originally sourced at: www.mexico21.org.mx (accessed 21 November 2000).

[33] *Ibid.*

[34] Coco Fusco has examined the trajectory of human ethnographic display, which encompassed exhibition at World's Fairs. She particularly noted the move from live performance to ethnographic film: "the popularity of these human exhibitions began to decline with the emergence of another commercialized form of voyeurism – the cinema – and the assumption by ethnographic film of their didactic role ... performed for camera." Fusco (1995), p.49. Through juxtaposition with two other exhibitions in the Mexican pavilion at EXPO 2000, the World's Fair, Germany, *Soul of Mexico* fitted neatly into a interpretation ethnographic film, capturing contemporary, indigenous "real" Mexican specimens.

[35] *Orfeo Indígena* (2007) Directed by Elisa Lipkau. Performed at Primer Festival de Danza en Espacios Urbanos "URBE Y CUERPO," and XXII Festival de México den el Centro Histórico, Mexico City.

[36] *Mil gracias*, many thanks to: the many families of the Lake Pátzcuaro villages and islands with whom I have spent time over the years (so many extraordinary memories); to the Ramírez-Tinoco family; to Clarissa and Juliana for their amazing hospitality; and to Elisa for her generous and provoking interactions.

CONSUMING CULTURE:
THE JAPANESE WAY OF TEA

MICHELLE LIU CARRIGER

Chanoyu
is conveyed through the mind,
through eye
and ear –
without a single stroke of the brush.
—Sotan

When one goes to tea, one must first "shake off worldly dust" and prepare to "leave the mundane world."[1] Then one enters the tea room, a special place removed from, or rather deep within, the everyday, where the simple, ordinary gestures of sharing food and drink are codified and abstracted to the level of art and ritual. In this place, social hierarchies are momentarily leveled, personal identities are obscured, and all participants submit themselves to an elaborate structure of bodily and mental discipline that culminates in the exchange of a small sweet and a few sips of bright green powdered tea, whipped into a froth by the host and drunk by the guests in turn.

Tea is a practice that balances paradoxically between the instantaneity of an unrepeatable, flawed performance and long-preserved memories of Japaneseness; artistic accomplishment; and spirituality, particularly Zen Buddhism. Guests and hosts alike simultaneously embody and express these memories by disciplining their bodies to perform the carefully taught and preserved behaviours that culminate in the creation of the bowl of tea, a momentary pleasure imbued with meaning, and then literally consumed. Tea's status as an embodied, repertoire-based performance practice allows it to carry multiple, sometimes contradictory messages. These unstable meanings are transferred from body to body through performance, raising questions about how bodies themselves affect the messages, and revealing that the philosophy of Tea is thoroughly imbricated with its physical practices. I argue that bodily Tea practices do not *express* a history or culture; they in fact *create* ideologically-charged versions of history and culture precisely through the appearance of immanence and "tradition." This occurs through bodily performance that most certainly looks very similar to the way it did 500 years ago, but whose connoted meanings are constantly in flux.

The three organizing principles of "performance," "embodiment" and "cultural memory" help us to conceptualize the ways in which Tea practice poises paradoxically between two temporalities – the instantaneity and disappearance of the Tea event that correspond to Peggy Phelan's theories of performance and the chain of memory maintained through the repertoire and practices of surrogation, as performance studies scholars like Diana Taylor and Joseph Roach have written. I argue that these two temporalities in concert enable the practice of Tea to remain a vehicle for apparently unchanging cultural memories while also adapting to new audiences and messages. After general background and description of what Tea practice and events entail, this essay is split into three major parts, addressing in turn the role of embodiment in transmission of Tea practice and values, the types of cultural memories that are transmitted in performance, and finally the performance of Tea, in which I will further discuss the two temporalities that govern the Tea gathering, dual temporal modes which enable fluid expressions of cultural memory through embodiment.

The Way of Tea

In Japan, it is said that the Buddhist monk Daruma cut off his eyelids while meditating in a cave in order to keep from falling asleep. He threw them outside the cave, and where they fell the tea plant (*camellia sinensis*) sprung up, yielding the leaves that ground or steeped in water enable monks to stay awake while meditating. *Maccha*, the type of tea used in Chanoyu, was probably brought to Japan by Eisai, the man who also is credited with introducing Rinzai Zen to Japan in the late 13th century CE.[2] *Maccha*, unlike most teas, consists of steamed, dried, and powdered tea leaves that are mixed with hot water and whisked into a froth, usually just a few sips per serving.[3] The enjoyment of tea, both steeped and *maccha*, spread from China to Japan and from Buddhist monks to the population at large. The aristocrat and warrior classes in particular developed and organized many events in which to enjoy tea, such as contests to name varieties of tea, opulent gatherings for showing off Chinese utensils, or poetry and tea parties.[4]

The Way of Tea as it is now practiced in Japan was codified from these earlier practices in the 16th century, largely through the influence of a single man, Sen no Rikyu, a merchant-class *chajin* ("tea person") who gained prominence solely through his mastery of Tea, becoming a favoured guest and teacher of daimyo Hideyoshi and earning fame as the "father" of Tea, although not its progenitor.[5] Although he did not invent it, he revolutionized his preferred style of Tea (*wabicha*, a heavily Zen-influenced practice that favours combinations of the old, repaired, and austere with the opulent) and his ensuing popularity helped ensure that it became virtually the only strand of tea ceremony that continues to be practiced.[6] The practice is known in Japanese as *chanoyu*, literally "hot water for tea," *chado,* or *sado*, both variations on "the way of tea." The term *chado* favors the Zen and Taoist connotations of Tea as a "path" or "way" of spiritual practice. In English, *chanoyu* is often called "tea ceremony," a term which certainly captures the highly stylized and sometimes solemn nature of the proceedings, but which is generally considered rather misleading.[7] In this essay I use the terms "Tea" and "Chanoyu" for the practice and "tea" to refer to the beverage.

Zen Buddhism undergirds the entire philosophy and aesthetic of Chanoyu, to the extent that Sotan, the grandson of Rikyu and one of the most highly revered Tea philosophers after Rikyu, is credited with coining the famous aphorism: "The taste of Tea and the taste of Zen are the same."[8] Generally speaking, Zen is concerned with the breaking down of the mental distinctions that keep humans locked in a cycle of karmic illusion; a key part of this process is realization of the "nonduality of mind and matter."[9] Daisetz T. Suzuki, one of the most important scholars to write on Zen in English, emphasizes the importance of thwarting the intellect by stating baldly, "Zen is a discipline and not a philosophy, it deals directly with life."[10]

The process of attaining this realization can take many forms, but Tea is considered an ideal vehicle for Zen-infused physical practice, because it focuses practitioners' attention on their material surroundings and encourages the equal value of (and therefore non-distinction between) the old and new, repaired and opulent, low and high. Further, although speech is used in Tea gatherings, the participants' actions are primary; this corresponds with Suzuki's observation that in Zen, language is recognized as "a treacherous instrument...always liable to make us take the symbol for reality."[11] Physical embodiment emerges as a means to circumvent the intellectual tool *par excellence*, language, as alluded to in the Sotan poem that serves as this chapter's epigraph. However, in keeping with Zen principles, to confound the intellect does not mean a simple binary swing to privilege the bodily, but rather to realize the fundamental unity of mind and body: nonduality. The means to achieve this in Zen (and in Tea) is practice – that is, through repeated performance.

As with most of the traditional Japanese arts, Chanoyu is maintained through a patrilineal chain called the *iemoto* system. *Iemoto*, often translated "grand master," translates more closely to something like "family head."[12] Through the *iemoto* system, Rikyu's scions inherited custodianship of the practice and continue to hold the highest places in the Tea world. Descendants of Rikyu are now *iemoto* of the three largest Tea schools: Urasenke, Omotesenke, and Mushanokojisenke. (The "senke" in their names means "Sen family.") The *iemoto* of the different schools are the final authorities both for the bodily movements that make up the practice and the philosophical content – the "why" to go with the "what" of tea making. Urasenke has many more students than any other school of Tea; this may be primarily due to top-down initiatives propounded by active *iemoto*, especially Ennosai, the 13th *iemoto* (1872-1924), Tantansai, the 14th *iemoto* (1893-1964) and Hounsai, the 15th *iemoto* (b.1923).[13]

During the Meiji restoration when the traditional arts faced devastating drops in participation, Urasenke under the leadership of Ennosai was the first Tea school to compensate by beginning a concerted effort to bring women through its doors and grant them teaching licenses. Tantansai and Hounsai expanded this policy fifty years later, shortly after the end of World War II, with an official campaign to extend Chanoyu to practitioners around the world. This essay focuses on examples from Urasenke, because of its special commitment to women and non-Japanese practitioners, and because it is the school I have studied with the longest.[14] Although the different schools all have different *iemoto* and therefore different final authorities, they do share common roots and an archive of historical information; most of the practices I outline are generalizable across schools.

Tea is both an event and a practice, the former describing a momentary and unique happening, a gathering of people which can never be repeated, the latter the means by which the event was enabled to occur. It takes sustained study with a teacher to produce people who share a codified knowledge of the bodily actions required to make and receive tea; in fact, most Tea practitioners spend the vast majority of their time doing Tea today during lessons. The codes of behaviour (called *temae*) learned by students of Tea share basic similarities across the different schools and amongst the varieties of procedures for thin and thick tea and the different seasons, rooms and utensils (there are about 800 such procedures in Urasenke and 500 or so in Omotesenke).[15]

The gathering called the *chaji* is generally considered the standard from which all other types of Tea events are derived. The *chaji* is generally about four hours long, and includes a host, perhaps a helper called a *hanto*, and a few guests. Four guests are often considered the ideal because with the host, the people in room comprise five persons, an auspicious number.[16] Guests arrive promptly at the time indicated by the invitation, entering through the garden which has been carefully prepared, along the path that has been splashed with water to give a feeling of freshness. They are greeted by the host and then enjoy a light meal and sake. The host serves the guests, but does not eat with them. After the meal and a sweet, the guests retire to a waiting room while the host prepares the tea room for *koicha*, thick tea. *Koicha* is the most solemn part of the gathering; the guests share the tea from a single bowl passed hand to hand.[17] Then the host adds charcoal to the hearth and the mood lightens with the beginning of the thin tea (*usucha*) procedure.

Usucha is the portion of the *chaji* that is most often excerpted in tourist demonstrations and the large gatherings called *chakai*. In any gathering save those tailored expressly as demonstrations for non-practitioners, guests have many duties to fulfill and must have been instructed as meticulously as hosts, so that together guests and host can bring a gathering to satisfactory completion. There are endless variations on the basic template of *chaji*, depending on the season, the guests, utensils, and space, guaranteeing that each Tea meeting will be a unique event, enabled by participants schooled in a centuries-long tradition of embodied practice and philosophy.

Embodiment

When one begins studying Tea, one can continue learning for life, advancing through higher and higher levels of a network administered and maintained by the direct descendents of Sen no Rikyu. At the same time as inhabiting this elaborate hierarchical structure, in a meeting of practitioners everyone should be interchangeable; all behaviour – from verbal exchange to the drinking of the tea to the placement of the feet as one walks and kneels – is dictated by the rules of *temae*, and therefore regularized enough so that any one practitioner can take over from anyone else at any moment. This rigorous bodily discipline can be explained in Zen terms as a means to eliminate pre-occupation with the self. As the Noh theorist and performer Zeami asserted that the greatest actor will perform "without any distinctive qualities," so too does the Tea practitioner rehearse the choreographies of movement that allow all the members of the gathering to produce a harmonious whole.[18]

A tea gathering is a highly controlled event that relies on each participant's adherence to an all-encompassing set of regulations in order to be completed. The complexes of bodily behaviours of which Tea procedures consist are called *temae*. Virtually every aspect of both host and guest behaviour in the tea room is accounted for by *temae*, including the way to lay the charcoal under the kettle; the way to enter, exit, and move around a room for both hosts and guests; how to give and receive sweets and tea; how to clean and use utensils; and how to measure and prepare the tea. While a large amount of supplementary archival information exists, these written records are always only ancillary to body-to-body transmission and moreover the information contained in these documents is itself most often orally shared in the form of stories and anecdotes. Chanoyu thus consists of an embodied, physical practice that always culminates in the exchange of food and drink, a bodily act of consumption that cannot be mediated.

It should be no surprise, in light of the importance of each performance, that *temae* is very consciously and explicitly maintained via a network of teachers, each of whom maintains a bodily knowledge of *temae* obtained from his or her own teacher(s). Virtually all teachers continue studying Chanoyu for life from higher-ranking teachers in a chain of hierarchy that ends with the current *iemoto*. While these networks of shared knowledge spread diachronically back in time as the elder teach the younger in meticulous imitations, new knowledge about *temae* is also periodically issued from the *iemoto*, the only person who can and does occasionally mandate changes in procedure. There is no substitute for body-to-body contact in teaching *temae*. While there are plenty of archival materials that supplement Chanoyu study, both in its philosophy and *temae*, photographs are unable to convey all the nuances of the movements required for each moment. While videos also exist, it requires a second, knowledgeable eye to identify where the learner deviates from prescribed behaviours and stop her. As in the teaching of dance, teachers tend to take an interactive approach to teaching, using a variety of methods including physical modeling, verbal description, admonishment, and actual body-to-body contact as one hand grabs another to shape it more perfectly, pushes a knee into place, or taps a back to remind it to straighten. Tea practice is thus a bodily discipline in a strict sense of the word, willingly undertaken by the student despite pain and discomfort from kneeling for long periods, the expense of utensils, lessons and supplies, and the necessity of submitting oneself to a rigidly hierarchical system of authority.

Temae may be usefully considered in the terminology of the "scenario," as elucidated by Diana Taylor in her book *The Archive and the Repertoire*. For Taylor, the scenario is "a paradigmatic setup that relies on supposedly live participants, structured around a schematic plot, with an intended (though adaptable) end."[19] The scenario "requires us to wrestle with the social construction of bodies in particular contexts," and they are "passed on and remain remarkably coherent paradigms of seemingly unchanging attitudes and values" but "adapt constantly to reigning conditions."[20] Like the scenarios of conquest discussed by Taylor, the basic outline of the Tea event has proved remarkably durable although, as I will discuss in more detail later, the connotations of the physical practice subtly shift. Certainly, the traditional appearance of Chanoyu and its centuries-old pedigree lend authority to its changing messages. Tea, like the scenario, "both keeps and transforms choreographies of meaning."[21]

The Chanoyu scenario preserves (and creates) a sense of historical and cultural continuity, a sort of living history that practitioners tap into when they submit their bodies and minds to the strictures of the Tea performance. Etsuko Kato goes so far as to give the subtitle "Bodies re-presenting the past" to her book, *The Tea Ceremony and Women's Empowerment in Modern Japan*. Kato examines how women came to make up the overwhelming majority of Japanese Chanoyu practitioners, a 20th century innovation that has vastly altered the face of Tea and especially foreign perceptions that revolve around the figure of the geisha. Chanoyu became part of girls' educational curricula in the early 20th century, primarily as a means of inculcating *sahō* – that is, etiquette or bodily discipline, rather than the philosophical aspects of Tea. Kato tracks how the influx of women into the previously male domain of Chanoyu sparked denunciations of women's Tea as superficial and calculated only toward making themselves attractive to men, rather than based on an interest in the philosophical, religious, cultural import of the practice.[22] This troubled transmission reveals anxieties about the ways bodies can affect the repertoire while also highlighting how an embodied practice can simultaneously serve many purposes in a society. Although the label of superficiality was unfairly leveled only at women, without a concomitant examination of men's motives in studying Tea, the critics who complain that some practitioners are more interested in form than content recognize that embodied practice delivers multiple messages, that bodies can shape those messages, and that power can be transferred to the bodies that take on these knowledges.

In Kato's analysis, cultural memory or the "re-presented past" and women's social bodies are mutually constituted via Chanoyu. Kato uses Linda Hutcheon's theory of "re-presentation" to categorize the performances of Chanoyu practitioners who use "mythological" sources and embodied transmission to create the present-tense practice that Kato calls "bodies re-presenting the past."[23] That is, women's embodiment or "active making of their own bodies in social space" is tied up with the perpetuation of Chanoyu as a practice that is perceived to preserve knowledge of the past, with each affecting the way the other is perceived.[24] On the one hand, embodying and re-presenting the past through Tea is a means of obtaining power within the society that values that past, but on the other hand, women have already been traditionally held responsible for preserving and maintaining "tradition," a role which may certainly include perpetuating the "living history" of Chanoyu.[25]

When the ethnic boundaries of the practice become blurred, then a new confusion comes to the fore – what exactly are non-Japanese people "re-presenting" from a past that is firmly marked as Japanese? Are non-Japanese Tea practitioners just a new version of "colour-blind casting" which asks us not to notice that the "wrong" people are performing? Is this a moment of cultural appropriation in which foreigners borrow, yet again, the things that catch their eye as appealing? Or are there perhaps ways in which non-Japanese people access cultural "memories" that they can "authentically" own, such as ideas about peace, community, or Zen practice? These non-Japanese bodies too "re-present" ideas, the diversity of bodies contributing to the diversity of "meanings" conveyed, be they about Zen, Japanese history, or peaceful communion.

Cultural Memory

The Tea scenario is the medium for myriad messages, about Japan, Zen, history, aesthetics, any number of which may be in play at a given moment. One or many ideas may be "sent" by a participant, but others received by other participants or observers. Although practitioners all strive to learn the same Tea scenario(s) that make them interchangeable participants in the event, they have recourse to a variety of explanations of what they are doing and why. Authors of works on Tea tend to focus on orthodox hermeneutic readings, generally through Zen, but also in anthropological-structuralist terms as "ritual" or semiotics.[26] There are also several ethnographic accounts of Tea which tend to focus on the material practices of practitioners rather than ideal practices as in hermeneutic works.[27]

My point in describing these different approaches to "explaining" Tea is to assert that all of these messages come into play, not just any one, and that the bodies involved moderate meanings. This section is primarily concerned with how cultural memories, both the mundane and ideal, are preserved and shared, particularly in considering what it means for non-Japanese practitioners to embody a practice that is generally identified as a uniquely and quintessentially Japanese phenomenon. This is not an attempt to exhaustively enumerate the "true meaning(s)" of Tea, but rather an attempt to examine the ways in which bodies contribute to the messages they relay. Etsuko Kato's account of the influx of women into official Chanoyu structures sets the stage for a consideration of the influx of "foreigners." In these examples, we can see how shifts in message accommodate (or fail to accommodate) changes in the demographics of Chanoyu practitioners.

In Japan, Chanoyu is classified as *sōgō bunka* ("cultural synthesis," that is, "an amalgamation and ultimate expression of Japanese culture," made up of many other arts, such as ceramics, flower arranging, cuisine, and so on).[28] Anthropologist Kristin Surak documents how it is designated as the quintessence of Japanese culture but simultaneously separate from everyday life and therefore "difficult to learn."[29] Only a small proportion of Japanese people have studied Chanoyu and it is often considered quite an arcane and inaccessible practice. My own experience while living in rural Japan bears out Surak's assertions: many coworkers and acquaintances remarked to me that I, an American of European and Chinese descent, was "more Japanese" than they were themselves because I practiced Chanoyu.

Despite the small numbers of actual practitioners, the distinctive gestures of Tea carry cultural cachet both within Japan and abroad, and often serve as a conveniently metonymic symbol for an essential and sublime Japan. For example, Nakasone Yasuhiro had himself photographed making tea on the day he became prime minister of Japan.[30] *The Karate Kid Part 2* brings its Okinawan love scene between American kid and Japanese girl (as well as between kid and Japanese culture) to a climax over a bowl of tea during a typhoon. Surak's informants from the Los Angeles-area Urasenke group, of both Japanese and non-Japanese descent, describe (sometimes unhappily) the way in which Tea presented for non-practitioners becomes a display of cultural difference, largely evacuated of its deeper philosophical meaning.[31] All these representations (and re-presentations) help contribute to a certain glorification of Tea as a uniquely Japanese practice, simultaneously generalized as the baseline of "traditional Japan" and rarified as the acme of civilization. For many people, Japanese and non-Japanese, Tea thus functions as a sort of living history or reenactment – a memory – of Japan's feudal past, for some an orientalist artistic mystery "to be admired, not comprehended," as Jennifer Anderson notes.[32]

For many (perhaps most) practitioners, the prospect of embodying Japanese classical culture is certainly part of the appeal of Chanoyu, a source of pleasure and a means of obtaining cultural capital as well.[33] Clearly however, the formula of "re-presenting" the Japanese past as a means of making oneself in public space becomes a much more complicated and problematic prospect when the individuals involved are not ethnically Japanese. While certainly non-Japanese kimono-clad people serving tea can seem like a strange, "inauthentic" juxtaposition and cultural appropriation is a real phenomenon with material ramifications in today's world, this does not necessarily mean that Chanoyu is a practice that should be reserved for Japanese people. By looking at how Tea is described to and by foreigners, we can see how long-standing ideas about Tea have shifted in the last fifty or sixty years to legitimate the participation of practitioners of non-Japanese origin. I do not mean to insinuate that the strands of thought which now "explain" Chanoyu as an appropriate expression of Zen or universalist communal practice were not previously present in Tea practice and lore, rather that subtly shifting one's focus on extant lore and documents comes to provide reasoning for demographic changes in practice.

Although foreigners had attended teas as early as the 16th century CE, when Catholic authorities suggested that Portuguese missionaries prepare tea rooms to help further their Christian mission in Japan, one of the most famous and influential English treatises on Chanoyu is Okakura Kakuzo's 1906 work, *The Book of Tea*.[34] Okakura attempts to translate the principles of Chanoyu into terms that Westerners will understand. He calls Chanoyu a "religion of daily life" and suggests that alimentary exchange is the first and most successful means of intercultural communication: "Strangely enough, humanity has so far met in the tea-cup. It is the only Asiatic ceremonial which commands universal esteem. The white man has scoffed at our religion and our morals, but has accepted the brown beverage without hesitation."[35]   In the case of Chanoyu, the beverage in question is bright green *maccha* and was largely surpassed in popularity by the steeped teas that attained much wider usage both in Asia and as an export (although in the last few years a certain fad has developed in Japan and the U.S. for *maccha* in ice cream and green tea lattes from coffee shops).

Okakura's small elision about types of tea is made in service of a plea for Western recognition of Japanese cultural achievement. A consumable commodity like tea holds a very complicated position in an economy of cultural exchange. In Okakura's formulation, tea was not entirely detached from its "ceremonial" signification when adopted by "the white man." The unspoken intimation is that while traders may have thought they were just importing a desirable commodity, in fact they may have imbibed a little of the "Asiatic religion and morals" along with their favoured beverage. *The Book of Tea* makes the imbrication of commodity and ideology explicit through the example of Chanoyu. In the years since Okakura's apologia, the Western world has become more receptive of Asian culture, generally speaking, a shift which the Urasenke school of Tea has used to its advantage. Now the case is made for the value of the ideology of Tea *over* the tea's commodity value; some even say that the reason there are only three and a half sips in a bowl of tea is to emphasize that tea consumption is not the point.

In 1950, Sen Soshitsu XV, the young man who would later become the *iemoto* Hounsai, was sent to the United States by his father, Tantansai, the 14th *iemoto*. Japan was still reeling from the catastrophic end of World War II and Hounsai himself had been conscripted as a kamikaze pilot, although he never flew.[36] His father had even created a new *temae* during the last days of the war so that his son could make bowls of tea in the field for departing kamikaze.[37] Now he found himself on a very different mission to the Americans: spreading "peace through a bowl of tea."[38] This journey connected foreign students of Chanoyu who were scattered through the United States, and after decades of unceasing labour, has culminated in twenty-one official branches of Urasenke on six continents and a special separate school in Kyoto for training non-Japanese students, who are expected to go back to their home countries and continue spreading Chanoyu.[39] In his foreign publications, Hounsai acknowledges Tea's relation to Zen, but generally focuses on Tea as a secular expression of peace and communion, "timeless and applicable to everyone."[40]

Urasenke's "unprecedented commitment to the advancement of the Way of Tea" was, according to the San Francisco Urasenke website, "sparked by the realization that although the Way of Tea is a distinctly Japanese cultural form, its basis is a set of values and concepts that could be followed by anyone, regardless of nationality." The San Francisco description reveals a hermeneutic sleight of hand in the use of the term "realization." It indicates that although the universalist themes of unity and peace were always present in Chanoyu, it was only in the twentieth century discovered how these things were universally applicable beneath the veneer of Japanese uniqueness. It is through this subtle shift of focus that Chanoyu comes to be recognized as a means of accessing knowledge that applies to all people, despite a superficial "Japanese form." The terminology of discovery suggests that Tea doctrine is essentially unchanged, although the face of Chanoyu may shift with the induction of non-Japanese, just as it did earlier in the twentieth century as women became the majority of the Tea establishment.

Practitioners thus have a variety of reasonings to call upon when asked why they study Chanoyu. Explanations may include accessing and preserving one's own culture, or a foreign but admired culture and history, or participation in a universally applicable means of sharing goodwill amongst humans, a message that has been subtly retooled from Zen teachings on Tea during the twentieth century.[41] Examining the way that messages shift to accommodate practitioners reveals that there is no single, inherent "truth" to Tea; rather, practitioners enact various truths that are contingent on many other factors. This is not to say that Tea could mean anything at all, but rather that, like the scenario, it "allows for a continuity of cultural myths and assumptions" while "adapt(ing) constantly to reigning conditions."[42]

Most importantly, Tea people express these reasonings primarily through their bodily actions, not through reading books or sharing ideas intellectually. Non-Japanese practitioners, then, embody and perpetuate

"Japanese culture" but their performing bodies reveal "culture" to be a learned and performed construct, rather than an innate one. Participants gather together to share food, drink, scents and art objects, making their bodies the centerpiece of a unique, fleeting exchange that gains value from its disappearance, enabled by a centuries old performance tradition. As I will argue in the next section, Chanoyu's balance of memory with change is ensured by the dual temporalities enabled by the mode of performance.

Performance

According to Diana Taylor, "A scenario is not necessarily, or even primarily, mimetic. Although the paradigm allows for a continuity of cultural myths and assumptions, it usually works through reactivation rather than duplication....Rather than a copy, the scenario constitutes a once-againness."[43] In Tea as well, although every action is a repetition, there is no originary; every movement reaches not back toward recapturing a past but forward to a momentary goal – the suspension of *maccha* in water and its consumption. Taylor's formulation of "re-activation" is particularly apt for a Zen-infused practice such as Chanoyu, which rejects the "artifice" suggested by the copy and focuses on truly inhabiting the physical world at every moment. The codified behaviors of Tea force the mind to truly inhabit the actions required for the mundane task of making tea, rather than wandering out of the present. A popular Zen Tea phrase that encapsulates this idea is *ichigo ichie*, "one time, one meeting." This phrase inspires Tea participants to practice non-attachment to the physical trappings of the Tea event, destined to disappear, but simultaneously to savour every second of a gathering precisely because it can never be repeated with the same group of people, space and utensils. These constant performances may be meticulously rehearsed and planned, yet little differences remain amongst practitioners. Although a host almost invariably makes one or two mistakes in carrying out *temae*, in a Tea gathering (as opposed to lessons), teachers say there are no mistakes; instead, inevitable mishandlings and pauses all contribute to the ephemeral uniqueness of the moment.

Etsuko Kato writes that the term *temae* denotes both the rules that govern bodily movements and the movements themselves, "as if they were inseparable," indicating semantically that she believes the abstract rules and their physical iteration are independent.[44] However, I contend in a practice maintained entirely within the repertoire of the performed, these things *are* inseparable. Chanoyu does not exist outside its doing, so short of the performer being judged illegitimate, in fact any bodily iteration of *temae is* both the "abstract entities of the rules" and "their physical presentation at one time."[45] The being and the doing of the repertoire are one and the same.

While some do-ers may be judged more reliable records than others, due to experience and ability, since there are no complete records of the movements that make up "true" Chanoyu, the "abstract entities of the rules" cannot exist without constant (re)iteration in physical contingency. Tea schools' elaborate systems of control aim at domesticating practitioners' bodies into a single structure, licensing both teachers and students. This indicates that the authorities recognize the vital importance of every individual performance. Practitioners enter into a physical relation with not only each other, but centuries of previous practitioners, passing knowledge as well as tea, from hand to hand in an unbroken chain. Tea's reputation as *sōgō bunka* and status as a cultural apotheosis is abetted by the appearance of "tradition" – by the very ontology of Chanoyu as a repertoire-based transmission (my father did it, his father, his father…) Things look the same or, at least, don't look new, occluding the shifts that do happen constantly in people's ideas about what Chanoyu is and does.

Many Tea practitioners would agree with Peggy Phelan's now axiomatic statement that performance (or Tea) "becomes itself through disappearance."[46] However, simultaneously, each contingent, unrepeatable performance is linked to the next and the one before in a chain. These performances are rife with singularities – small mutations – yet overall knowledge is transmitted from body to body, performance to performance, in a remarkably stable manner. The meanings vary, the physical performances vary, yet the Way of Tea endures as an instantly recognizable lineage. The individual and the collective, the message and the medium are all intertwined. Neither schools nor individuals fully control the messages they transmit along with a bowl of bright green tea. Rather, messages are activated by physical presence and the actions of the body, performed according to a carefully preserved (although sometimes judiciously altered) script, with inevitable mistakes and obstacles.

Because Chanoyu is constituted in the moment, over and over again, it perhaps only contains those aspects of symbolism, spirituality, or sociality that the practitioners bring to it or read in it. The exchange of tea whisked into hot water is a time-limited operation that can exist only in the few moments that the water continues to steam and the tea powder remains suspended in the mixture. However, paradoxically, practitioners learn these messages through repetition, through years spent studying with each other. Certainly there are many items in use in the unrepeatable moment that have a much longer – admirably long – duration, such as thousand year old bowls and rooms preserved for centuries. Chanoyu as a practice is suspended between these opposing temporalities – the ancient and the instantaneous – and it reflects back to practitioners the values that they bring to it. For me, there are many acceptable, "true" messages which might be delivered through a bowl of tea, which is not to say that Chanoyu can mean anything. It is an expression of the highest realization of Japanese culture, courtesy, and aesthetics; it is a living historical artifact; it is an effective means of social and Buddhist communion.

When a guest receives a bowl of tea from a host, she places the bowl between herself and the guest who drank before her and bows, saying, "*Goshoban itashimasu*" ("I will join you"). Then she places the bowl between herself and the next guest and says, "*Osaki ni*" ("Excuse me for drinking before you"). Finally, she places the bowl before her and bows to the host, saying, "*Otemae chōdai itashimasu*" – "I receive this *temae*." In describing the bowl not as "tea" but as *temae* – the actions taken to produce the tea – the sentence acknowledges that the exchange between host and guest consists of more than tea in hot water. In this bowl, passed from hand to hand, there is a whisked suspension of water and powdered *maccha*, but there is also a sharing of performative practice, knowledge and belief that is imbibed with the tea, through eyes and ears, hands and mouth. The tea becomes a part of the guest who drinks it, inseparable, and so does the history, the memory, and the bodily discipline that makes up Chanoyu.[47]

Works Cited

A Chanoyu Vocabulary: Practical Terms for the Way of Tea (2007) Kyoto: Tankosha Publishing Co.

Anderson, J. (1991) *An Introduction to Japanese Tea Ritual*, Albany: State University of New York Press.

Hirota, D. (1995) *Wind in the Pines: Classic Writings of the Way of Tea as a Buddhist Path*, Fremont, CA: Asian Humanities Press.

Kato, E. (2004) *The Tea Ceremony and Women's Empowerment in Modern Japan: Bodies Re-presenting the Past*, London: Routledge Curzon.

Kondo, D. (2005) "The Tea Ceremony: A Symbolic Analysis," in Howes, D. (Ed.) (2005) *Empire of the Senses: The Sensual Culture Reader*, Oxford and New York: Berg, pp.192-211.

Mori, B. L. R. (1992) *Americans Studying the Traditional Japanese Art of the Tea Ceremony: The Internationalizing of a Traditional Art*, San Francisco: Mellen Research University Press.

Narayan, U. (1996) *Dislocating Cultures*, New York: Routledge.

Nhat Hanh, T. (1995) *Zen Keys: A Guide to Zen Practice*, New York: Doubleday.

Okakura, K. (1964) *The Book of Tea,* New York: Dover Publications.

Phelan, P. (1993) *Unmarked: The Politics of Performance*, London and New York: Routledge.

Plutschow, H. (1999) "An Anthropological Perspective on the Japanese Tea Ceremony," *Anthropoetics*, 5.1.

Roach, J. (1996) *Cities of the Dead: Circum-Atlantic Performance*, New York: Columbia University Press.

Sadler, A. L. (1963) *Cha-No-Yu, the Japanese Tea Ceremony*, Rutland, VT: C. E. Tuttle.

Schneider, R. (2001) "Performance Remains," *Performance Research*, 6.2, pp.100-108.

Sen XV, S. (1979) *Tea Life, Tea Mind*, New York: The Urasenke Foundation, Kyoto by Weatherhill.

Surak, K. (2006) "'Ethnic Practices' in Translation: Tea in Japan and the US," *Ethnic and Racial Studies*, 29:5, pp.828-855.

Suzuki, D. T. (1974) *The Training of the Zen Buddhist Monk*, Berkeley: Wingbow Press.

—. (1958) *Zen and Japanese Buddhism*, Tokyo: Japan Travel Bureau.

—. (1970) *Zen and Japanese Culture*, Bollingen Series 64. Princeton, NJ: Princeton University Press.

Taylor, D. (2003) *The Archive and the Repertoire: Performing Cultural Memory in the Americas*, Durham: Duke University Press.

Urasenke Foundation, San Francisco, "The Urasenke Tradition," at: http://www.urasenke.org/tradition/kyoto.php (accessed 16 July 2008).

Varley, P. and I. Kumakura (Eds.) (1989) *Tea in Japan*, Honolulu: University of Hawaii Press.

Notes

[1] Dennis Hirota (1995) *Wind in the Pines: Classic Writings of the Way of Tea as a Buddhist Path*. Fremont, CA: Asian Humanities Press, p.219; Soshitsu Sen XV (1979) *Tea Life, Tea Mind*, New York: Weatherhill, p.27.

[2] *Maccha* is sometimes spelled "matcha"; the double "c" is a literal translation from the Japanese, the "tc" helps indicate pronunciation.

[3] *A Chanoyu Vocabulary: Practical Terms for the Way of Tea* (2007) Kyoto: Tankosha Publishing, p.137.

[4] *Ibid.*, pp.15-20.

[5] *Ibid.*, p.34.

[6] *Ibid.*, p.195.

[7] Howard Plutschow (1999) "An Anthropological Perspective on the Japanese Tea Ceremony," *Anthropoetics*, 5.1; Jennifer Anderson (1991) *An Introduction to Japanese Tea Ritual*, Albany: State University of New York Press, p.xv.

[8] Sen (1979), p.61.

[9] Clearly, it is beyond the scope of this essay to adequately address Zen Buddhism or even the relationship of Chanoyu and Zen. For more on these topics see for example: D.T. Suzuki (1970) *Zen and Japanese Culture*, Princeton, NJ: Princeton University Press; Hirota (1995); Sen (1979).

[10] Daisetz Teitaro Suzuki (1974) *The Training of the Zen Buddhist Monk*. Berkeley: Wingbow Press.

[11] Daisetz Teitaro Suzuki (1958) *Zen and Japanese Buddhism*. Tokyo: Japan Travel Bureau, p.4.

[12] I will use the word *iemoto* throughout this essay, following the Japanese grammar by using the word for both singular and plural forms.

[13] Urasenke Foundation, San Francisco, at: http://www.urasenke.org (accessed 16 July 2008).

[14] I have now studied under Urasenke teachers for about seven years in California, Colorado, Kansas and Massachusetts. I studied with an Omotesenke teacher for two years in Ehime Prefecture, Japan.

[15] To an untrained eye, practitioners of different schools may look as if they are doing the same thing, but to students of one school or another the differences may seem quite pronounced; for instance, in Omotesenke, one usually turns the bowl counterclockwise, while in Urasenke, it is almost always turned clockwise.

[16] Because so much of Tea lore is shared orally, I have documented a few assertions by reference to my most recent teacher, tea master (kyoju) Glenn Sorei Pereira of Boston, Mass.

[17] Tankosha (2007), p.117.

[18] Hirota (1995), p.77.

[19] Diana Taylor (2003) *The Archive and the Repertoire: Performing Cultural Memory in the Americas*, Durham: Duke University Press, p.13.

[20] *Ibid.*, p.29 & p.31.

[21] *Ibid.*, p.20.
[22] Etsuko Kato (2004) *The Tea Ceremony and Women's Empowerment in Modern Japan: Bodies Re-presenting the Past*. London: Routledge Curzon, p.13 & pp.65-66.
[23] *Ibid.*, p.54.
[24] *Ibid.*, pp.13-14.
[25] Uma Narayan (1996) *Dislocating Cultures*, New York: Routledge; Kato (2004), p.66.
[26] See Paul Varley and Isao Kumakura (Eds.) (1989) *Tea in Japan*, Honolulu: University of Hawaii Press; Plutschow (1999); Dorinne Kondo (2005) "The Tea Ceremony: A Symbolic Analysis," in David Howes (Ed.) *Empire of the Senses: The Sensual Culture Reader*, Oxford and New York: Berg, pp.192-211; Suzuki (1970).
[27] See Barbara Lynne Rowland Mori (1992) *Americans Studying the Traditional Japanese Art of the Tea Ceremony: The Internationalizing of a Traditional Art*, San Francisco: Mellen Research University Press; Kristin Surak (2006), "'Ethnic Practices' in Translation: Tea in Japan and the US," *Ethnic and Racial Studies*, 29: 5, pp.828-855; Kato (2004).
[28] Surak (2006), p.835.
[29] *Ibid.*
[30] Anderson (1991), p.220.
[31] Surak (2006), pp.840-1.
[32] *Ibid.*, p.220.
[33] Kato (2004), p.3.
[34] Varley and Kumakura (1989), p.105.
[35] Kakuzo Okakura (1964) *The Book of Tea,* New York: Dover Publications, p.5.
[36] Anderson (1991), p.71.
[37] I am once again indebted to Glenn Pereira for this point.
[38] Sen (1979), p.81.
[39] Urasenke Foundation, San Francisco, at: http://www.urasenke.org.
[40] Sen (1979), p.81.
[41] See for example Surak (2006), Kato (2004), Mori (1992), Pereira (2006).
[42] Taylor (2003), pp.31-32.
[43] *Ibid.*, p.32.
[44] Kato (2004), p.2.
[45] *Ibid.*
[46] Peggy Phelan (1993) *Unmarked: The Politics of Performance*, London and New York: Routledge, p.146.
[47] I would like to acknowledge my many teachers and peers in Chanoyu, from whom I have learned much of what is written here. Thanks especially to my teachers: Glenn Pereira, Michael Ricci, Dale Slusser, Tokuko Kameda, and Glenn and Carol Webb.

No Sweat:
Performance and the Care
of the Singapore Self

Paul Rae

iDesire

Are you sitting comfortably? Then we'll begin. If you want to understand the relationship between performance, embodiment and cultural memory in the Southeast Asian city-state of Singapore, I advise you lie back and submit to the ministrations of the OSIM iDesire, "the world's 1st intelligent full body massage chair." Go on, *relax*: sink into the black synthetic leather, whose anti-bacterial coating ensures "that the surface is hygienic from different users" [*sic*], and run through the pre-set massage healthcare programmes that range from "full body relief" to "acupressure." Don't sweat the cuffs now encircling your wrists: the air-bags around your arms will "firmly squeeze to release any tightness," while the "audio therapy" will soothe you by piping music through the "superior speaker" in the remote. Discomfited? Rest assured that the "intuitive display…keeps you in the know at every stage of your massage experience so that you may have the ultimate control."[1]

Now then, as you enjoy your "massage of unprecedented realism," perhaps you can already intuit some of the different kinds of performance exemplified by your experience. In fact, let's start with that idea of "unprecedented realism," which seems to promise both more and less than "the real thing." The "simulacrum" analysis of hi-tech Singapore has arguably been over-stated by Euro-American pundits in the past,[2] but such scrupulous restorations of behaviour do point to some distinctive features of why "performance," in several senses, is such an important watchword in the local context.

Chief among these is Singapore's ambivalent relationship to its past. An outpost of the Riau-Johor Sultanate from the fourteenth to nineteenth centuries, a British colony (1819-1943, 1945-1963), and lynchpin in Japan's "Greater East Asia Co-Prosperity Sphere" (1943-5), Singapore seceded from the British Empire in 1963 to join Malaysia. Political tensions with the federal government in Kuala Lumpur resulted in the effective ejection of the state from the Federation two years later, and on 9 August 1965, Singapore became a nation in spite of itself. With few natural resources and a densely-packed population of politically and religiously diverse and sometimes restive ethnic groups (most notably of Chinese, Malay and Indian origin), the long-term viability of the island Republic was far from given.

However, Singapore was strategically located within a volatile but potentially profitable region, boasted a relatively well-educated workforce, and was led by an ambitious government under the bullish Prime Ministership of Lee Kuan Yew. Lee had come to power when Singapore was granted self-government in 1959, and combined parliamentary advantage, tactical cunning and the deployment of Emergency-era security laws not only to out-manoeuvre his rivals at the time, but to lay the groundwork for the overwhelming political dominance that his People's Action Party (PAP) enjoys to this day.[3]

Lacking both a domestic market large enough to stimulate and sustain the local economy, and a hinterland that could ensure self-sufficiency, Singapore nailed its colours to the mast of global competitiveness early on. From the late 'sixties onwards, multinational corporations were aggressively courted, the port and other trans-shipment facilities continued to grow, and the government invested heavily in developing the island's infrastructure, as well as in industries such as tourism, communications, armaments, semi-conductor manufacturing and financial services.

Economically, this approach would serve the city-state well. Today, Singapore has one of the highest per capita GDPs in the world, up from US$512 in 1965 to US$35163 in 2007.[4] To maintain this position in a globalizing world, however, means that there is no let-up in the obligation to improve performance: as Singapore moves up the "value chain," it must find ever more innovative ways to boost productivity. OSIM, a Singaporean company, represents one such response to this imperative. With manufacturing outsourced, the Singapore operation is free to focus on design and branding, typically "value added" activities in a so-called "knowledge-based economy." Indeed, in 2007, the Prime Minister of Singapore officially presented U.S. President George W. Bush with US$450 worth of OSIM products. And yet, such imprimaturs notwithstanding, as the name "iDesire" makes abundantly clear, what is being sold is at once product and promise. The affluent consumers of Singapore and elsewhere in OSIM's global sales network will be pampered, but they will never be satisfied: like an ache that even the most refined massage machine cannot soothe, the "real thing" will always remain just out of reach.

Speaking of which, how are you feeling? Have you got to the part yet where "a vibrator sends soothing vibration around your tailbone region"? No? Let's switch to a different setting. Because it's all very well talking about technical, economic and even diplomatic performance, but we can't realistically understand the significance of the iDesire without bringing embodiment into the picture. In a place where human capital is of paramount importance, you can't just magic productivity out of thin air, although in some respects, independent Singapore began with little more than that. An unexpected state, it had few default resources for building a national identity. Not only did it lack a coherent pre-colonial history, a racial or cultural "essence," or even an independence struggle to lionize, but the push to be a "global city" potentially threatened what attachment to the local that its inhabitants *did* share.

Instead of looking to the past, then, the PAP government began to invent a national identity that would be constituted both in and through economic productivity. From the late 'sixties onwards, a comprehensive program of legislation, surveillance and propaganda was introduced that sought to produce workplace compliance and uniform behaviour as defining features of Singaporean-ness. Myriad aspects of social and cultural life were engineered, many of which centred on the bodies of the populace, including language and speech, personal hygiene and procreation habits, and interpersonal and inter-ethnic relations. Infrastructural development was bound up with the regulation of public and private space, and a national ideology resulted in low-level militarization through a Swiss-style "Total Defence" program. This was underwritten by a resolutely future-oriented rhetoric of pragmatism that privileged actions over words, and brooked few objections on grounds of abstract ideological principle or historical precedent.

To put it another way, if the OSIM iDesire is an exemplary Singaporean product, in combining a responsiveness to and shaping of the body, it is also emblematically productive *of* Singaporeans. Modern Singapore and the modern Singaporean have been, to a significant extent, performatively produced. But if Singaporean *is* as Singaporean *does*, the nature of that doing, as well as its relationship to what has been done before, is subtle and complex. Beyond popular clichés of the city-state's economic successes and authoritarian excesses, the contingent and adaptable qualities of nation-oriented performativity mean that it intersects with diverse religious, ethnic and class identities so as to inform, rather than override, them. The diverse cultural means by which these behaviours, meanings and identities are transmitted and expressed, is the larger subject of this chapter.

iDocile?

These complexities notwithstanding, for observers schooled in more liberal political traditions, the widespread acceptance of pervasive, indeed invasive, levels of social control in as modern and cosmopolitan a place as Singapore can seem anomalous, even contradictory. For you, switching between the nine different kinds of massage actions, the better to commit your personal programme to the iDesire "memory function," it is less so:

> To begin with, there was the scale of the control: it was a question not of treating the body *en masse*, 'wholesale,' as if it were an indissociable unity, but of working it 'retail,' individually; of exercising upon it a subtle coercion, of obtaining holds upon it at the level of the mechanism itself – movements, gestures, attitudes, rapidity: an infinitesimal power over the active body. Then there was the object of the control: it was not or was no longer the signifying elements of behaviour or the language of the body, but the economy, the efficiency of movements, their internal organization; constraint bears on the forces rather than on the signs; the only truly important ceremony is that of exercise.[5]

Thus Michel Foucault on the production of "docile bodies" in eighteenth-century France, where, he proposes, the invention and institutionalisation of techniques for normalizing, training and correcting the body increased its economic utility while diminishing the likelihood of dissent.

Can the same be said for modern Singapore? Certainly, in its culturally diverse, economically differentiated, fast-changing and densely populated urban environment, bodies are sites of focused attention by state and commercial interests alike. Normative bio-political surveillance – compulsory identity cards include fingerprints, blood type and "race" – finds its corollary in the prevalence of corporeal discipline within the judicial system. Over thirty offences are punishable by caning in the Republic, which has one of the highest *per capita* prison populations in the Asian region, and, allegedly, one of the highest *per capita* execution rates in the world.[6]

At the same time, one of the great attractions of the city to visitors and inhabitants alike is its service-oriented user-friendliness. Its notorious cleanliness and efficiency facilitate access to the plethora of sensible pleasures available in its miles of malls and ethnic quarters. Singapore's many so-called "High Net Worth Individuals" make extensive use of its designer shops and restaurants; but the scope and extent of similar opportunities for ordinary consumers is a striking feature of urban life. Food culture, high-street fashion, beauty and "wellness" treatments, and the sex industry are all integral to the ways in which diverse demographics and markets experience and interpret Singapore.[7] The high degree of overlap between leisure and consumption is reflected in a theatricalised aesthetics of presentation and demonstration. "Concept" food courts recreate nostalgic versions of 1950s Singapore, complete with servers in period dress and fake reclamation décor. Meanwhile, most of the major malls have an atrium design, with amphitheatre-like spaces left open in the centre for product launches, promotional events and roadshows. OSIM is a regular presence in such venues. With its head, back and full body massage machines, and eye-catching fitness products like the uSurf and uGallop, shoppers are only too happy to try out the merchandise, and in so doing present an attention-grabbing spectacle for others.

The resulting relationship between somatic wellbeing and social discipline has not gone unremarked by Singaporean commentators, and it is telling that in *Singapore, the Air-Conditioned Nation: Essays on the Politics of Comfort and Control*, the former journalist Cherian George should use it as the framework for a collection of wide-ranging articles on governance, civil society and national identity. Justifying his choice of title, George notes that Lee Kuan Yew once cited the air-conditioner as the most influential invention of the last millennium, and writes: "Think of Singapore as the Air-conditioned Nation – a society with a unique blend of comfort and central control, where people have mastered their environment, but at the cost of individual autonomy, and at the risk of unsustainability."[8] As he expands on the image, it begins to lose its somatic anchoring in favour of more widely applicable metaphorical uses; but it is significant that where George brings embodied experience back into his analysis, it is with reference to memory. In the chapter "Lost at Home: A Nation's State of Geographical Confusion," he reflects on the fact, widespread in space-scarce and development-intensive Singapore, that "…the place you grow up in will not be the place you grow old in, and that you can never go back, because what was there then is here no longer."[9]   George   recounts   the   disappearance   of   his   childhood neighbourhood, demolished to accommodate an expressway sliproad, and how he salvaged a small piece of tiled floor from the rubble of his house. It is a detail he returns to at the close of the chapter: "Conservation protects only the most widely shared of memories…Memories recorded self-consciously always miss the mundane. It is the things one takes for granted that disappear most irretrievably – like the feel of small mosaic tiles beneath one's small, bare feet."[10]

Taken in the context of George's wider thesis – that in Singapore "comfort is achieved through control"[11] – this conclusion complicates some common assumptions in the literature on performance and cultural memory. Where performance is often described as playing a politically progressive role in processes of collective remembering, for George it is the most personal and least mediated memories that have suffered greatest under Singaporean modernity. And yet, given the scope and scale of Singapore's development, this phenomenon is itself widely shared, while the disappearance of so much material history means that bodies are all the more   significant   as   repositories   and   representations   of   memory. Sometimes, it can feel like the oldest and most durable things in Singapore are Singaporeans themselves.

As a result, when it comes to questions of the past, performance is at once a privileged mode of behaviour and a problematic means of cultural expression. This in turn feeds into a high level of self-awareness on the part of Singaporeans about their condition, especially amongst the sizeable middle class. George's commentary itself first appeared as a column in the influential English-language broadsheet, *The Straits Times*, while in Singapore's most vibrant local art form, theatre, there has been no shortage of works that have dealt with the theme of rapid development and its consequences for Singaporean selfhood.[12]

For the performance scholar, this poses an interesting methodological challenge, because it means that the contrasts between what Jon McKenzie describes as "normative" and "resistant" performativity are more than usually blurred.[13] It is appealingly neat to suggest that state-mandated performative behaviour in Singapore has erased cultural memory in favour of producing docile bodies, but it is also an over-simplification. Nor, on the other hand, should we take the prevalence of cultural products that have provided a reflexive commentary on this situation as amounting to efficacious critique simply by default. Certainly, some plays have been explicitly critical of the pace and price of urbanization in Singapore; but arguably the most significant are those that have articulated the ambivalence with which many Singaporeans triangulate themselves in relation both to the past, and to those in power. While there is more to be said, then, about the role of Singapore theatre in representing and reconstituting the past, the distinctive points of intersection between performance, embodiment and cultural memory in Singapore require a slightly different approach. Rather than separating out the theatre from other performative practices, in what follows I shall pay attention to several different areas where they are mutually informing.

iCare

A good example of this ambivalence regarding self, past and power can be found at the opening of one of Singapore's best-known plays, *Descendants of the Eunuch Admiral* (1995) by the late Kuo Pao Kun:

> I have come to realise of late that dreaming has become the centre of my life.
>
> Yes, dreaming. Dreaming all by myself. Alone, painfully alone, and floating away.
>
> But this loneliness is a potent one; it is an inviting loneliness. There is a vast space all around me. Endless. Haunting. Unknown. But promising. And seemingly reachable.
> ...
> In these dreams, being alone, I was able to look at myself, look inside myself and look through myself. And as I dived deeper and deeper into the stark loneliness of myself, I felt I had become closer and closer to him, closer to this 600-year-old legend of a molested and incarcerated man.
>
> Yes, each night, through my own fear and uncertainty, I discover more agony in him, more respect for him, and more suspicion of him.[14]

Over the course of the play, Kuo develops this association between the unnamed voice of a contemporary Singaporean corporate employee and Zheng He, a Chinese Muslim eunuch who commanded an imperial armada on seven expeditions between 1405 and 1431, sailing as far as Africa and India for purposes of trade and diplomacy, and in a show of military might and cultural pre-eminence. A prominent strand of the text outlines a range of traditional Chinese castration methods, including one where a nanny would regularly massage the testicles until they were completely crushed, although it would be "received by the subject as comforting, enjoyable and even highly desirable."[15]

By bringing themes of corporate performance, political control and pleasurable constraint together within the context of Chinese Imperial power, Kuo used a historical figure to throw the Singapore condition into sharp relief. And yet, the very fact that he could do so, and that he, like Cherian George, could count on an audience for whom his interpretation would resonate, signals an additional degree of complexity. In the passage above, for instance, the speaker expresses a self-awareness of impotence that is itself generative; the figure of the Eunuch is at once seductive and salutary. In particular, the line "I was able to look at myself, look inside myself and look through myself" recalls Foucault's later nuancing of his concept of "docile bodies" in favour of what he called "the care of the self." Noting that it would later be eclipsed, with the rise of Christianity, by a moralising version of the command to "know thyself," Foucault saw in the care of the self discussed by Socrates, Xenophon and others an ascetic practice of self-formation by the subject, "an exercise of the self on the self by which one attempts to develop and transform oneself, and to attain a certain mode of being."[16]

Such "techniques of the self" were more concerned with on-going processes of living than prohibitions, though this is not to say they were entirely self-derived: "They are models that he [the individual] finds in his culture and are proposed, suggested, imposed upon him by his culture, his society, and his social group."[17] For Foucault, these wide-ranging practices fell between two poles: *exercitatio* – physical exercises by which one established one's independence relative to the external world – and *meditatio* – "progressive exercises of memorization" by which one assimilated and tested one's grasp of the "relevant true discourses" in order to respond ethically in the face of such challenges as life may present.[18] Foucault went on to suggest that the concept of an "ethical subject" might provide a means of thinking about power "on the basis of freedom, strategies and governmentality," rather than the more familiar "legal concept of the subject" that derives from understanding power solely in terms of political institutions.[19]

To the extent it is applicable across contexts, this suggests a more subtle approach to the relationship between performance, embodiment and cultural memory in Singapore than the "docile body" model, and once again, an OSIM massage chair provides a focal point for the discussion. I'm handing you a copy of *The Straits Times* from 28 March 2005. Today, a sidebar on the front page features taxi driver Kee Lek Khim, who saved for over a year to purchase her iSymphonic AV.[20] She is pictured reclining on the still partially shrink-wrapped chair in her bedroom, where there is air-conditioning "so it won't get spoilt." Citing the backaches she gets from long shifts in the taxi, Madam Kee states: "Every night, before I go to bed, I have to sit on it. After half an hour, I'll feel very relaxed and sleepy and then I can just go to sleep." The article goes on: "Like her, many other Singaporeans have embraced the massage chair…A growing health consciousness on the one hand, and increased stress at the workplace have combined to enhance their appeal." However, "while retailers keep hoping the massage chair will catch on in the West, they concede readily that up till now it has had a peculiarly Asian appeal."[21]

Now, this human-interest story cum industry snapshot hardly amounts to a parable of the "care of the self" *à la* Foucault. However, it does provide a starting point for re-thinking the two poles of *exercitatio* and *meditatio* in the Singapore context. First, although the article points out that the massage chair phenomenon is relatively recent, it also makes clear that there is a cultural dimension to their popularity that is, in part, historical. And while it pays to be wary of essentialised, culturalist conceptions of Asianness, it is nevertheless fair to say that the "care of the self" is today better exemplified in certain aspects of South, East and Southeast Asian philosophies than in those of the Western tradition.[22] In Singapore, martial arts and meditation, massage and acupressure, and traditional medical treatments and healing therapies, make up a widely available and philosophically-informed set of somatic practices originating in China, Japan, Korea, India and the Malay world. Moreover, their influence can be felt far beyond the specific domains of health and sport. Even younger, English-educated Singaporeans, who may well see themselves as highly "Westernised," tend to manifest such sensibilities in their lifestyle choices and consumer behaviour, especially with regards to diet.

In fact, we might go so far as to say that if the OSIM iDesire exemplifies the way in which bodies in Singapore are disciplined through pleasurable constraint, it also represents a particularly visible manifestation of a more subtle kind of oversight: a mode of self-monitoring that is acutely sensitive to the ebbs and flows of bodily states in relation to the environment. Similarly, while Madam Kee's decision to keep her massage chair under wraps in an air-conditioned room may seem to bear out George's characterisation of an air-conditioned nation, her anxiety about the corrosive effects of Singapore's hot and humid climate is far from misplaced. Singapore's can be an unexpectedly hostile environment, where the simple act of passing in and out of doors involves substantial variations in temperature and humidity. In response, its inhabitants have developed a repertoire of coping techniques, including clothing choice, supplementary nutrition and frequent re-hydration. From a pragmatic point of view, this serves to regulate body temperature, and protect against infection. But a secondary effect, often only tacitly understood by individuals, is that such practices constitute an important means by which cultural memory is transmitted; a point reinforced, in my own experience, at extended family gatherings and other social events, where inter-generational conversation revolves to a significant degree around assessments of – and prescriptions for – the health and well-being of family members and interlocutors.

Remembering to Forget

Nuancing an interpretation of bodies in Singapore as objects of social discipline, then, is their status as privileged sites of cultural memory, enacted performatively through exercises and strategies that enable individuals to constitute themselves as subjects in a cosmopolitan, capitalist society. Bodies are all the more significant a repository of memory in light of Singapore's rapid urban transformations, future-oriented ideology, and novelty-obsessed economy, which have seen the destruction of much of its built heritage, and the discarding of its material history.

It is therefore tempting, at this point, to refer to Diana Taylor's compelling discussion of embodied memory as a repertoire of meanings and actions that lie in dynamic relation to the more durable and stable objects of the archive.[23] But here we come to one of the most distinctive aspects of the care of the Singapore self, one that departs from the Foucauldian schema: the role of forgetting. Foucault described some of the exercises that contributed to the *meditatio* pole of the care of the self as a "mnemotechnical formula."[24] In Singapore, we might more usefully identify an *amneso*technical formula, deriving from diverse historical sources, and manifesting itself in various cultural and expressive media.

In part, this forgetfulness is ideologically motivated. Writing in 1999, Hong Lysa and Huang Jianli identified a 1964 account of the PAP's first ten years by then Minister for Culture S. Rajaratnam as the template for interpreting the period that "has not moved one iota" since. They went on:

> The plotting of the PAP story as Singapore's history has not seriously been challenged either by professional historians or by former political actors, who have been doubly defeated. The latter certainly lost the political game and, having done so, also lost their voice as agents of history because of the institutional and political constraints on them. Their narrative of betrayal and undemocratic practices on the part of Lee's faction of the PAP has been unable to find a place in the story of contemporary Singapore.[25]

However, it is also noteworthy that at times the Singapore establishment has been disarmingly open about the need to forget – Hong and Huang cite Rajaratnam on the importance of "collective selective amnesia" to effective nation building – and I would argue that this very openness indicates that there is more to the story of Singapore's self-forgetting than propaganda. In terms of embodiment, there is an epistemological dimension – Singapore's varied cultural traditions have different ways of remembering, including oral and other kinds of performances – and, perhaps paradoxically, there is also a historical dimension. Massage chair owner Kee Lek Khim's statement that "Every night, before I go to bed, I have to sit on it. After half an hour, I'll feel very relaxed and sleepy and then I can just go to sleep" is curiously redolent of the opening speech in Kuo's *Descendants of the Eunuch Admiral*, and indeed it is tempting to posit that both bespeak an otherwise mute cultural memory of oblivion.

In the efficient and hi-tech knowledge-based economy of modern times, it is easy to overlook the sheer amount of back-breaking physical labour that has been and continues to be required to effect the transactions and transformations that have propelled Singapore's development for almost two centuries. Today's sizeable population of migrant workers from South Asia, China and elsewhere in Southeast Asia has its precedent in the waves of convict and immigrant labour of the colonial period, "a river of muscle and bone," as the historian Carl A. Trocki memorably describes the vast numbers of Chinese coolies who entered Singapore in search of a better life.[26] Illiterate, often indentured, these rickshaw pullers, plantation workers, coal heavers and stevedores were the mainstay of the Singapore workforce at least until the 1930s, toiling through forgotten lives in the service of a small number of wealthy Chinese and European merchants. Forgotten, moreover, not only by the historical record, but also to themselves. As Trocki points out, the free port of Singapore was unusually reliant for revenues on the taxation of "luxury" items such as cannabis, coconut toddy, betel nuts and, most of all, opium. With few other distractions, many labourers became opium addicts, locking themselves into a system of debt from which they never escaped. For Trocki, this sustained the local economy throughout the nineteenth century, while the trans-shipment of opium between China and Europe "is what made Singapore the trading nexus between the global economy and the local economies of Southeast Asia."[27]

It is predictably ironic that Trocki's broad thesis concerning the centrality of opium to the founding and development of modern Singapore is revisionist, granting an underlying rationale to its economic history that he believes to be lacking in other scholarly accounts. This paradox of the forgetting and recovery of forgetting itself is indicative of a phenomenon that the writer Janadas Devan has identified as a structural condition of Singapore:

> The history of Singapore, in particular, is a series of forgettings. This is nobody's fault. That is how the history of Singapore unfolded: as forgettings, as leavings, as partings, as separations, as sudden, unaccountable breaks…To put it simply: Singapore, in many ways, is the product of forgettings. Singapore occurred, and continues to sustain itself, as a result of recurrent acts of forgettings. Forgetting is the condition of Singapore.[28]

Clarifying that he is not concerned with the "accidental" forgettings of forgetful people, Devan goes on to specify two dynamic modes of Singaporean forgetting. One is political, and derives from the abruptness of Independence; a largely unforeseen and unwanted event that only came to be desired by Singaporeans *ex post facto*, and marked a fundamental break with the pre-1965 past. The other concerns the personal implications of this for Singaporeans who wished to define themselves as such. Devan parses a poem, "My Country and My People" (1980) by Singaporean Lee Tzu Pheng, which begins: "My country and my people/ are neither here nor there, nor/ in the comfort of my preferences,/ if I could even choose."[29] He identifies in it a series of deliberate forgettings and rememberings of forgettings – of loss, homelessness, ethnicity and difference – by which

Lee is able to reconcile herself to her discomfiting homeland. He concludes that maintaining an awareness of these complexities is key to avoiding the "lies" to which coherent stories of the past invariably give rise: "Forgetting is necessary. Forgetting is also inevitable, for our history forgets. But pray do not let the forgetting be of the other kind: the forgetting that presumes to remember a mythical origin, a hegemonic history."[30]

Productive Paradox or Double Bind?

Devan's analysis of how Singaporeans "remember to forget" suggests a mode of subject formation that we might call the care of the Singapore self. However, while in its combination of embodied practice and discursive reflection, as well as in its political dimension, it follows the broad contours of Foucault's formulation, it also possesses significant differences. Clearly, it arises out of specific historical, geographic and cultural conditions that influence the precise form it takes – given the particularities of Foucault's own primary frames of reference (Ancient Greece and post-war Western Europe), such variations are only to be expected. But there are also *peculiarities* in "remembering to forget" that relate closely to its conjunction of embodiment and cultural memory, and that may represent a more substantial divergence from the Foucauldian schema.

Most notably, Foucault's description of the care of the self in progressive terms as a "mode of action"[31] is not necessarily borne out in Singapore, where the strange temporality of "remembering to forget" is experienced as a mix of change and stasis. Rapid urban transformation and the fast pace of city life are offset by a pervasive sense in Singapore of baseline predictability. Not only is change itself a constant – construction is an integral part of the cityscape – but in a seasonless climate where the sun rises and sets at almost the same time year-round, one experiences neither the sudden nor cyclical transformations characteristic of environments further from the Equator. Something similar might be said of the political climate. In 2009, the PAP celebrated half a century in power, with no serious challenge to its record of parliamentary dominance in sight. One consequence of this is a perception amongst some "post-65ers" – Singaporeans born after independence – that they have missed out on history; that the important work was done by the "Pioneer Generation" of Lee Kuan Yew and others, and that it only remains for them to live out the rewards in harmony and prosperity. Others suggest the opposite: that for as long as modern Singapore's "founding father" remains in the Government, history cannot begin.

Either way, this sense that history is elsewhere (or elsewhen) has itself contributed to a growing interest in the past amongst younger Singaporeans. Typically, theatre-makers have played a leading role in this development, yet, once again, their work cannot easily be disentangled from state discourses, or from other modes of presentation and performance.

A good example of this concerns the fate of Singapore's history museum, which is run by a branch of the Ministry of Information, Communications and the Arts. In the late 'nineties, it looked set to realise precisely the outcome that Devan warned against in his description of "the forgetting that presumes to remember a mythical origin, a hegemonic history." In 1997, then Deputy Prime Minister Lee Hsien Loong announced the introduction of a National Education initiative centring on the "Singapore Story," which was not "an idealised legendary account or a founding myth" but "objective history, seen from a Singaporean standpoint."[32] A multi-media exhibition version of the Singapore Story was duly installed in the Singapore History Museum, which was compulsory viewing for all school students.[33]

However, although some individual voices spoke up in criticism of the initiative – it was in this context that Hong and Huang, cited above, bemoaned "the plotting of the PAP story as Singapore's history" – the main challenge came from its intended audience. The scope and consistency with which the Singapore Story was propagated through the school system and civil service was unprecedented. But within a few years, concerns were being expressed by the Ministry of Education that young Singaporeans were not as receptive to it as had been hoped – indeed, they were suspicious of it. It was clear that a generational shift was underway, and that for young, techno-savvy Singaporeans, the turbulent independence period was distant, abstract and, in light of their scepticism towards national narratives, unknowable.

In 2003, the museum closed for a major refurbishment. This involved a complete overhaul of the exhibits, and a complete re-branding exercise. Partly with an eye to the tastes of the younger demographic, and partly in compensation for the paucity of material culture that was actually available for display, the new exhibits were to be experiential and immersive. The renamed National Museum of Singapore (NAMOS) opened in December 2006. It features four "Lifestyle Galleries," which track social and cultural history through photography, fashion, food and film and theatre, and feature multi-sensory displays and video installations. Meanwhile, exhibits in the main History Gallery are viewed to the accompaniment of a hand-held audio companion, which contains over seven hours of narration, analysis, sound effects, archival material and dramatic reconstructions. This marked a shift in the means by which historical objects and interpretations would be encountered in Singapore; in contrast to the extensive use of explanatory placards and a single narrative thread in earlier displays and other state-run museums, embodied experience and visitor choice would now be paramount.

And so it was that when it needed to re-imagine Singapore history for a new generation, the state called upon its theatre-makers and visual artists. Several of Singapore's most established playwrights produced treatments for the rooms and sub-sections of the gallery, and scripted both the factual descriptions and fictional scenes. Two prominent local actors were selected as the narrators, and over fifty others voiced the cacophony of stories and experiences that make up the audio experience. Up-and-coming film-makers were commissioned to create innovative works that both documented specific events or periods, and commented upon their representation.[34]

In my own experience, the result condenses several of the performance modes I have discussed above, from the behavioural to the presentational. As the first narrator introduces himself through the headphones, the listener follows a spiral path deep into the bowels of the museum; already one has the sense of being prompted to act in certain ways – choreographed, as it were, by a combination of instructions, narrative and the physical environment. This is experienced as a removal from the present, of physically travelling back in time and down into the historical substratum. After viewing a multi-screen film by the artist Ho Tzu Nyen, which presents Singapore's pre-colonial history in a wordless diorama of cross-cultural arrivals, departures and contestations, the visitor can choose from a series of snaking pathways through the dimly-lit and irregularly-shaped galleries. In response, perhaps, to the resulting spatial disorientation, my personal experience is that one focuses one's attention all the more thoroughly on the exhibits to hand, which are very precisely picked out through the careful positioning of pinspot lighting. The accompanying audio serves either to explain or "stage" whatever one is looking at; without the audio, one's understanding of the artefacts would be severely hampered. But at the same time, one is, oneself, "staged" in at least two ways. The dense layering of the soundtrack – with fast edits, diverse modes of address, a range of vocal textures and personalities, background sound and music, and the use of binaural effects – acts upon the body of the listener so as to suture them into a relation with the objects of their attention. At the same time, the set-like design of many of the small rooms provides a diminutive theatrical environment for each encounter.

Imagining and rendering characters and scenarios; arranging objects, bodies and meanings in space and time; anticipating and heightening the recipient's encounter with the material: all these skills were brought to bear by theatre-makers upon the representation and transmission of Singapore's history. In so doing, they reaffirmed the social significance of an art form that has often been viewed with suspicion by the authorities. The innovations paid off for the Museum, too. In a blog posting shortly after the opening, the Minister for Foreign Affairs, George Yeo, wrote enthusiastically about his visit: "[Lee] Chor Lin, Director of SHM [Singapore History Museum (*sic.*)], told me that teenagers love the [audio] companion. In the multi-media age, information, education and entertainment go together…The ability to make education entertaining is the key to success in the knowledge economy of the 21st century."[35] In 2008, Lee topped the annual "Arts Power List" in *The Straits Times*, which noted that "[u]nder her direction, the museum has revamped itself as a hip lifestyle location."[36]

While the NAMOS refurbishment granted many theatre-makers an important national platform, in light of the foregoing discussion, the "lifestyle" tag and the seamlessness with which Yeo incorporated his response into a larger lesson about success in the knowledge economy, raises some pointed questions: Is the NAMOS experience a new way of remembering to forget? To what extent does it alter the dynamics of Singaporean subjectivity? Is theatricality in the museum a real innovation, or simply an expansion of state performativity into the cultural domain? Or, to put it another way, is cultural performance the new iDesire?

Certainly, "culture" has become increasingly desired by the Singapore state in recent years, as it seeks to boost its economic competitiveness by improving innovation and creativity. In 2008, MICA published the third instalment of its ambitious *Renaissance City Plan*, which maps out the Republic's arts and heritage policy to 2015, and performance – as both cultural practice and metric of efficiency – is central to this project.

However, in the space that remains, and in place of a conclusion, I would like to discuss an artwork that exemplifies several of the often contrasting ways in which performance, embodiment and cultural memory intersect in Singapore.

Film-maker Royston Tan's *Sin Sai Hong* (2006) is a 35 minute cinematic portrait of the eponymous Hokkien-dialect Chinese opera troupe, and a compelling meditation on the process of cultural transmission. Commissioned by NAMOS to make a film for its opening festival, Tan spent a year researching the project by performing walk-on roles for the group in their performances at temples and other entertainments. However, although the film opens with a short narrative summary of its hundred-year history by an elderly former troupe leader, the result is more document than documentary. The temporary bamboo-scaffold stage where open air *wayang* (street opera) is normally performed, was reconstructed in a studio. Shot largely in the backstage area, where actors make up and wait to go on, the camera pans slowly back and forth before the troupe, who are already fully made up, and stand resplendent in their wigs, headdresses, false beards and costumes of sequins and silk.

They remain almost static as they sing their way through a repertoire that spans the twentieth century, and harks back to a much older Chinese folkloric tradition and narrative corpus, one populated by doomed lovers, corrupt magistrates, filial sons, stern parents and ageless sages. The presence of the entire ensemble in the compact space, and the range of themes and emotions they cover – from blushing courtship through comic interludes to pious devotion and tear-jerking bereavement – suggests that the cast is not so much backstage at a performance by Sin Sai Hong, as at a parade of the entire Hokkien popular imaginary. This spatial concentration is matched by the slow pace at which the style of the music changes over the course of the film, and by the stateliness of the tracking shots and of the performers' regal bearing. The result is a compressed sense of gradual and continuous transformation over time and across generations.

In one regard, then, *Sin Sai Hong* is an affectionate portrayal of a local performance tradition that, while no longer as popular as it was, retains some currency in certain socio-cultural contexts. Yet the NAMOS context begs a question about the cultural status of Sin Sai Hong and the art form that it practices; is or isn't it a "museum piece"? This issue is addressed in a number of ways by the film itself. The fact that it is shot backstage implies that there is something hidden or obscure about the colourful world that is represented, and the film closes on a note of profound ambivalence. After a "curtain call" sequence presented *on*stage, most of the lights are switched off, and the viewer is given to believe that the film has finished. Then, however, the ensemble are presented once more backstage, wearing only the under-garments of plain white trousers and tunics, and packing away their make-up boxes (although their faces remain made-up). Music begins again, and, turning directly to the camera, they sing in Hokkien:

> *(Maudlin)*
> The golden years are over
> We do not know what the future holds for the troupe
> We'll always remember this tradition, passed down by our forefathers
> Through trials and tribulations we have aged
> It's been 96 years, it's hard to keep it going
> This is the fourth generation of the opera troupe
>
> *(Upbeat)*
> Thank you everyone for your support
> You watch an opera, and the culture is preserved
> Never forget this tradition, let it be passed on
> Let Sin Sai Hong be remembered through the generations
> In the National Museum of Singapore.

We then see a final wide shot of the stage. The remaining lights are shut down with a loud "thunk," the screen goes dark, and the credits begin to roll.

This two-part epilogue is deeply perplexing. We are informed that the culture has been preserved simply by dint of our watching the film, and implored to sustain its transmission. Even taking into account, however, the tradition of patronage by which temples and other institutions engage opera troupes to perform, the appreciation shown to NAMOS in the last line is deeply ironic; all the more so, given the film has only been shown in public on a handful of occasions. Pro-Mandarin language policies in Singapore mean that the use of other Chinese dialects in the public realm are heavily regulated, and anecdotal evidence suggests that this may be the reason the film has not enjoyed wider distribution.

By this token, the visceral shut-down at the end of the film both depicts and enacts a process of erasure. Blackout. And yet, I contend that that very viscerality is what compels me to write here, as instructed by the song, against this forgetting. After all, I have no personal stake in the vitality of Hokkien culture. I do not understand the language, share in the underlying belief system, or recognise the characters beyond their typologies. But, lacking though I am in the cultural competencies of the aficionado, or even of the fan, I nevertheless respond to an affective quality in *Sin Sai Hong* that is irreducible to signifying systems or personal identifications. By filming in mid-shot performers who are dressed and made up to be seen from a distance, by placing them in proximity where normally they are spread out, and by maintaining an almost constant pace and focus as the troupe sings its way through their repertoire, Tan has created a film that does not *look* very much like an ordinary *wayang* performance, but captures the visual, aural and emotional intensity of the form in a way that is specific to his own medium. The costumes texture the screen, and fill it with blocks of bright, contrasting colours; the broad, bold whites, pinks and blacks of the mask-like make-up accentuate the distinctive features of each face, resulting in a sort of abstracted intimacy; the singing is full throated, the language direct: "All the shared memories are gone/ We cannot be together in this life"; and when they cry, I cry.

uSpace

In 2008, a new massage chair succeeded the iDesire as OSIM's flagship product. After mounting the uSpace, "the world's first Well-Being Chair,"[37] a domed white hood extends over the user in order to provide them with a range of programmes combining massage, mood lighting and synchronised music. Retailing at approximately US$6500, and prominently displayed in its own nature-themed vitrine in malls across Singapore (see *Figure 1*), the uSpace reflects changing times. Where the appropriative iDesire was all sleek black leather and wrist cuffs, the concessionary uSpace is a "personal sanctuary of holistic well-being"; more Huxley's "feelies" than Kafka's "In the Penal Colony." The publicity copy's promise that it will "restore and maintain the delicate balance and harmony between your mind, body and soul" seeks to soothe contemporary eco-anxieties, while expanding the iDesire's "full body" remit to encompass the whole existential package.

Figure 1: uSpace, on display in VivoCity Mall, Singapore. Photo: Paul Rae.

Certainly, the self is to be well and truly cared for; but what kind of subject is thereby presupposed? Slide in. The massage will "renew your body naturally." As you select a colour palette from the lighting menu in order to regulate your body's "inner rhythms," specially modulated "sound pulses" create "entrainment": "a tendency of brainwaves to adjust to our sound environment so that they vibrate in harmony." Cocooned now in your own private theatre of the self, all that remains is to forget. Relax. Sleep. Recharge. Harmonise…*all the shared memories are gone…*

Except one. Where have you heard that line before? It triggers the sensed memory of another embodied state, the one you felt when you watched that *wayang* film. The one whose colours and sounds have somehow bedded down in your experience of the world, and inflect, however slightly, your relation to it. You carry that disposition with you now, and all the amnesiac "entrainment" and "therapeutic use of light and colour" in Singapore won't dislodge the configuration of body, memory and action that the earlier experience has installed so singularly and yet so durably. If you thought about it harder, you could trace some of the reasons for this – the unbroken process of transmission that lends a density, an easeful solidity, to the performances; the highly selective absorption of a century and more of trends and technological developments into the songs; the echoing of long-told narratives of loss and rebirth through the life course of the aging performers…But for now, you are content to let the uSpace "cradle your body into a supine position." The associations of "supine" with "failing to act or protest as a result of moral weakness or indolence" (OED) may trouble you; but as long as *Sin Sai Hong* and other such memories remain wedged into that same body, resolutely aslant of the version the uSpace is programmed to act upon, the resources exist to act otherwise. You will remember how to perform. No sweat.

Works Cited

Alfian Sa'at (2006) *Homesick*. Unpublished playscript. Singapore.
Amnesty International (2004) *Singapore: The Death Penalty – A Hidden Toll of Executions*, at:
    http://www.amnesty.org/en/library/info/ASA36/001/2004.
Brookstone (2009) *OSIM iGallop Core and Abs Exerciser* product brochure, at: http://www.brookstone.com.
Capgemini and Merrill Lynch (2008) *Asia-Pacific Wealth Report 2008*, at:
http://www.capgemini.com/resources/thought_leadership/asia_pacific_we alth_report_2008__english/.
Chia, A. (2008) "Feel the Power," *The Straits Times*, 4 December, pp.2-6.
Devan, J. (1999) "Forgetting to Remember," in Kwok, K. W. *et al.* (Eds.) *Our Place in Time: Exploring Heritage and Memory in Singapore*, Singapore: Singapore Heritage Society, pp.21-33.
Foucault, M. (1984) "Docile Bodies," in Rabinow, P. (Ed.) *The Foucault Reader*, London: Penguin Books, pp.179-187.
—. (1997) *Ethics: Subjectivity and Truth*, ed. Paul Rabinow and trans. Robert Hurley and others, New York: The New Press.
George, C. (2000) *Singapore: The Air-Conditioned Nation - Essays on the Politics of Comfort and Control 1999-2000*, Singapore: Landmark Books.
Gibson, W. (1993) "Disneyland with the Death Penalty," *Wired*, September/October, pp.51-5 & 114-16.
Hong, L. and Huang, J. (2008) *The Scripting of a National History: Singapore and Its Pasts*, Singapore: Singapore University Press.
Koolhaas, R. (1995) "Singapore Songlines: Portrait of a Potemkin Metropolis…or Thirty Years of Tabula Rasa," in Koolhaas, R. and B. Mau (Eds.) *S,M,L,XL*. Monacelli Press and Taschen: New York and Cologne, pp.1008-1089.

Kuo, P. K. (2003) *Two Plays by Kuo Pao Kun: Descendants of the Eunuch Admiral* and *The Spirits Play*. Singapore: SNP Editions.

Lee, H. L. (1997) *Speech by BG (NS) Lee Hsien Loong, Deputy Prime Minister, at the Launch of National Education at Television Corporation of Singapore (TCS) TV Theatre on Friday, 17 May 1997 at 9.30am*, at: http://stars.nhb.gov.sg/stars/public/ (accessed February 2005).

Lee, K. Y. (1998) *The Singapore Story: Memoirs of Lee Kuan Yew*, Singapore: Singapore Press Holdings.

McKenzie, J. (2001) *Perform or Else: From Discipline to Performance*, London and New York: Routledge.

MHA (2004) "The Singapore Government's Response to Amnesty International's Report 'Singapore – The Death Penalty: A Hidden Toll of Executions,'" Singapore: Ministry of Home Affairs, at: http://www.mha.gov.sg/basic_content.aspx?pageid=74 (accessed November 2008).

MICA (2008) *Renaissance City Plan III*, Singapore: Ministry of Information, Communications and the Arts.

OSIM (2004) "iDesire Brochure," at: http://www.osim.com/SG/product/idesire.aspx?category_id=5CC7C642-A1F3-4CC6-8BBF-290DEE474BA3.

OSIM (2008) "Massage Chairs," on the OSIM homepage, at: http://www.osim.com/SG/category/massage_chairs.aspx (accessed November 2008).

OSIM (2009) "Innovative Fitness," on the OSIM homepage, at: http://www.osim.com/SG/category/innovative_fitness.aspx (accessed January 2009).

Shusterman, R. (2008) *Body Consciousness: A Philosophy of Mindfulness and Somaesthetics*, Cambridge: Cambridge University Press.

Statistics Singapore (2008) "Per Capita GDP at Current Market Prices" (November 2008), at: http://www.singstat.gov.sg/stats/themes/economy/hist/gdp.html.

Taylor, D. (2003) *The Archive and the Repertoire: Cultural Memory and Performance in the Americas*, Durham: Duke University Press.

Trocki, C. A. (2006) *Singapore: Wealth, Power and the Culture of Control*, London and New York: Routledge.

Walmsley, R. (2007) *World Prison Population* (Seventh Edition), London: King's College International Centre for Prison Studies, at: http://www.kcl.ac.uk/depsta/law/research/icps/.

Wong, K. (2005) "More buying a chair way to heaven," *Straits Times*, 28 March, pp.1-2.

Yeo, G. (2006) "Singapore History Museum," *Beyond SG*, 24 December, at:
    http://beyondsg.typepad.com/beyondsg/2006/12/singapore_histo.html
    (accessed November 2008).

Notes

[1] OSIM (2004) iDesire Brochure, at:
http://www.osim.com/SG/product/idesire.aspx?category_id=5CC7C642-A1F3-4CC6-8BBF-290DEE474BA3.

[2] The best-known examples, both with broadly self-explanatory titles, are science fiction author William Gibson (1993) "Disneyland with the Death Penalty", *Wired*, September/October,   pp.51-5 & 114-16; and architect Rem Koolhaas (1995) "Singapore Songlines: Portrait of a Potemkin Metropolis…or Thirty Years of Tabula Rasa," in Koolhaas and Mau (Eds.) *S,M,L,XL*. Monacelli Press and Taschen: New York and Cologne, pp.1008-1089.

[3] Lee served as Prime Minister from 1959-1990. He has since remained in the Cabinet, first as Senior Minister (1990-2004), and subsequently as Minister Mentor. From 1966-1981, the PAP enjoyed total parliamentary dominance. Since then, the number of elected opposition seats has fluctuated between one and four. At the time of writing, the opposition holds two elected seats out of 84.

[4] Statistics Singapore (2008) "Per Capita GDP at Current Market Prices" (November 2008), at:
http://www.singstat.gov.sg/stats/themes/economy/hist/gdp.html.

[5] Michel Foucault (1984) "Docile Bodies," in Paul Rabinow (Ed.) *The Foucault Reader*, London: Penguin Books, p.181.

[6] See Walmsley, R. (2007) *World Prison Population* (Seventh Edition), London: King's College International Centre for Prison Studies, at:
http://www.kcl.ac.uk/depsta/law/research/icps/, and Amnesty International (2004) *Singapore: The Death Penalty – A Hidden Toll of Executions*, at
http://www.amnesty.org/en/library/info/ASA36/001/2004. Singapore's Ministry of Home Affairs responded robustly to Amnesty's report in MHA (2004) "The Singapore Government's Response to Amnesty International's Report 'Singapore – The Death Penalty: A Hidden Toll of Executions,'" Singapore: Ministry of Home Affairs, at: http://www.mha.gov.sg/basic_content.aspx?pageid=74

[7] Singapore's population of High Net Worth Individuals (people with over US$1 million in financial assets) is amongst the fastest growing in the world, and stood at approximately 77,000 in 2007. See Capgemini and Merrill Lynch (2008) *Asia-Pacific Wealth Report 2008*, p.3, at:
http://www.capgemini.com/resources/thought_leadership/asia_pacific_wealth_report_2008__english/.

[8] Cherien George (2000) *Singapore: The Air-Conditioned Nation - Essays on the Politics of Comfort and Control 1990-2000*, Singapore: Landmark Books, p.15.

[9] *Ibid.*, p.190.

[10] *Ibid.*, p.194.

[11] *Ibid.*, p.18.

[12] An indicative list would include: Kuo Pao Kun (1985) *The Coffin is Too Big for the Hole*; Stella Kon (1986) *Emily of Emerald Hill*; Haresh Sharma (1992) *Still Building*; Leow Puay Tin (1996) *The Yang Family*; The Necessary Stage (2002) *Close – In My Face*; Ho Tzu Nyen (2008) *House of Memory*; and Jean Tay (2008) *Boom*.

[13] In *Perform or Else*, McKenzie identifies a paradox in the fact that, although numerous key theories of performativity – including those of Marcuse, Lyotard and Butler – have focused on how it serves to standardize and enforce certain behavioural norms, many performance practitioners and performance studies scholars articulate the significance of cultural performance in terms of progressive or radical political efficacy. For McKenzie, the prevalence of such interpretations is so common, that he coins the term "liminal norm" to describe how the expectation of political "resistance" has itself become standardized. McKenzie (2001) *Perform or Else: From Discipline to Performance*, London and New York: Routledge.

[14] Kuo Pao Kun (2003) *Two Plays by Kuo Pao Kun: Descendants of the Eunuch Admiral* and *The Spirits Play*. Singapore: SNP Editions, p.38.

[15] *Ibid.*, p.64.

[16] Michel Foucault (1997) *Ethics: Subjectivity and Truth*, New York: The New Press, p.282.

[17] *Ibid.*, p.291.

[18] *Ibid.*, pp.100-1.

[19] *Ibid.*, p.300.

[20] The iSymphonic is another massage chair in the same range as the iDesire: "OSIM iSymphonic is the first of its kind to provide massage and music therapy at the same time. It is relaxation therapy both physical and mental, bringing harmony and peace to your body and soul." OSIM (2008) "Massage Chairs," at: http://www.osim.com/SG/category/massage_chairs.aspx (accessed November 2008).

[21] Kelvin Wong (2005) "More buying a chair way to heaven," *Straits Times*, 28 March, pp.1-2.

[22] For a brief discussion of the ways in which "East-Asian philosophy has insisted on the bodily dimension of self-knowledge and self-cultivation" in ways analogous to Foucault's "care of the self," see Richard Shusterman (2008) *Body Consciousness: A Philosophy of Mindfulness and Somaesthetics*, Cambridge: Cambridge University Press, pp.17-18.

[23] Diana Taylor (2003) *The Archive and the Repertoire: Cultural Memory and Performance in the Americas*, Duke University Press.

[24] Foucault (1997), p.238.

[25] Hong Lysa and Huang Jianli (2008) *The Scripting of a National History: Singapore and Its Pasts*, Singapore: Singapore University Press, p.50.

[26] Carl A. Trocki, (2006) *Singapore: Wealth, Power and the Culture of Control*, London and New York: Routledge, p.3.

[27] *Ibid.*, p.182.

[28] Janadas Devan (1999) "Forgetting to Remember," in Kwok Kian Woon *et al.* (Eds.) *Our Place in Time: Exploring Heritage and Memory in Singapore.* Singapore: Singapore Heritage Society, p.22.

[29] *Ibid.*, p.23.

[30] *Ibid.*, p.33.

[31] Foucault (1997), p.225.

[32] Lee Hsien Loong (1997) *Speech by BG (NS) Lee Hsien Loong, Deputy Prime Minister, at the Launch of National Education at Television Corporation of Singapore (TCS) TV Theatre on Friday, 17 May 1997*, p.11, at: http://stars.nhb.gov.sg/stars/public/ (accessed February 2005).

[33] *The Singapore Story* is also the title of the first volume of Lee Kuan Yew's memoirs, published during the same period (1998).

[34] In the interests of transparency, I should state that, in my capacity as a theatre-maker, I, too, was involved in producing treatments and scripts for some of the rooms in the History Gallery.

[35] George Yeo (2006) "Singapore History Museum," *Beyond SG*, 24 December, at: http://beyondsg.typepad.com/beyondsg/2006/12/singapore_histo.html.

[36] Adeline Chia (2008) "Feel the Power," *The Straits Times*, 4 December, p.2.

[37] OSIM (2008).

PIANOLA KARAOKE AND OTHER ATTRACTIONS: RESISTING THE HOMOGENISATION OF CULTURAL MEMORY ATTACHED TO MATERIAL SITES

MINTY DONALD

Concealed behind a crumbling façade, above a functioning, contemporary amusement arcade, in a building that sits on a busy shopping street on the cusp of Glasgow's regenerating Merchant City district and its deprived East End, lie the decaying remains of one of the UK's oldest surviving music halls. Now known as the Britannia Panopticon, combining two titles from its previous manifestations as an entertainment venue, the building has been subject to changing functions and fortunes since its earliest-recorded existence, as a warehouse, in the mid-1850s. Following its demise as a popular venue for live performance, its roles included indoor carnival and cinema, before the premises were occupied by a succession of retail businesses, leaving the vestiges of the music hall abandoned, hidden above a false roof in the building's upper floors.

Since 1997, a group of volunteers, operating as the Board and Friends of the Britannia Panopticon Music Hall Trust and sanctioned by the building's current owners (the Mitchell family, who run the amusement arcade on street level), have worked to uncover the fabric of the old music hall, raise funds for its preservation and, above all, publicise its existence.[1] In the limited space that remains publicly accessible, they continue to mount a programme of performances, tours and exhibitions, which regularly features their own amateur music hall re-enactments alongside a more erratic and eccentric schedule of poetry readings, experimental music and film, and screenings of Laurel and Hardy movies[2] – all situated within a semi-permanent display of memorabilia, artefacts found in the building and assorted bric-a-brac. Meanwhile, below the decrepit auditorium, the amusement arcade attracts a stream of regular punters.

Read in this context, the site is one of multiple, competing narratives, bound up in the social and cultural fabric of Glasgow. It is a site in which the varied interests and investments of those who use and remember it are interwoven, and whose histories and potential futures are open to debate. Given its location in an area designated for gentrification as the city's "cultural quarter," it is, however, highly susceptible to drives to formalise, contain or close down its varied functions and meanings, stemming the proliferation of anecdotes and imagined histories it propagates.[3]

Focussing, as a case study, on a suite of site-responsive artworks – events or interventions – which I developed in the Britannia Panopticon building in October 2007, this essay considers the efficacy of artworks which employ performance[4] and other embodied[5] practices to critique impetuses to circumscribe, unify and regulate the uses and readings of such rich, productively unresolved "heritage" sites. It reflects, in particular, on their potential to resist the restriction and homogenisation of the individual and shared memories generated by such sites. The Britannia Panopticon artworks were collectively titled *Glimmers in Limbo*, in a (mis)appropriation of Gaston Bachelard's *The Poetics of Reverie* which discusses the way we experience memories, especially those linked to space and place, as unresolved memory-images that interleave past and present.[6]

Performance, Embodiment, Memory and Heritage

This essay proposes that engaging with ideas of heritage through performance and embodied practices dissolves perceived boundaries between material and intangible culture. It suggests that by focusing on heritage as a "multi-layered performance" and on-going "cultural process,"[7] we can challenge tendencies among those charged with its stewardship (often characterised as "the heritage industry") to promote heritage as static, as separate from and unavailable to contemporary culture. By doing so, it proposes, we can offer a critique of situations where heritage serves to perpetuate the ideologies it can be seen as representing. I will argue that performance and embodied practices can destabilise the fixed meanings and functions that consolidate around material sites and objects, opening them up to operate as stimuli for creative acts of individual and collective memory – imaginative rememberings – which allow us to continually re-visit, re-think and re-imagine relationships between past and present, evading the potential of heritage to be used to maintain and endorse dominant beliefs and power structures.

Figure 1: Façade Fruitmachine. Photo: Alan Dimmick.

Pianola Karaoke, Façade Fruitmachine, Shoebox Archive and *Real Estate?* – the four events or interventions I staged at the Britannia Panopticon – took place simultaneously and varied significantly in form and the media they employed. My intention was to mirror and emphasise the multivalency of the site by delivering what one commentator described as "a hotch potch of entertainments to diverse audiences."[8] In this essay, I will focus primarily on *Pianola Karaoke,* one of the two artworks which took place inside the building, referring more briefly to the other interior work, *Shoebox Archive,* and to one of the external works, *Façade Fruitmachine* (See *Figure 1.*)

Pianola Karaoke

For *Pianola Karaoke,* the work in which performance figured most overtly and in the most commonplace understanding of the term, I invited eleven people to choose the song that they would like to sing in the old music hall, requesting that their choices were inspired by their personal responses to the building but making no further stipulations, other than to suggest that I was not trying to re-create "old time music hall." Specially-commissioned accompaniments to the songs were then converted into paper rolls for a 1920s pianola – a mechanised piano which, using pedal-operated bellows, draws air through a perforated paper scroll, causing the keys to function. The domestic-style pianola is one of many items that have been accumulated by the Friends of the Britannia Panopticon Trust during their stewardship of the music hall. Though historically inauthentic and slightly incongruous, it is one of the building's most popular attractions, visitors regularly commenting on its ability to evoke for them what they describe as the sound and atmosphere of the music hall. The songs were performed live, by the song-choosers (or, in the case of choir mistress Janis F. Murray, by The Parsonage Choir), for one night only, on the evening of 18 October 2007.

I made a considered decision not to record the live event. It was documented only through still photographs (and in a bootleg video of Hanna Tuulikki's performance of *Wuthering Heights*, captured by an audience member on their mobile phone). The documentation was intended to function primarily as "a spur to memory, an encouragement of memory to become present."[9] My wish was for the event to have an after-life, following the live performance, only through the incomplete, "unreliable" and contradictory memories of those who had attended, and in the imaginations of those who had heard partial accounts, seen fragmentary images, or listened on-line to the versions of the songs recorded by the singers on a separate occasion.[10] I did not want the event to persist, through its documentation, as another site-related artefact preserved as though for posterity and subject to (ab)use in promoting a particular perspective. I did not want it to "participate in the circulation of representations *of* representations."[11] Instead, I wanted to orchestrate an occasion that would be in itself memorable, that would generate multiple new stories and reminiscences. In doing so, my intention was to allow the site, through the proliferating memories and accounts of the event witnessed there, to continue to participate in the continual cultural process of heritage, extending the significance of the site beyond its physical and temporal boundaries and beyond its value as a relic of former times, thus evading its potential to function in perpetuating specific values and ideologies.

My main intention in *Pianola Karaoke* was to discover if, and how, people might relate to material culture through music and song. In line with the overall *Glimmers in Limbo* project, it was led by research objectives. However, as the artist responsible for its inception and orchestration, I had a (perhaps unavoidable) investment in the "success" of the live event. My hope was that both audience members and singers *would* feel a personal connection with the site, that the live performances would encourage them to participate in imaginative rememberings or re-imaginings, that the event would re-invigorate and re-articulate the productive disjunctures between interpretations, images and experiences of past and present which the site has the potential to engender. I also, undoubtedly, wanted everyone to have a good time. As such, my commentary on the event, while countered, corroborated and enriched by the observations of other participants and audience members, is clearly subjective and deeply invested.

My reflection also comes from the perspective of a key participant, or performer, as I took on the role of pianola "player" throughout the performances, inserting a perforated paper roll of music for each new song and pumping, with demonstrable physical effort, the creaking pedals that operate the pianola's bellows. My experience of *Pianola Karaoke* was, therefore, a strongly embodied one, located at the heart of the event.

The invitation to select a song in response to the site inspired a wide range of choices, from Kate Bush's *Wuthering Heights* to traditional ballad *Unfortunate Rake*. Many of the songs selected alluded to the singers' own memories, relating to different times and places in their lives, triggered as a response to the context of the crumbling music hall, with its idiosyncratic assortment of artefacts and occupants. The singers' reasons for making their choices suggested that the site had a rich capacity to generate diverse associations and creative reminiscences.

For instance, Ross Sinclair, who picked the song *Wan Light,* written by Glasgow post-punk band, Orange Juice, said of his choice:

> The words seemed to suggest this idea of the music hall being this other place. The first line [of the song] is, 'there is a place which no-one has seen where it's still possible to dream.'

He spoke of a cluster of associations around his selection: memories of the abandoned theatres and cinemas he had explored when a student, thoughts about his own practice as an artist, memories of listening to the song at various times over a twenty-year period and of a recent television documentary following the lead singer of Orange Juice, Edwyn Collins, as he recovered from a brain hemorrhage.

Figure 2: Ella Finer sings *After Hours* by The Velvet Underground. Photo: Stephen Robinson.

Ella Finer, who chose The Velvet Underground song, *After Hours*, did so because she said, "it *celebrates* the enclosed and dark nature of the space rather than highlighting it as a ghostly or sad place" and that this reminded her of times when she had wanted "a place where you can shut out the light and have your own private time to contemplate whatever in your life, or love and everything." (See *Figure 2*.)

These reflections, along with other singers' comments on the ideas connected with their choices, suggested that the invitation to respond to the site through song induced a kind of poetic, associative contemplation, or daydreaming, in relation to the physical space, akin to that characterised by Gaston Bachelard as "reverie." This quality of interaction with material sites that "imagines while remembering" problematises "the historian's memory"[12] – the official, factual record – by allowing the site to function as a stimulus for personal, heterogeneous reminiscences and associations. Thus, the Britannia Panopticon building could conjure, for one singer, places of private sanctuary and comforting seclusion while, for others, it suggested occasions of communal celebration or images of neglect, decay and disenfranchisement. Based on the singer's experiences, it appears that engagement with material sites through a state of "poetic reverie" encourages interactions which are expansive and inclusive, allowing individuals to make their own imaginative connections that range across time and space, and which resist drives to circumscribe or determine the uses and readings of tangible heritage.

For the live performance, the stalls level of the auditorium – the only part of the music hall accessible, on health and safety grounds, to the public – was left open, with no seating and no raised stage or clearly demarcated area for the singers. It remained in virtual darkness, with the exception of a spotlight focussed on the pianola, while the textures of the atmospherically peeling paintwork, charred wooden beams and aged, encrusted theatrical fittings of the unreachable upper levels were picked out and made palpable through sensitive lighting. The pianola occupied a central position, facing what had been the music hall's stage. During the performances, audience members gathered around the pianola in an irregular arc, those at the front sitting on the floor, while the performers simply emerged from the crowd to take up their chosen positions by the pianola.

In doing so, we (audience, singers and pianola player) "performed" and were "performed by" the space, our spatial configurations echoing the architecture of the music hall (mimicking the stage and seating arrangement which once occupied the auditorium) while evoking, for myself and other audience members, memories of the informal settings of domestic living rooms, where friends and family gathered to perform and listen to one another's "party pieces." Through our embodied performance of the space (and its "performance" of us) we were induced to access collective, cultural memories – of the layout of the many theatres and performance venues that we knew or had visited, and of our actual, inherited or imagined, experiences of family sing-songs and similar events.

In *Pianola Karaoke,* the interweaving of individual and collective memories – the singers' personal and idiosyncratic memories evoked by the material site, and the shared cultural memories prompted by audience members' spatial "performance" – suggested that embodied practices may offer us the potential to move fluidly between personal and communal responses to material culture, allowing neither to dominate, thus providing a strategy for resisting homogenisation.

The fact that the performances were musical ones – experienced more through the aural, than visual, sense – was highly significant in terms of the quality of the embodied experiences which the event produced for both performers and audience.

> In human sensing, whereas sight distances, hearing envelops… Sound, by its enveloping character, brings us closer to everything alive. Hearing musical sounds … makes us especially aware of proximity and thus connectedness.[13]

As Leppert here proposes, the peculiarly physical, visceral and emotional impact of sound, and musical performance in particular, is resistant to the kind of measured analyses, and subsequent closing down of interpretation, that the visual image allows. Operating through irrational and bodily affects, live music refuses such regulation and encourages engagement and a kind of "knowing" that is individual and experiential – that is, it is beyond-representational.

The embodied, affective practice of listening to and performing live music is often attributed with inducing involuntary memories – the type of unregulated, unbidden reminiscences triggered by sensory encounters that is identified famously in the work of Proust, and taken up by Benjamin. This effect, commented on by several audience members, was described by Karen Lury in her reflections on the event:

> I am allowed access to, or possessed by, a host of different temporalities – the regular pulse of the pianola which Donald pedals industriously; the performer's voice pulling and tugging at the orchestration of the music; the recollection (a sonic echo) of earlier versions of the song, my knowledge of why the performer chose the song, my own feeling about the song – a coalescence of their memories and mine.[14]

In her comments, Lury points to the event's ability to evoke multiple, over-lapping timeframes, to invite audience members to entertain the co-existence of numerous individual and collective memories, but to judge none of them as having authority over others. This occurrence – the capacity of the event to encourage participants to access multiple unresolved memories – may, she suggests, be attributable to the embodied nature of our engagement with, particularly live, music.

The complex relationship between live, embodied performance and its recording as static, inanimate artefact is embedded in the concept of *Pianola Karaoke*. The pianola is a device that allows music to be stored in a permanent material form – as a perforated paper roll – and then endlessly and unchangingly reproduced. The phenomenon of karaoke is based on its participants' wish to perform their own cover versions of favourite songs, to produce countless sonic echoes and an accumulation of layered memories. As such, *Pianola Karaoke* exemplified approaches towards the recording and re-enactment of live performances which have been characterised by Diana Taylor as "archive" and "repertoire." Taylor suggests that although there is a tension between the two – the archive frequently being taken to represent fixed, authoritative and enduring versions of the past, while the repertoire is viewed as personifying transient, mutable knowledge passed on through embodied practice – they, in actuality, "exist in a constant state of interaction."[15] *Pianola Karaoke* played with this tension.

While acknowledging material culture's susceptibility to being perceived as permanent, official archive, it allowed it to function as a stimulus for an on-going cultural process that folded together reminiscence, imagination and lived experience, where both individual and shared pasts were continually performed and renegotiated in the context of the present, and where the here-and-now was played out amid physical reminders of the there-and-then.

Sound, as Susan Smith argues, "is highly participatory, for performers and for those in earshot."[16] In *Pianola Karaoke*, the requirement for participation by the listener was increased by the informal spatial arrangement of the venue – the audience were obliged to play an active role in positioning themselves in order to both hear and see – their need to concentrate, to listen intently, made even more acute by the singers performing without amplification. Rather than finding this disconcerting or frustrating, both audience and performers responded positively. Audience comments suggested that it made them feel that they were involved in a shared enterprise, that they were "part of something… special." Stevie Jackson, an experienced professional musician, and one of the singer-song-choosers, remarked:

> I think I learned something about projection and presenting material in a certain way… To present music without amplification… well people

reached out to it and were entertained and fulfilled by it, you could totally feel it.

Though unquantifiable and wholly partial, my own overwhelming impression, while I sat pedalling the pianola with the audience behind me and the singers to one side or in front of me, was of a collective will for the performances to succeed, for the evening to "work."

One factor on which several visitors commented, and that may have contributed to this sense of communality, was a shared awareness of an element of risk and uncertainty running through the event – a feeling that we were all in it together, but that we did not know exactly what "it" might turn out to be. In their exposure to both the relentless, unyielding mechanics of the pianola and to the judgement of an audience – demonstrated in the initial nervousness some singers displayed – the singers' risk-taking was evident. But the audience too had opened themselves up to chance, attending an occasion with no prior knowledge of what to expect and whose loose structure gave them little guidance on how to behave. They had taken a risk in placing themselves in a physical setting which was disconcerting and unsettling in its collisions of style: contemporary gaming room and nineteenth century music hall, authentic Victorian jewellery and "fancy dress" costume, 'sixties pasteboard partitions and ornate plaster cornices.

Risk-taking extended also into my shaping and organisation of the event: not simply in the deliberately open-ended approach and light touch I had taken in directing the evening's proceedings, but also in the real physical hazards presented by the dilapidated fabric of the building and in the fact that, through the popularity of the event and the generosity and enthusiasm of the volunteer door-keepers, audience capacity limits agreed with the licensing authorities had been exceeded. While hardly extreme or endangering, the element of risk-taking inherent in the event, and the relaxed, irreverent attitude towards the music hall as a heritage site that it implied, ran counter to more typical approaches towards material culture where heritage sites are strictly regulated, with visitors' experiences rendered risk-free and the potential for unplanned occurrences strictly limited.

Through exposure to risk, to the physicality of the site and the performances, the event encouraged encounters where both audience and performers' sensory experiences were foregrounded. Memories of the event were, as later discussions with participants revealed, closely associated with specific corporeal sensations – the smell, temperature and quality of sound were all notably commented upon. The event was, in this sense, "remembered" through the body, invoking a form of memory which, in its lived, experiential nature, was unique to each individual. As such, it was resistant to the archiving strategies (recording through written or other means) which Taylor and others argue can render cultural memory susceptible to regulation.[17]

Whether attributable to a feeling of shared risk or not, the impression of a supportive rapport between singers and audience members that characterised *Pianola Karaoke* was undoubtedly pleasurable. And the perception of the event as a positive, communal experience, described by those attending as "life-affirming" and "up-lifting," was certainly gratifying to my desire for the occasion to be "a success." Once the moment of the live event had passed, however, I was left with a faint unease that this perceived sense of unity, of shared celebration and sentiment – among what was, predominantly, a white, middle-class and "arty" contingent – was an illusion, perhaps functioning to erase difference, ignoring exclusions and opposing voices, rather than to promote the productively dissonant multivalency of the site.

It could equally be argued, though, that what occurred in the fleeting semblance of unity was a *performance* of communality – a utopian moment, as characterised by Jill Dolan:

> Live performance provides a place where people come together, embodied and passionate, to share experiences… that can describe or capture fleeting intimations of a better world.[18]

It was also a moment which (as typifies the unsustainability, or unattainability, of utopias) began to dissipate as soon as the last note was struck and sung, exposing the messy and complex realities of our relationships with the site and with one another.

Departing audience members may have been heard to comment on the "fabulous" and "moving" night that they had just experienced, but they did so as they left the building past the punters in the amusement arcade, past drug-users' discarded syringes at the side-lane exit and past the East End of Glasgow's own crowded karaoke bars. And while the overheard remark of one visitor, "I think we'll all remember this as a great Glasgow night," hinted that the event had allowed the crowd to form, in the moment of the live performance, a sense of collective identity, its transience (reinforced by the lack of documentation of the performances) ensured that their memories would not be unified or homogenised. This feeling, Simon Frith has suggested, is characteristic of live music's ability to allow us to experience identity not as fixed, but as continually in process – as "a becoming not a being."[19] Sensing identity through performance in this way – as always in flux, forming and re-forming, moving between the personal and the communal – offers an alternative to circumscribed and static models which can serve to maintain existing power structures and perpetuate dominant ideologies.

Pianola Karaoke appeared to create a situation where audience and performers were able to slip in and out of, or simultaneously entertain, a cluster of experiences: a sharp awareness of existing as a distinct individual, while feeling a sense of collective identity or communality (as one audience member described it: "the experience was very personal. It feels like you are alone in the space yet the music creates a very communal atmosphere"). A strong sense of being "present" in the unique here-and-now of the physical environment, while travelling, through memory and imagination, to the multiple temporalities evoked by the songs, the space and the occasion. A brief utopian moment, punctured by the contingencies of the specific location.

Following the night of the live performance, recorded versions of the singers' renditions – accompanied by other traces of the event, such as projections of fragmented scrolling lyrics and paper pianola rolls printed with singers' comments – acted as a soundtrack, a ghosting of *Pianola Karaoke*, for the second artwork I wish to consider.

Shoebox Archive

For *Shoebox Archive*, I installed six hundred shoeboxes in the auditorium of the music hall (See *Figure 3*). The boxes referred to one of the building's previous roles as a shoe warehouse, and were inspired by the recollection – quite possibly a false memory – of my first visit to the space and the piles of boxes I "remember" filling the stalls area. In one hundred and fifty of the shoeboxes I placed one of the many artefacts that have been excavated from under the floorboards of the Britannia Panopticon: everyday detritus from the 1860s to the 1930s – ticket stubs and spent matches, a whelk shell and a baby's dummy – which had lain discarded for decades.

Figure 3: Shoebox Archive. Photo: Stephen Robinson.

Although the mass of white, stacked boxes created an imposing image in the space, they were not intended to be interpreted as solely representational. Visitors were encouraged to interact with them[20] – to rummage through the boxes, discovering what they contained and connecting with the objects in an intimate, personal, tactile and imaginative way – as a counterpoint to the labelled artefacts on display under glass in the Britannia Panopticon's more permanent exhibition. As one visitor observed, highlighting the sense of present-ness and ownership they felt through the experience, "it's like finding the lost items yourself." In the remaining four hundred and fifty empty boxes, labels fixed in their bases invited visitors to "please leave something in the box." Over the duration of the intervention more than three hundred items were left in the empty boxes by visitor-participants.

The accumulated items – historical and contemporary artefacts – formed an unruly jumble, a collection that resisted categorisation and ordering. While it was possible to speculate that some items had been consciously selected to set up correspondences – for example, a set of headphones for an MP3 player was left beside a programme for the music hall – the choice was limited to what the donor happened to have about their person and so was arbitrary, not pre-meditated: a ticket from the national museum in Istanbul, a tiny architectural scale model of a human figure or, more often, the mundane junk that we carry around in our pockets – loose change, till receipts, paper clips.

This shambolic assortment of everyday objects – a collection, but one which encouraged interaction and random additions, and which was presented in the homely, domestic containers of the shoeboxes – functioned as critique of the controlled meanings promoted through the heritage industry's common curatorial practices, and a stimulus for the kind of involuntary associations and fragmentary, elusive memories that Joe Moran describes (referring to rubbish) as a "memory surplus which is neither purposive nor easily recuperable by dominant ideologies."[21] As one visitor remarked: "it reminded me that every person who visits leaves something behind, takes away or experiences something different." Another wrote of the piece:

> Given that the layered history of the building is still present in the wooden beams and projection room, the installation, for me, disturbed the way in which we try to 'read,' understand and pigeon-hole chronologically… It raised questions about such sites and whether we do not actually do them a disservice through period restoration, through display boxes, through meta-narratives that tell some stories and silence others. For me, it highlighted the value of disruption, of discovery, of lessening narration in favour of imagination, of constructing our own stories about the place, of fiction but a very living fiction. I liked the not-knowingness of it all, but that not-knowingness coming from something that was very real. I don't think that the power of the fragment should be underestimated.

When the installation was dismantled, the historical objects were returned to the care of the Britannia Panopticon Trust, while the donated items were secreted around the building, creating a new layer of rubbish: rubbish with the potential to prompt the type of everyday, dispersed memories that, Joe Moran argues, escape "formal mechanisms of remembrance"[22] or evade the official memorialising of the heritage industry.

Inside Out

While *Pianola Karaoke* and *Shoebox Archive* engaged with the Britannia Panopticon's interior, the remaining two interventions, *Façade Fruitmachine* and *Real Estate?*, interacted with the exterior of the building. They sought to consider its identity within the context of its ever-changing urban environment, and to engage with audiences additional to those who chose to enter the building. In *Real Estate?* photographs of details of the building's interior were mounted in the shop front window of the amusement arcade, mimicking the displays in estate agents' windows. They were installed to form a permeable layer through which the two existing window displays – the Britannia Panopticon Trust's music hall memorabilia and Mitchell's Amusement Arcade's neon advertising signage – could be glimpsed.

In *Façade Fruitmachine* an animated sequence was projected in the windows of the inaccessible second floor of the building, making reference to signage on the façade from the past one hundred and fifty years of its existence (using the range of fonts recorded in photographs of its exterior over this period) and to its current function as an amusement arcade. In the animation, letters spun like the drums of a coin-operated fruit machine, sometimes, momentarily, resolving into words that pointed to the building's former roles as music hall, tailors' warehouse, waxworks and cinema.

As I had anticipated, the constituent audience for this intervention had little overlap with the audience who experienced the interior works. Many of the people who came to the opening event, or who visited the exhibition during the following week, did not notice the exterior projection, as it was visible only after dusk and from the opposite side of the street. Those who did witness both the internal artworks and *Façade Fruitmachine* spoke of how the animated projection had shifted and extended their perceptions of the building. They remarked on the transition from the "private" secluded interior of the music hall into the "public" arena of the lively city street, and how this movement altered both their physical and conceptual relationships with the site. As one observer put it:

> The light work on the exterior of the building... made me look up... It forced me to see the building as a built object that had a role in the cityscape beyond – or maybe before – its commercial, entertainment and 'heritage' one.

The effectiveness of the work in dislocating the building from its heritage, as well as other, identities – in encouraging spectators to form their own imaginative relationships with it in the context of the contemporary urban environment – was borne out by additional responses.

The most concentrated audience for the intervention – and one on whose conversations it was easy for me to eavesdrop inconspicuously – consisted of waiting passengers at the bus stop facing the Britannia Panopticon building. Remarks overheard from this loose community of incidental spectators revealed that a relatively small number had linked the animation's rotating letters with the building's function as an amusement arcade, while an even smaller group – who clearly had prior knowledge of the site – recognised some of the building's former titles in the animation. (The words Britannia, Panopticon and the local nickname for the music hall, "pots and pans," were all spelt out.) The majority of viewers appeared to remain unaware of the animation's relationship to the site's commercial, heritage and entertainment identities.

This general failure to recognise the connection between the projected words and the building's histories opened up the site's multiple possibilities – spawning conjectures and imaginative propositions about the building's past, present and future roles – rather than functioning as the exercise in naming, or labelling, it might have become had the link been more clearly identified. Instead, spectators entered, through the work, into a playful interaction, or performance, with the site – participating in a (word) game with no discernable rules, played out in the context of their routine activities on the city street.

Through the intervention, the spectators' relationship with the Britannia Panopticon building diverged from more customary engagements with heritage sites – generally marked off from their surroundings as special and valuable. It became an everyday – albeit extraordinary – encounter; the cold, the rain, the passing buses and bustle of the busy shopping street formed a web of competing experiences, of which the flickering animation in the darkened windows of the music hall was just one component. As in the unregulated, hands-on interaction with the uncategorised artefacts in *Shoebox Archive*, the connection to heritage made by the spectators of *Façade Fruitmachine* was left open and unexplained, located firmly within the context of their day-to-day existence. The work invited spectators to engage in an enactment of the proposition that heritage sites should not, and cannot, be separated from contemporary life, that material culture cannot be contained, controlled and preserved for posterity, that the past remains very much alive in the present.

Concluding Remarks

Reflecting on the project in light of my own observations, and those of audience members, other visitors and participants, it appears that *Glimmers in Limbo* at the Britannia Panopticon demonstrated the potential of performance and associated embodied practices to activate relationships between material culture and cultural memory, dissolving perceived distinctions between tangible and intangible heritage and mobilising heritage as a living, ongoing, creative process. The embodied nature of the *Glimmers in Limbo* artworks – their emphasis on sensory engagements with the site, the uncertainty, or risk, inherent in the live performances, and their transience – worked against the impetus to control and regulate interactions with material culture, opening it up as a site of multiple possibilities. Their integration of space, place and performance activated and generated both shared and personal memories – inviting participants to play out individual and collective identities that coalesced and dispersed, complemented and contradicted, but which refused resolution or homogenisation.

Allowing the material culture of the building to "perform" and to be performed unlocked its potential to play unlimited roles, to inspire numerous competing, yet overlapping, reminiscences and re-imaginings, to foster a dynamic relationship between past and present where the world might be considered as, in Nigel Thrift's words, "a heap of highly significant fragments... contingent and complex, a space for opportunities and events."[23]

Works Cited

Bachelard, G. (1971) *The Poetics of Reverie: Childhood, Language, and the Cosmos*, Boston: Beacon Press.

Bowers, J. (2007) *Stan Laurel and Other Stars of the Panopticon*, Edinburgh: Birlinn.

Dolan, J. (2005) *Utopia in Performance: Finding Hope in the Theatre*, Ann Arbor: University of Michigan Press.

Frith, S. (1996) "Music and Identity," in Hall, S. and P. du Gay (Eds.) *Questions of Cultural Identity*, London: Sage.

Leppert, R. (1993) *The Sight of Sound: Music, Representation and the History of the Body*, Berkeley, CA: University of California Press.

Lury, K. (2008) "Glimmers and Limbo: Following the 'Path of Reverie' and Locating the Ghosts of the Everyday." Paper presented at the *Art – Site – Audience* symposium, 26 October, in Glasgow, U.K.

Maloney, P. (2007) *The Britannia Music Hall and the Development of Urban Popular Entertainments in Glasgow*. PhD dissertation, University of Glasgow.

Moran, J. (2004) "History, Memory and the Everyday," *Rethinking History*, 8, pp.51-68.

Phelan, P. (1993) *Unmarked: The Politics of Performance.* New York and London: Routledge.

Smith, L. (2006) *Uses of Heritage*, London and New York: Routledge.

Smith, S. (2000) "Performing the (Sound)world," *Environment and Planning D*, 18, pp.615-637.

Taylor, D. (2003) *The Archive and the Repertoire: Performing Cultural Memories in the Americas*, Durham and London: Duke University Press.

Thrift, N. (2003) "Performance and…" *Environment and Planning A*, 35, pp.2019-2024.

—. (2004) "Performance and Performativity: A Geography of Unknown Lands," in Duncan, J., N.C. Johnson and R. Schein (Eds.) *A Companion to Cultural Geography*, Malden MA: Blackwell Publishing.

—. (2008) *Non-Representational Theory: Space/Politics/Affect*, London and New York: Routledge.

Notes

[1] Despite the efforts of the Trust, its official status "of special historic interest" (as designated by Historic Scotland in 2008) and its presence on Scotland's Buildings at Risk Register, no secured funding for the building's conservation and maintenance, or coherent plans for its future currently exist.

[2] Stan Laurel allegedly made his debut, as a boy, at the Britannia Music Hall.

[3] Two recent works demonstrate the richness and diversity of the testimonies, stories and myths that the Britannia Panopticon has generated. Paul Maloney's PhD thesis *The Britannia Music Hall and the Development of Urban Popular Entertainments in Glasgow* (2007) contains a substantial collection of first and second-hand testimonies of the latter years of the Britannia Panopticon's existence as a public entertainment venue, while *Stan Laurel and Other Stars of the Panopticon* (2007) by Judith Bowers, founder of the Britannia Panopticon Trust, provides her own personal, highly anecdotal, account of the music hall's history.

[4] I use the term "performance" within the essay to refer to a spectrum of activities that can be read as marked off from everyday, unconsidered behaviour through a degree of intentionality – either on the part of the "performer," who is consciously performing a task, action or role, or on the part of the commentator, who designates the behaviour as "performance." This ranges from commonplace understandings in which the term refers to situations where audience and performers play clearly designated roles within conventional theatrical or

entertainment settings, to less specific usages, such as Nigel Thrift's where "performance" is taken to mean a physical "doing". See Thrift (2003) "Performance and…" *Environment and Planning A*, 35, pp.2019-2024; and Thrift (2004) "Performance and Performativity: A Geography of Unknown Lands," in J. Duncan, N. C. Johnson and R. Schein (Eds.) *A Companion to Cultural Geography*, Malden MA: Blackwell Publishing.

[5] Within the context of the essay I define "embodied" as that which is understood or enacted primarily through somatic, expressive and non-discursive means, where sensory and corporeal experience takes precedence over cognitive comprehension. While acknowledging that embodied experience cannot be separated from intellectual engagement, the essay takes the position that the body can "know" in ways distinct from rational thought and that this type of knowing is more resistant to control and regulation than discursive epistemologies. Significantly, in terms of this essay, embodied practice is also, as Diana Taylor argues, key to shaping, transmitting and re-negotiating cultural memories and identities. Taylor (2003) *The Archive and the Repertoire: Performing Cultural Memories in the Americas*, Durham and London: Duke University Press, p.16.

[6] Gaston Bachelard (1969) *The Poetics of Reverie: Childhood, Language, and the Cosmos*, Boston: Beacon Press, p.112.

[7] Laurajane Smith (2006) *Uses of Heritage*, London and New York: Routledge, pp.3, 44-84.

[8] Responses to the artworks/interventions were gauged and recorded using a variety of methods: participant observation, informal conversations, structured group discussions, interviews, questionnaires and invited written responses, from which all quotations and paraphrased comments used in the essay are derived.

[9] Peggy Phelan (1993) *Unmarked: The Politics of Performance,* New York and London: Routledge, p.147.

[10] The songs were recorded on-site at the Britannia Panopticon in the week preceding the live performance. Singers had, therefore, one very brief rehearsal, or run-through, of their song with the pianola before facing an audience.

[11] Phelan (1993), p.147.

[12] Bachelard (1969), p.119.

[13] Richard Leppert (1993) *The Sight of Sound: Music, Representation and the History of the Body,* Berkeley CA: University of California Press, p.29.

[14] Karen Lury (2008) "Glimmers and Limbo: Following the 'Path of Reverie' and Locating the Ghosts of the Everyday." Paper presented at the *Art – Site – Audience* symposium, 26 October, in Glasgow, UK.

[15] Taylor (2003), p.21.

[16] Susan Smith (2000) "Performing the (Sound)world," *Environment and Planning D*, 18, p.624.

[17] See, for example, Taylor (2003), p.17.

[18] Jill Dolan (2005) *Utopia in Performance: Finding Hope in the Theatre*, Ann Arbor: University of Michigan Press, p.2.

[19] Simon Frith (1996) "Music and Identity," in Stuart Hall and Paul du Gay (Eds.) *Questions of Cultural Identity,* London: Sage, p.109.

[20] The outside of the boxes were marked with labels informing visitors that the box might contain an artefact, while invigilators in the music hall gently suggested that the boxes could be opened and searched through.

[21] Joe Moran (2004) "History, Memory and the Everyday," *Rethinking History*, 8, p.58.

[22] *Ibid.*, p.66.

[23] Nigel Thrift (2008) *Non-Representational Theory: Space/Politics/Affect*, London and New York: Routledge, p.125.

NOISE, MEMORY, GESTURE:
THE THEATRE IN A MINUTE'S SILENCE

ROSS BROWN

The dead, the never-born, the locked-out souls
Are scratching on the thin shell we have grown
Around ourselves. Listen, the afternoon
Is dark already, and there is a moon [1]

At 12 noon on 7 July 2006, London observed a two minute silence to mark
the first anniversary of the terrorist attack on its public transport system.
On pavements outside workplaces, in shopping centres and in tube
stations, people paused in their journeys, set down their bags, and adopted
familiar poses of silent remembrance. A strange thrall descended, to which
the urban permadrone, distant sounds of building works and individual
locomotive events, formed a distant perimeter. The two minutes passed,
but outside my workplace people did not move. The two minutes became
five, before people gently moved away. I tried to imagine a piece of silent
theatre comprising nothing more than the same sublime, anxious thrill of
pause, in which nothing is said, but in which the mundane becomes
monumentally strange and yet fond; in which audience becomes
performance; in which the body tingles with memory and sound; in which
noise and stray thoughts are allowed to be exquisite rather than guilty
interruptions.

This thought provided the impetus for a two-year practical investigation of
the minute's silence as theatre. This chapter is not about that research, but
offers some thoughts derived from it pertinent to the themes of this book.
It looks at the minute's silence as a modern ritualised practice of cultural
remembrance, and in particular at the ways in which it connects the inner
selves of participants, through the energetically inscribed tissue of the
body, to the external environment. As a cultural practice the silence faintly
remembers other ritual group practices in which participants enter
trancelike states of "oneness" with environment and with others through
vibration or sonic analogy. As is well established, sound has played a key

role in funereal and other ritual practices since at least the Stone Age, often through acoustics designed to create a feeling of corporeal vibration, which seems to link the inner self to the resonance of the room.[2] The energising effect of silence is less easily explained by physics but is commonly experienced in religious congregations and by mourners, protestors and theatre audiences.

However, since empirical "silence" is neither acoustically nor psychoacoustically silent, but a continuum or plenum of local environmental noise, then its effect, phenomenologically speaking, is not one of silence, nor negatively of sound, but of present noise and the body's relationship with it. This chapter's main proposition is that the "thrall" experienced in the minute's silence and other theatrical pauses is an aural embodiment of moment, made possible by the suspension of everyday activity, and the conventional constraints of having to hold the body still in a particular way. It also proposes that, within a formal silence, memories and other thoughts are experienced aurally, within the body, as a kind of noise.

Whilst this conceptualisation of the aural body is phenomenological, it is conditioned by a historical progression that has come to be known recently as sensual culture. In particular it recalls different hearing cultures in which sound is ontology,[3] and the human body a microcosmic extension of a universe understood through sonic tropes – the Upanishad mantra *nada brahma*, "the universe is sound", or Boethius' conceptual trinity of *musica mundana* (the sound of the material universe), *musica humanis* (the sounds of the human microcosm) and *musica instrumentalis* (sound which is heard.) These are analogical philosophies – appropriately so since sound exists only in analogue forms (in air, flesh, neural impulse, voltage modulations and so on) whose originary event was a kinetic disturbance within a medium, but not, in itself and without human ears to hear it, a sound.

How might the street theatre of the memorial minute's silence, which places memory and the performing body within an aural trope, help us better to understand concepts such as sound, noise, immersivity, embodiment and the phenomenology of memory in relation to theatre practice?

Memory and Circumstance

Culturally, the minute's silence is a political event, but the civic honour made to the deceased or the missing is largely a performance made discursively *around* it: in the scheduling, the preparation and the traces left afterwards. The dedication might be to the deceased, but the act of remembrance that resonates more in the individual psyche is transacted in a live, fleshbound moment of being "alone in a crowd" and in an aural and mnemonic circumstance which one experiences in a solitary dialectic between body, perception and noisy environment.

Entering this personal state in the company of others is a pleasure, but in a thrilling, not a mawkish way. The "football silences" that have been a growing cultural phenomenon during the early twenty-first century, although genuinely intentioned and usually faithfully observed, also function a little like preludinal cheerleaders or fireworks, ramping up the theatrical excitement before the game. Silence – or perhaps more particularly the absence of anything programmatic to listen to other than background noise – seems somehow to forefront *liveness* in the crowd and occasion.

One might be tempted to cite this kind of "energy in mere presence" as a retort to Auslander's scepticism about "clichés and mystifications concerning the aura, presence and the 'magic of live theatre,' etc.,"[4] but it should be recognised that the convention of the minute's memorial silence, in its twentieth-century history, was from the very beginning also a media(*tised*) event. The memorial Armistice Day silence, introduced in Britain in 1919 in order that domestic survivors might honour those who had perished in the distant, terrifying noise of the Great War, originated in a London newspaper campaign for

> a very sacred intercession, [...] church services, too, if you will, but in the street, the home, the theatre, anywhere, indeed, where Englishmen and their women chance to be, surely in this five [*sic*] minutes of bitter-sweet silence there will be service enough?[5]

The words "bitter-sweet silence" themselves suggest that the tribute was conceived as a pleasurable sensual experience, despite its solemn occasion. The campaign proved so popular that the government had to move quickly to endorse and control it. The initial idea of a populist *ad hoc* five minute silence was subtly modified (the idea of tools downing, or cessation of daily travail, carried obvious threats): five minutes became two, and the idea of a secular, civilian Armistice Day, eleventh hour, eleventh day event was transformed into a national showing, with heavy militaristic and religious overtones, receiving celebratory media coverage and promoted by official rhetoric about "united Empire." The "official" silence became a state-sponsored media event – some might say a propaganda exercise.

In cinema newsreels and, from 1923, as an immensely popular "live" outside broadcast, it became intertwined in the public consciousness with hierarchically regimented scenes of the Remembrance Sunday service in Whitehall, with wreath-laying, twenty-one gun salutes, uniformed bodies stood to attention by rank, salutes, and the monolithic centrepiece of the Cenotaph. That whole scene, it should be noted, was dramaturgically orchestrated and monumentally designed in haste by Sir Edwin Lutyens, to an urgent cabinet brief, and made ready for the November 1919 event in response to the May newspaper campaign.

Political subtext and pomp aside, it is clear that the experience of collective silence at the heart of the ceremony – even when experienced through the media, in cinema seats or gathered around the radio at home – achieved its bitter-sweet effect. Reviews of the 1919 event remarked on its potency, and the silence became an annual moment of shared, and mediatised, human experience. As a broadcast, the silence was anything but "dead air." An early BBC radio technician wrote:

> …here is one of the great paradoxes, that no broadcast is more impressive than the silence following the last dashing strokes of Big Ben. Its impressiveness is intensified by the fact that silence is not a dead silence, for Big Ben strikes the hour, and then the bickering of sparrows, the crisp rustle of falling leaves, the creasing of pigeon wings as they take flight, uneasy at the strange hush, contrast with the traffic din of London some minutes before. Naturally, vigilant control of the microphone is essential. Audible distress near to the microphone would create a picture out of perspective as regards the crowd's solemn impassivity and feelings. Our job is to reduce all local noises to the right proportions, so that the silence may be heard for what it really is, a solvent which destroys personality and gives us leave to be great and universal.[6]

BBC broadcasts show the minute's silence not to be a period of acoustic inactivity – far from it – nor a generic two minutes of ambience, but an ambience energised by static corporeal energy (literally the energy of bodies standing).[7] Even on the radio, their presence is palpable in the "strange," noisy hush.

Its latter history (after "Diana" and 9/11) has seen the "dramaturgy" of state-sponsored silences like the 7/7/06 event return to the initial premise of the *ad hoc*, culturally immersive event. Simultaneous memorial tableaux taking place nationwide fill the news-cycle with images of local contexts of a country getting on with its life, accompanied by the now familiar "soundbite" of the open-microphone relaying nothing but ambience.

In the pictures, it is hard to judge the extent to which the characteristic arrangements of the body – hands held loosely together in front, heads bowed in semi-secular supplication, eyes shut, or staring into the vague distance – have become a self-imitative "genre" propagated through news media. From a detached position of non-participation, the scenography of memorial postures might be said to "remember" nothing more than other news montages of politicians standing shoulder-to-shoulder with the public; parents clasping children to their sides; shopping bags set down temporarily on the floor; fire-fighters, tube-workers, sports teams, hand-linked in circles to show that through teamwork they will overcome.

The occasional old soldier in ceremonial red may salute, but these days there are fewer images of massed, ceremonial ranks. The plain-clothed public, whom contemporary minutes' of silence more frequently mourn, stands in irregular congregations of individual silence, eyes front or down or closed, never meeting. There is no certainty in the way such *ad hoc* ceremonies are oriented; like the new wars that increasingly form their context, they have no clear *front*. Bodies no longer "stand to attention" but display a kind of meekness, and stand askance from one another.

Perhaps this is a display of individuality – that their silence is private. Or perhaps this is the body-language of a public immersed in potential peril; in homeland insecurity. The scenography of remembrance – flowers or personal items tied to railings or lampposts, particular organisations of the limbs, heads and eyes – are not designs like Lutyens's stone Cenotaph, but visible traces of aural states. The performers of the minute's silence are not playing statues, they are not posing, or organising themselves into tableaux in order to be observed. They stand still to address the space and time of their everyday circumstance.

The Aural Body

So what is happening *subjectively* within this memorial scenography? As a street or place-specific theatre, the silence is wholly an event of audience participation; its bodies are objects *and* subjects, performers and audience. While postures of silence are performed according to generic convention (even if occasionally in a display of resistance to it), the corporeal attentiveness to circumstance experienced subjectively by the performer belongs to a genre-related state of *audience*.

When sitting as part of that congregation called *a theatre audience*, one is similarly required, by convention, to perform a corporeal attitude (to stay silently still, except when allowed to clap, laugh or cough; to sit and behave in prescribed ways). This regime, and the nearby presence of others governed by it, produces a corporeal engagement with circumstance perhaps not dissimilar to that in the minute's silence. This awareness is part of the excitement of being in a live audience. Whilst it becomes more noticeable during pauses, it is there throughout. Even when one's attentive gaze is focused in the direction of the *mise en scène*, one is aware of one's material surroundings – through the occasional sideways glance, but mainly through the "skin/air" senses of hearing, smell, touch.

Even though the word has specific associations with the ear, I describe the sum of this circumstantial sensual awareness as *aural*, because the etymology of the word connects with the Latin word *aura* (breeze or zephyr – that airborne, tactile, mnemonic sense of place). This synaesthetic, general background awareness of ambient environment, of noise, resonant space and others, *is* the atmosphere within which any perception is made, and modifies the meaning of any received communicative signal. It is a perceptual experience of the whole body and one which creeps more into the perceptual foreground during moments of pause.

I wish, also, to implicate the auditory imagination and memory within my holistic concepts of *audience* and the *aural body*, but I realise that for many people this would seem to be stretching the meanings of *audition* or *aurality* a little too far. But I am going to persist with this, because my experience as a theatre sound practitioner leaves me in no doubt that hearing has an interdependent relationship to the imagination, memory, and a synaesthetic air/skin sense of corporeal placement in ambient environment. This cannot, in my view, be discounted from any full definition of the term *hearing*; a position legitimised, perhaps, by the fact that sound has historically not always been defined exclusively as *that which is heard*. Recent studies of sensual culture in any case challenge the modernist categorisation of perception into discreet senses and the attendant categorisation of the phenomenal universe into objects grouped according to the senses (sounds, smells and so on).[8] The "meaning" of a sight, it is proposed, cannot be disassociated from the ambience of its place of reception, which is experienced synaesthetically within the *sensorium* (a mediaeval concept revived as a trope for holistic sensual perception.)

Not only does one sense impinge on and affect the others, but perception is affected by cultural histories associated with the senses. As David Howes explains:

> To a greater or lesser extent, every domain of sensory experience, from the sight of an artwork to the scent of perfume to the savour of dinner, is a field of cultural elaboration. Hence the necessity of adopting an anthropological approach to the study of the sensorium.[9]

Contemporary perception of sound is affected by a complex and multifarious cultural history which can, very broadly, be summarised in two major narratives. The first of these is the *objectification* of sound and the narrowing of its definition from earlier, more holistic concepts of analogically sonic ontology. In this narrative, vision and the visually-orientated tropes of the Enlightenment are often portrayed as culprits in the denigration of sound as the softer sense of the dominant pair – the "touch feely" sense, so to speak; the sense of spirituality and emotion but not of rational thought or detached observation.[10] The second major narrative is the history of growing opposition between culturally "wanted" *sound* (music, clear speech and so on) and *noise*.[11]

Together these narratives describe the modernisation of hearing. However, as Veit Erlmann suggests:

> The modern sonic self is defined by complex dialectical processes insecurely poised between the modern and the 'primitive,' between the rational and the affective, the discursive and the embodied.[12]

For Erlmann there is a residual cultural memory in the modern psyche, of a time when sound was more than packets of communication delivered through auditory apparatus, or the medium of the verbal idea or the musical artwork. In various "primitive" understandings, sound is an analogical concept by which existence is understood.[13]

As Bruce R. Smith notes, the culture change from a pre-modern culture defined analogically by sound to the visualist concepts and terminologies of the Enlightenment is nowhere more manifest than in the theatre and theatres of Shakespeare's London.[14] The transition from an oral/aural – and therefore body-centred – culture of analogical understandings, to a culture of intellectualism and transcribed ideas is traced in the dialectic between the soniferousness and sonic trope of early modern drama, and its ideological wordplay. Smith describes how the *technê* and theatre architecture of the time also reflect the transition from a world culturally understood though aural effect to a world explained by rational ideas which speak to the intellect rather than the body.

Smith uses the concept he calls "o" to describe a circular connectivity, the body as a resonant sonic instrument, linking into the acoustic environment as a place where cultural and "natural" transactions resonated together, linking back into the body again as a resonant receptor. This connectivity was perhaps more noticeable in daily life before the *permadrone* of the city raised the noise-floor and compressed the dynamics of the sound-world above it. The soundscape of burgeoning modernity, contained by the soft resonance of the wood, thatch and plaster of London, offered the urban dweller an aural positioning system of parish bells and commercial and artisanal districts, just as the Vitruvian acoustics of the wooden Os organised one's aural relationship to drama within the encircling resonance of the theatre.

What is more difficult to understand today, perhaps, is the degree to which early modern subjects understood their aural state to be representative of their internal health, emotional disposition, and the environmental "health" of the whole universe. As David Lindley points out, the public would bring to the theatre an ontologically aural understanding of a universe in which they were connected through sound to those of others and to the cosmos as a whole.[15] In Boethius' 6th century scholarly iteration of the long, Pythagorean tradition of aural theory, *musica instrumentalis*[16] – music which is heard – was merely the audible part of a universal sonic eco-system. The balance of dissonance and harmony evident in the soundscape was the audible manifestation of the balance of order and chaos in the universe (*musica mundana*, the macrocosm) and the human condition (*musica humanis*, the corporeal microcosm.)

Music and *sound* were more than auditory concepts. Within this theorem of sound, matter, fate, spirituality and health interconnected. Acoustic sound was its manifestation, a symptom of something bigger, but through it one could alter or affect natural processes. By intervening within *musica instrumentalis* – for example, by formally dancing, or playing harmonic music in the face of chaos or disharmony – it was possible to provide a cure for noisy cosmic or microcosmic imbalance.[17] Attali suggests that music, in this pre-modern sense, was a form of sacrificial act rather than an artistic or entertainment commodity.[18]

Perhaps the analogical, aurally-corporeal culture of *musica humana* is dimly remembered in modern conventions of *audience* and memorial silence. But the concept of the *aural body* is not merely part of an analogy – the body is also an acoustic place. Processes of hearing and vocal production take advantage of the resonant properties of organs and cavities within the body, which the body has evolved to maximise where useful. Most obviously, vocal resonance happens around the throat, and in the nasal, oral and chest cavities, while auditory resonance happens predominantly within the ear canals and in nearby nasal and other head cavities. But many different parts of the body also have measurable dominant resonance frequencies.[19] Most of these are at inaudible, infrasonic frequency levels but nevertheless represent significant energetic activity within the body. The body, as a whole, measurably resonates at 2Hz when lying down, between 4-5Hz when standing (relaxed) and at 5-6Hz when sitting. Heads will resonate at between 20-30Hz (within the hearing range) and eyeballs at 40-60Hz. Chest walls resonate, typically, at 60Hz, spinal columns at 8Hz, pelvic areas at 8Hz and so on.[20]

The body is thus mapped in sound – in sympathetically resonant response to external, air-based acoustic energy, and in the sound that it produces through its organic processes. This can be deliberately communicative (vocal or kinetic sound production) or it can be involuntary. We live in the flesh but also the sound of our own bodies; we all continually inhabit our own breathing, wheezing, rumbling, swallowing, sniffing, coughing and so on. Sound is kinetic, so it follows that hearing is very close to tactile sensations such as itches, or to physical pleasure or pain. The sound of a low bass frequency is defined as much by the tingling vibration it causes within the chest and lower body as it is by its auditory appearance. A shrill sound can hurt. Try swallowing some saliva. Where does the sound end and the tactile sensation begin?

Listening Through the Mnemonic Body

The aural body is the intimate theatre we live in, and all wider theatres are experienced through it. Listening out from the point of sentient awareness that is the constant, blinking cursor point of *me being awake* (located, it seems, somewhere behind my sinuses), I have largely learned to be deaf to my own constant noise, only becoming aware of it in moments when I am alone or silent. But when I am alone or silent I am also aware that there is sensation other than acoustic sound within my aural body – the ghosts of sounds and sounds yet to happen.

Partly this is *phonomnesis* – imagined or recalled sound: the sounds of these words in my head as you read this sentence. These are within your body as thoughts, but have the potential to be spatial. I can imagine a sound to my left or right; above me or below me. I can remember the sound of my parents downstairs as I lay in bed as a child and the imagined sounds come from the direction *down*. In the workshops I ran as part of my research into noise and memory, I asked participants to remember sounds such as these. I then asked them to listen to something in the room and remember something else at the same time, which proved impossible, as if trying to remember was the same as listening (and whilst one may hear polyphonically, one cannot listen to two things at the same time.)

But the sonic ghosts are not only in my head; there are also bodily sensations, corporeal imaginings of aural feelings: the recollection of the internal vibration of standing by the sea or the roadside; the impetus to wince remembered from a shrill sound; the complex emotional arrangement of vibration, flushes, prickling skin and adrenal activity of engaging with music. Augoyard and Torgue describe a phenomenon they call *anamnesis*: the physical recollection – literally the re-*membering* – of sound through the body.[21] This might be triggered empathetically by sensual perception or through imagined or remembered sound. One might remember music in one's head (phonomnesis) and also experience its effect in the body (anamnesis). Anamnesis is produced either by sound or memory; indeed, one might view it as an embodied form of memory experienced in the aural body. This is how, in my reckoning, memory is aural and how, in that they are both transacted through the aural body, hearing and remembering interdepend and, in their wider definitions, overlap.

This overlapping is evident in the following "trace," composed from the "keyword" or "keyphrase" testimonies of people who took part in a series of "flashmob" memorial silences which I convened in order to research into the aurality of the minute's silence:[22]

> underground voices condensing walls not rush yet voices animated tourists
> near images in papers strewn and imagined people dying faces

commemorate lost life lives counted body the rhythm of city walking
breathing pace calming muted chaos angel gates shut tube instead walk
angry blares sound sun shining good london time transport clank tube
grunt slowing american russell square beep yeah green park change clink
eros early friend waiting energy boost inspiration waiting teacher next
direction cacophony school french laugh tease push am middle whirl
fifteen year-olds perch step getting stand lillywhites exposed breathe nose
separateness noise increase travel deeper find my spot shade rails
piccadilly regent st buses warm chest shake rattle tremor alone breathing
slowly staring space trying sleep record needle dust flecks curtains front
door voice mother's home breathe hands pockets shut hard eyes flex toes
head down blanket pillow block light lost virginia gun traffic exit tube time
calm cacophony foreign and visiting very far away sounds inside me pretty
little clumsy glasses a million knew shaft measles something going to
happen there more than statue pavement downstairs steps and human life
immersed in my the statue walk right into me as if covering them camera
invisible lost child watching my daughter[23]

Memories, noises and thoughts combine as the environment within which
the minute's silence is personally experienced. When I asked participants
to reflect separately on the things they heard and the things they thought
about or remembered, each of them felt a strong inclination to merge the
categories. Some reported that the "deeper" they went into the personal
aural state of silence, the further away the general noise of the place
became, while specific sonic intrusions (someone walking close to them,
talking; the loud air brakes of a bus; a siren; a tannoy announcement)
seemed to relate more closely to the things they were thinking about than
to their auditory sense of location. This tendency towards a trancelike state
seemed to increase significantly after about thirty seconds, but to dispel in
noisy places after about four minutes. In quieter places (places with a
lower level of acoustic energy – for example, Broadgate Circle), the state
seemed to sustain longer. Our flashmob minute's silence lasted a good ten
minutes at Broadgate.

I employed two physically trained performers to take part, because I
wanted them to be particularly alert to the relationship and possible
tensions between the gestural postures of standing in silence. I also wanted
them to be able to show me, through movement, some of the embodied
sound and memory that they experienced. This outward expression of
subjective aural feeling developed as an unforeseen "bonus outcome" of
the project. Two different forms of training (Laban and butoh), and two
very different personalities, manifested two very different aural personae
in the form of "danced" aurality.

The Dance of the Silent Body

These improvisations showed the aural state produced in the dancers' bodies by the memorial silence. The silence they showed had spiky, gestural qualities. It did not have smooth surfaces or continuous lines but consisted in transient shapes, anecdotal sequences and staccato events. In a game of charades, one might not have guessed them, because silence is not supposed to be an anxious, noisy place of circumstantial and mnemonic incident. But are those silences of serenity or oblivion any more than unattainable *ideals*? Acoustic silence is an empirically impossible proposition, as is well known through John Cage's work. Those who promote ideals of silence usually do so for political reasons,[24] or they really mean to suggest a lack of speech or distraction, rather than a lack of sound.

Utter silence only exists in theory and in places where there are no ears. Cage pointed out that even anechoic chambers are not silent when experienced subjectively. These almost-totally noise-cancelling, isolated rooms allow molecular level objective measurements to be made with minimal influence of environmental acoustic energy, but humanly they are experienced as oppressively noisy places. There is no separating self from environment, because the sound of the self fills the environment. In order to perceive them as silent, one has to discount unintentional sound, and therefore discount one's empirical self. As John Cage describes:

> one enters an anechoic chamber, as silent as technologically possible in 1951, to discover that one hears two sounds of one's own unintentional making (nerve's systematic operation, blood's circulation), the situation one is clearly in is not objective (sound-silence), but rather subjective (sounds only), those intended and those others (so-called silence) not intended. If, at this point one says 'Yes I do not discriminate between intention and non-intention' the splits: subject-object, art-life, etc., disappear, an identification has been made with the material, and actions are then those relevant to its nature.[25]

Think of silence more as a verb than a noun. To be silenced is to be stilled or shut up. Being silenced – either abruptly or by convention (in a theatre or a minute's silence) causes an adrenal rush, muscular tension, and social anxiety. It also recalls a primal state – the state of standing bolt upright and frozen to the spot when one hears a twig breaking in the forest or a noise in the house late a night. The body bristles with attentiveness (even if one affects a casual posture rather than literally standing to attention).

Staying *silenced* for a prolonged period of time is difficult, and a certain amount of potential noisy energy seems to build up in the muscles. Think of the fidgety energy and coughs released in the interlude between the movements of a symphony. Think of the anxiety of a prolonged theatrical pause. To remain still in a fidgety world is a tensile performance; an effort. Unless one is engaged in dialogue or rapt in concentration or meditation, the human inclination seems to be to fidget, to cough perhaps, to scratch, hum, whistle or move around.

But there is more to the strange thrall that seems to descend on theatre auditoria during pauses than the tension of withheld movement, and it has to do with a tension between the conventional imperative to be silent and still, and the sonic activity and anamnesis happening involuntarily within the aural body (the agent through which the theatre production is being watched and listened to). The body will not be told to shut up by convention; it resists. In prolonged theatrical pauses, the focus of theatrical energy seems to move out from the playing area, hover in the auditorium, and then, as the silence prolongs further, invade the throat and the chest, until the audient's own body becomes the epicentre of the theatrical energy. One's own subjective discomfort becomes the theatre, until the performance resumes. Circumstantial noises – the hum of the building, the whirring and ticking of lighting equipment, accidental coughs and car horns from outside – seem to assist this energy transference rather than disperse it. This theatre noise seems also to become embodied, feeding an almost sublimely anxious thrill. And then there is the heightened effect of being part of a silent crowd.

The Weight of Congregational Silence

Let us move back from the subjectively phenomenological experience of silence, and consider silence and noise in a more cultural sense.

In the "pre-modern" Boethian ontological analogy, noise was a necessary part of a balanced cosmos. As Attali and others have suggested, noise then became demonised as part of the process of commodifying music, and, as industrial noise levels increased in the environment, of commodifying "lifestyle." By casting noise as a bad thing, people pay to avoid it, or have it removed or abated. "Badness," though, is a cultural determination. Loudness, crassness, grunginess, cheesiness, offensiveness – none of these is an inherent quality:

> Noise is negative: it is unwanted, other, not something ordered. It is negatively defined – i.e. by what it is not (not acceptable sound, not music, not valid, not a message or a meaning), but it is also a negativity. In other words, it does not exist independently, as it exists only in relation to what it is not. In turn it helps structure and define its opposite (the world of meaning, law, regulation, goodness, beauty, and so on). Noise is something like a process.[26]

An unfashionable accent, a *faux pas* or grammatical error might, in certain contexts, be considered "noise," just as radio interference or thrash metal music might be considered noise in others.

Alphonso Lingis contends that sonic noise is essential in communications – both in the background and also in the internal imperfections of our messages to each other. While noise is often assumed, by definition, to be insignificant, it is inevitable and omnipresent, and our psychoacoustic and imaginatively discursive processes have come to rely on its ambiguities and interference as part of the negotiation of meaning. In short, "we" (as a plural collective) need it. Communities of individuals who may well have very little else in common form around the need to overcome noise in order to transact communications. Lingis goes even further than this, to suggest that the noise we make in our cities, as we go about our daily business, is not necessarily the environmental "pollution" that those who would politically idealise silence might claim it to be; it is, rather, a cultural performance:

> All these stammerings, exclamations, slurrings, murmurs, rumblings, cooings, and laughter, all this noise we make when we are together makes it possible to view us as struggling, together, to jam the unequivocal voice of the outsider: the facilitator of communication, the prosopopeia of maximal elimination of noise, so as to hear the distant rumble of the world and its demons in the midst of the ideal city of human communication.[27]

Communities make, allow and value noise like a masking scent, to block out the noise of *other* and the *beyond*, but also as the necessary evil which must be overcome within the daily travail in order to achieve ideal discourse. Perhaps this is another reason group silences are so particularly affecting. As a convention, they are an agreement to let down the everyday shield and brave, together, the *rumble* and *demons*. They are also an agreed respite from the constant struggle to locate discursive meaning in noisy meaninglessness – a powerfully unifying agreement that at this moment, nothing need be said.

A silent crowd is a powerful place. The symbolist playwright Maeterlinck wrote with fewer words and more scripted noises-off than his contemporaries, and had an influential effect on the development of theatre aurality. He understood the thrall of the silent audience, and the powerful way it would complete his verbally sparse texts in the moment of performance. Personally, he feared silence, and in particular the silence of a crowd:

> [T]he life of every day [is] replaced by a life of deepest earnest, wherein all are defenceless; a life in which laughter dares not show itself, in which there is no obeying, in which nothing can evermore be forgotten...

> And it is because we all of us know of this sombre power and its perilous manifestations, that we stand in so deep a dread of silence. We can bear, when need must be, the silence of ourselves, that of isolation: but the silence of many – silence multiplied – and above all the silence of a crowd – these are supernatural burdens, whose inexplicable weight brings dread to the mightiest soul. We spend a goodly portion of our lives in seeking places where silence is not. [28]

This *weight*, like the *thrall* mentioned earlier, is a tactile imposition from somewhere beyond the ideal city of human communications. It is almost like high atmospheric pressure, like weather. Memorial and other ceremonial or conventional silences thus take on a ritually sacrificial role just as music once did, by performing a submission to this cosmic weather which the "roof" of cultural noise usually keeps safely on the outside. [29]

Cultures are defined by their discourse and by their noise; silences say "none of that is important for now" and reveal underlying energies, as Bert States writes:

> The famous pauses in [the Moscow Art Theatre's] productions of Chekhov, [Osip Mandelstam] said, 'are nothing other than a holiday of pure tactile sensation. Everything grows quiet, and only a silent tactile sensation remains.' This is exactly right: what happens in a Chekhov silence is that the tactile world, the visible world (which the talk is aimed unconsciously at keeping at bay), this history-in-objects, quietly encroaches on the human, like the creeping vegetation in Sartre's Bouville. Suddenly you can hear the ticking of objects and the ceaseless flow of future into past: the world is no longer covered by conversation. [30]

Conclusion

The minute's silence thus speaks to embodiment, immersive environments, perceptual ambiguities, aural performance and subjective theatres of flesh, memory and noise – characteristically contemporary themes of theatre practice and research.

I know a scenographer who seems to derive her creative energy from a somewhat paradoxical disciplinary resistance to objectivity. In a world that expects models, pre-production decisions and plotted meaning, she finds herself detesting "miniature utopian visions – statuesque and deadly"; she would rather her audiences and performers "wander in space, undecided" than look-on from a perspective she has decided for them. She talks a lot about *immersive space* and the "*resonant space* between the self and the other." "Meaning," she says, "happens retrospectively if at all." She describes her own creativity as immersive and uses music (any music, not the opera she is designing) to enable her to spend "hours in an immersive [creative] space."[31]

Baz Kershaw uses concepts such as "paradoxology" and "the paradoxical primate – the human both as object and subject" and at one point, suggests that current criticism and dramaturgy are concerned with "energy not signs … not Brecht but Artaud."[32] He talks of energetic transfer within local eco-systems transacted within a macro environment. These are concepts of non-passive immersion in a deep-field of interrelational and interdependent exchange; in my view they are *aural* concepts of an analogical kind which remember concepts such as *theatrum mundi* (which Kershaw mentions) but also recall to me analogical aural concepts such as *musicae humanis, mundane et instrumentalis*.

I hear these theoretical tones resonating in the "immersive" theatre of UK companies such as Punchdrunk, and the interactive mind and body games of Blast Theory, which have transcended the fringe to achieve "international" platforms at national theatres and made theatres of "platform games" or aleatory systems. Audience participation is taken to a point where distinction between audience and performance becomes almost redundant. I hear harmonics of them in flashmobs, and social networking architectures – both virtually and in dramaturgically conceived club environments.

Interactive immersion in culturally noisy environments makes for a new
kind of theatre architecture; but if this chapter and my research have
anything to say to all of this, it is the following. Even in these new
theatres, remember the weight of silent pause and silent congregation.
Under their weight, the aural body becomes a powerful theatre in its own
right. When silenced by the conventions of a cultural moment, it dances
with personal memory and circumstance, on a cosmic stage.

Works Cited

Attali, J. (1985) *Noise, the Political Economy of Music*, trans. B. Massumi,
    Minneapolis: University of Minnesota Press.
Augoyard, J. and H. Torgue (2005) *Sonic Experience: a Guide to
    Everyday Sounds*, trans. A. McCartney and D. Paquette, Montreal &
    Kingston: McGill-Queen's University Press.
Auslander, P. (1999) *Liveness*, London and New York: Routledge.
Berendt, J. E. (1988) *The Third Ear*, Vermont: Destiny Books.
Devereux, P. (2001) *Stone Age Soundtracks: The Acoustic Archaeology of
    Ancient Sites*, London: Vega.
Cage, J. (1978) *Silence*, London: Marion Boyars Publishers.
Erlmann, V. (Ed.) (2004) *Hearing Cultures*, Oxford and New York: Berg.
Farley, P. (1998) *The Boy from the Chemist is Here to See You*, London:
    Picador.
Gregory, A. (2001) *The Silence and the History*, at:
    http://www.locusplus.org.uk/sempess.html (accessed August 2007).
Hegarty, P. (2007) *Noise/Music: A History*, New York: Continuum
    Publishing Group.
Howes, D. (Ed.) (2005) *Empire of the Senses*, Oxford and New York:
    Berg.
Ihde, D. (1973) *Sense and Significance*, New York: Humanities Press.
—. (1976) *Listening and Voice: a Phenomenology of Sound*, Athens: Ohio
    University Press.
Kershaw, B. (2007) *Theatre Ecology: Environments and Performance
    Events*, Cambridge: Cambridge University Press.
Lindley, D. (2006) *Shakespeare and Music*, London: Thomson
    Learning/Arden Shakespeare.
Lingis, A. (1994) *The Community of Those who have Nothing in Common*,
    Bloomington: Indiana University Press.
Maeterlinck, M. (1897) *The Treasure of the Humble,* trans. A. Sutro,
    London: George Allen.

Smith, B. R. (1999) *The Acoustic World of Early Modern England: Attending to the O-Factor*, London: University of Chicago Press.

States, B. (1985) *Great Reckonings in Little Rooms: On the Phenomenology of Theater*, Berkeley: University of California Press.

Sterne, J. P. (2003) *The Audible Past*, Durham and London: Duke University Press.

Notes

[1] From Paul Farley "A Minute's Silence", in P. Farley (1998) *The Boy from the Chemist is Here to See You*, London: Picador.

[2] See, for example, Joachim-Ernst Berendt (1988) *The Third Ear*, Vermont: Destiny Books, p.38; Paul Devereux (2001) *Stone Age Soundtracks: The Acoustic Archaeology of Ancient Sites*, London: Vega.

[3] While many of the examples discussed in this chapter relate to specific British cultural contexts, I hope they resonate beyond the local parish.

[4] Philip Auslander (1999) *Liveness*, London and New York: Routledge, p.55.

[5] "Appeal for a memorial silence on armistice day," *London Evening News*, 8 May 1919.

[6] *Radio Times*, November 1935, quoted by A. Gregory in *The Silence and the History*, at: http://www.locusplus.org.uk/sempess.html (accessed Aug 2007).

[7] For a collection of BBC broadcasts, see the CD *Kenataphion*, Charm/Locus + records, by Jonty Semper (2001).

[8] See, for example, David Howes (Ed.) (2005) *Empire of the Senses*, (Oxford and New York, Berg); Veit Erlmann (Ed.) (2004) *Hearing Cultures*, (Oxford and New York, Berg). Sensual culture is an emergent field, manifest in the recent Sensual Formation series of Readers published by Berg.

[9] Available at http://www.david-howes.com/DH-research.htm (accessed 6 Jan 2009).

[10] See, for example, Jonathan P. Sterne (2003) *The Audible Past*, Durham and London: Duke University Press, p.15.

[11] Jacques Attali (1985) *Noise, the Political Economy of Music*, trans. Brian Massumi, Minneapolis: University of Minnesota Press, and Paul Hegarty (2007) *Noise/Music: A History*, New York: Continuum Publishing Group, have described this as a more political story.

[12] Erlmann (Ed.) (2004), p.13.

[13] See Don Ihde (1976) *Listening and Voice: a Phenomenology of Sound*, Athens: Ohio University Press), and Berendt (1988).

[14] Bruce R. Smith (1999) *The Acoustic World of Early Modern England: Attending to the O-Factor*, London: University of Chicago Press.

[15] David Lindley (2006) *Shakespeare and Music*, London: Thomson Learning/Arden Shakespeare.

[16] Of which the famous "music of the spheres" was a part.

[17] Lindley (2006), pp.30-50 and *passim.*

[18] Attali (1985).

[19] that is, *standing-wave* characteristics

[20] Source: NASA-STD-3000/Vol1/Rev.A quoted in Devereux (2001), p.51.

[21] Jean-François Augoyard and Henry Torgue (2005) *Sonic Experience: a Guide to Everyday Sounds,* Montreal & Kingston: McGill-Queen's University Press, p.85.

[22] A *flashmob* (or *flash mob*) is a prearranged coming together in public place, to perform an unusual action for a brief time and then quickly disperse without any explanation or debriefing. As a genre of cultural performance flashmobs might be seen as a development of Happenings or earlier Surrealist or Dada performative events (they were also initially known as "Inexplicable Mobs"). The first flashmob, *per se* (by his own later account in *Harpers* magazine), was convened anonymously in New York by Bill Wasik, in May 2003. They have tended to be "fun" events rather than political protests, organised by email list or through networking facilities such as Facebook or MySpace. Famous examples include simultaneous worldwide pillow-fights on 22 March 2008 and a silent disco held at Paddington Station on 10 February 2007 (videos widely available, e.g. on YouTube).

[23] Extract from the "cut-up" trace-testimony of participants in *Five Minutes of Silence for My Lost Self,* a flashmob Piccadilly Circus on 18 April 2007, part of the author's AHRC project *Noise, Memory Gesture: The Theatre in a Minute's Silence.*

[24] See, for example, Attali (1985).

[25] John Cage (1978) *Silence,* London: Marion Boyars Publishers, pp.13-14.

[26] Paul Hegarty (2007) *Noise/Music: A History,* New York: Continuum Publishing Group, p.5.

[27] Alphonso Lingis (1994) *The Community of Those who have Nothing in Common,* Bloomington: Indiana University Press, p.105.

[28] Maurice Maeterlinck (1897) *The Treasure of the Humble,* London: George Allen, pp.1-22.

[29] One might, as an alternative to Attali's position that silent listening in the concert hall or theatre reinforces a capitalist economy that requires silence in order to commodify artistic product, instead see the establishment of silence, in certain "live" performance events, as a version of this ritualistic function, a kind of "saying of grace," a nod to the aural horizon for the crafted ideological discourse "we are about to receive."

[30] Bert O. States (1985) *Great Reckonings in Little Rooms: On the Phenomenology of Theater,* Berkeley: University of California Press, p.74.

[31] Joanna Parker, Central School of Speech and Drama Research Seminar, 22 October 2008.

[32] Baz Kershaw (2007) *Theatre Ecology: Environments and Performance Events,* Cambridge: Cambridge University Press.

KEY TEXTS

Assmann, J. and J. Czaplicka (1995) "Collective Memory and Cultural Identity," *New German Critique*, 65, pp.125-133.

Bal, M., J. Crewe and L. Spitzer (Eds.) (1999) *Acts of Memory: Cultural Recall in the Present*, Hanover: University Press of New England.

Bhabha, H. (1994) *The Location of Culture*, London: Routledge.

Butler, J. (1990) *Gender Trouble: Feminism and the Subversion of Identity*, London & New York: Routledge.

Carlson, M. (2001) *The Haunted Stage: Theatre as Memory Machine*, Ann Arbor: University of Michigan Press.

Connerton, P. (1989) *How Societies Remember*, Cambridge: Cambridge University Press.

De Certeau, M. (1988) *The Writing of History*, New York: Columbia University Press.

Diamond, E. (1996) *Performance and Cultural Politics*, New York and London: Routledge.

Donald, M. (2009) *Glimmers in Limbo*, Glasgow: Tramway/Glasgow School of Art.

Foucault, M. (1977) *Discipline and Punish: The Birth of the Prison* [1975], trans. A. Sheridan, Harmondsworth: Penguin.

Halbwachs, M. (1992) *On Collective Memory*, trans. & ed. L. A. Coser, Chicago: University of Chicago Press.

Hirsch, M. (1997) *Family Frames: Photography, Narrative and Postmemory*, Cambridge, Massachusetts and London: Harvard University Press.

Howes, D. (Ed.) (2005) *Empire of the Senses: The Sensual Culture Reader*, Oxford and New York: Berg.

Huyssen, A. (1995) *Twilight Memories: Marking Time in a Culture of Amnesia*, New York: Routledge.

Maufort, M. and C. De Wagter (Eds.) (2008) *Signatures of the Past: Cultural Memory in Contemporary Anglophone North American Drama*. Brussels: P.I.E. Peter Lang.

Miller, N. K. and J. Tougaw (Eds.) (2002) *Extremities: Trauma, Testimony, and Community*, Urbana: University of Illinois Press.

Nora, P. (1989) "Between Memory and History: *Les Lieux de Mémoire*," trans. M. Roudebush, *Representations*, 26 (Spring), pp.7-24.

Pearson, M. (2006) *"In Comes I": Performance, Memory and Landscape*, Exeter: University of Exeter Press.

Phelan, P. (1993) *Unmarked: The Politics of Performance*, London and New York: Routledge.

—. (1997) *Mourning Sex: Performing Public Memories*, New York and London: Routledge.

Roach, J. (1996) *Cities of the Dead: Circum-Atlantic Performance,* New York: Columbia University Press.

Rodriguez, J. and T. Fortier (2007) *Cultural Memory: Resistance, Faith & Identity*, Austin: University of Texas Press.

Schechner, R. (2006) *Performance Studies: An Introduction* [2002], New York and London: Routledge.

Silverman, K. (1996) *The Threshold of the Visible World,* New York and London: Routledge.

Taylor, D. (2003) *The Archive and the Repertoire: Performing Cultural Memory in the Americas*, Durham and London: Duke University Press.

CONTRIBUTORS

CARIAD ASTLES works at the Central School of Speech and Drama (UK) as Puppetry Tutor and Strand Leader of the Theatre Practice (Puppetry) BA. She trained at Exeter and London Universities and worked at the University of Plymouth prior to working at CSSD. She is a professional puppeteer and works in Catalonia for several months each year. Recent work includes directing puppetry for the Northcott Theatre's production of *Macbeth* (Exeter, UK) and performances of *Adama's Journey* in Molins de Rei, Catalonia as part of a collaboration with the Catalan intercultural project *Irenia*. She has published several articles in journals and edited collections on puppet theatre and national identity, Cuban carnivalesque and ritual performance and the body in performance within puppet theatre.

ROSS BROWN is Reader in Sound and Dean of Studies at the Central School of Speech and Drama, University of London (UK). He trained as a fine artist in Newcastle but later switched media from paint to sound. As a theatre practitioner he composed and performed for many productions by Red Shift, in the commercial West End, and for BBC radio drama, the Citizens' Theatre, Glasgow, Derby Playhouse, Lancaster Duke's Theatre, Shared Experience and the Royal Court. He has also collaborated in the composition of live scores for dozens of silent film screenings. At Central, he founded and taught the UK's only specialised degree in theatre sound design, and on the MA Advanced Theatre Practice. His 2008 project *Noise, Memory, Gesture: the Theatre in a Minute's Silence* was funded by the AHRC; his book *Sound: a Reader in Theatre Practice* (Palgrave Macmillan, 2009) is about the dramaturgy of sound.

MICHELLE LIU CARRIGER is a PhD student in Theatre and Performance Studies at Brown University in Providence, Rhode Island (USA). Her recent research projects include explorations of how people imbue space with historical and cultural meaning at Los Angeles' Olvera Street tourist attraction; clothing theory and historiography; Japanese performing arts and embodiment; and historical reeactment and affect. Her performance work includes *Cabaret Murderess* and *Mirror Stage*, created with Molly Flynn and Elise Morrison, exploring intersections amongst feminism, mediatization and the gaze. Her MA thesis about Victorian cross-dressers on trial was completed in 2006 at the University of Colorado. She has been practicing the Japanese Way of Tea for almost ten years.

COLIN COUNSELL is Senior Lecturer in Theatre Studies and Performing Arts at London Metropolitan University (UK). His research has focused on material performance practices, most of his writings dealing with modernist performance, English renaissance theatre, and performance and disability. In addition to numerous articles, he is the author of *Signs of Performance* (1996), co-editor (with Laurie Wolf) of *Performance Analysis* (2001), and editor of the "Classic Texts" series of plays for Nick Hern Books. His most recent research has focused on the body and movement in modernist performance.

MINTY DONALD is an artist and lecturer in Theatre Studies at the University of Glasgow (UK). She works in the area of critical spatial practice, adopting an approach developed from a background and extensive career in theatre/performance scenography. Minty was an AHRC Fellow in the Creative and Performing Arts, based at the Glasgow School of Art, from 2005-2008, where her practice-led research project, *Glimmers in Limbo*, was concerned with exploring the potential of spatial practices – using performance, sound and projected imagery – to engage with, critique and shape, conceptions and perceptions of the built environment. Current and forthcoming projects – including a multi-sited exhibition/performance on the River Clyde, Glasgow and a bookwork reflecting on *Glimmers in Limbo* – continue to investigate the role of spatial practices in interrogating relationships between, and definitions of, "art," "site" and "audience."

RUTH HELLIER-TINOCO is Senior Lecturer in Performing Arts at the University of Winchester (UK) and was recently a visiting lecturer in ethnomusicology at the University of California, Santa Barbara (USA). Her research is interdisciplinary in nature, encompassing performance studies, ethnomusicology, dance studies and dance anthropology, applied and community arts, theatre studies, and Latin American studies. Ruth's most recent publication is the forthcoming book entitled *Embodying Mexico: Tourism, Nationalism and Performance* (Oxford University Press), and she is editor of a forthcoming collection of biographical essays entitled *Female Singers in Contemporary Global Contexts*. She also works in the field of arts and disability and is the former director of *InterAct Theatre Workshop*.

RIC KNOWLES is Professor of Theatre Studies at the University of Guelph (Canada), editor of *Canadian Theatre Review*, and former editor (1999-2005) of *Modern Drama*. Among his books are *The Theatre of Form and the Production of Meaning* (1999), *Shakespeare and Canada* (2004), *Reading the Material Theatre* (2004), *Remembering Women Murdered by Men* (with the Cultural Memory Group, 2006), and *Theatre & Interculturalism* (2009). He is editor or co-editor of ten collections and anthologies, including two volumes of *Staging Coyote's Dream: An Anthology of First Nations Drama in English* (co-edited with Monique Mojica, 2003, 2006), and is general editor of two book series, "Critical Perspectives on Canadian Theatre in English" and "New Essays on Canadian Theatre." His current work is on intercultural performance and the semiotics of drama and theatre.

ROYONA MITRA is a trained classical and contemporary Indian dancer and a physical theatre practitioner who teaches at the University of Wolverhampton (UK). She has an MA in Physical Theatre from Royal Holloway, University of London and a BA (Hons) in Theatre & Performance from the University of Plymouth; she is currently undertaking a PhD at Royal Holloway. Royona's research interests include South Asian performance practices, the interventionist body in diasporic choreography and postcolonial studies. She has published in journals such as *Feminist Review* and *Women and Performance: A Journal of Feminist Theory*.

ROBERTA MOCK is Reader in Performance at the University of Plymouth (UK) where she also manages postgraduate programmes in the School of Humanities & Performing Arts. Her books include *Jewish Women on Stage, Film and Television* (Palgrave Macmillan, 2007) and, as editor, *Performing Processes: Creating Live Performance* and *Walking, Writing & Performance: Autobiographical Texts by Deirdre Heddon, Carl Lavery & Phil Smith* (both published by Intellect Books). She has contributed to a number of journals and edited books, most recently focusing on the application of Georges Bataille's ideas to specific performance events, and is currently writing a book entitled *Doing Performance Research* with Baz Kershaw and Gillian Hadley for Palgrave Macmillan.

PAUL RAE is an Assistant Professor on the Theatre Studies Programme at the National University of Singapore. He is the author of *Theatre & Human Rights* (Palgrave Macmillan, 2009), and the co-artistic director, with Kaylene Tan, of spell#7 performance (www.spell7.net).

BRYONI TREZISE lectures in Theatre and Performance Studies at the School of English, Media and Performing Arts, University of New South Wales (Australia). Her research intersects theories of cultural memory and contemporary performance practice and is published in *Performance Research*, *Australian Feminist Law Journal* and *Performance Paradigm*.